P9-AGP-884

HOW'D THEY DESIGN AND PRINT THAT?

HOW'D THEY DESIGN AND PRINT THAT?

WAYNE ROBINSON

Cincinnati, Ohio

A QUARTO BOOK

ISBN 0-89134-403-9

First published in the USA by
North Light Books, an imprint of F & W Inc.,
1507 Dana Avenue, Cincinatti, Ohio 45207

This book was designed and produced by
Quarto Publishing plc,
6 Blundell Street,
London N7 9BH.

Senior Editor Kate Kirby
Editor Lydia Darbyshire
Designer David Warner
Picture Researcher Peter Doherty
Illustrator Rob Shone
Photographer Paul Forrester
Assistant Art Director Chloë Alexander
Art Director Moira Clinch
Publishing Director Janet Slingsby

Typeset by QV Typesetting, London
Manufactured in Hong Kong by
Excel Graphic Art Ltd
Printed in Singapore by
Star Standard Industries Ltd

SECTION
ONE

■ PRE-PRESS

SECTION TWO

ON PRESS

SECTION THREE

FINISHING

CONTENTS

INTRODUCTION

This book has been written from a love of print and design and from a desire to see the imagination and creativity of designers fueled by a deeper knowledge and understanding of today's print industry. It is also informed by a wish to see an end to the typical relationship between printer and designer, which more often resembles war than the ideal of two parts of the same equation working together.

Print and design affect every aspect of our lives, both personal and corporate. No area of life today is devoid of printed matter in some form or other — whether we are at work, play, or rest, print is there. From the moment we are born and begin to use diapers (now presented in beautifully printed packages), to our first birthday card and plastic books, from eating baby food in colorfully labeled cans and jars, to the cartoon comics we read, from our schooldays to our work, through the rest of our lives, print plays a crucial role.

The birth of modern printing

Ever since Johann Gutenberg brought modern printing into the world when he invented movable type five centuries ago, print has to some extent been surrounded by an air of mystery. The general public knows little of any print processes, being content merely to enjoy the way print has facilitated the progress of civilization over the centuries. Designers, of course, know more, yet they cannot be expected to have kept up with all the developments that have occurred in recent years. Print has always been somewhat of an amalgam of art, craft, and science, of creativity, skill, and technology, and that has never been truer than today. The variety of printing techniques and the effects that can be achieved is growing continually as printers and their suppliers seek new methods of production.

Like most people involved in the printing trade, I step back from the day-to-day excitement from time to time and take a broad view of the industry, and I am always astounded by the incredible range of high-quality print that is part of our everyday lives. The quality has become possible largely because the printing industry has been in the vanguard of the technological revolution that has occurred over the last 20 years and that is continuing at an ever greater rate today. However, the revolution, which affects every area of print, has been hard enough for people in the trade to follow, let alone those people, such as designers, who are on the periphery of the industry.

The wonders of print

The purpose of this book is to communicate to you — the designer — the potential that exists within today's print industry. More than 60 different print processes are described on the pages that follow — everything from printing bank notes to magazines to T-shirts — and the text covers the whole of each print process from beginning to end. Each of these 60 or so techniques differs, and each has its own production parameters. If you are going to design successfully, imaginatively, efficiently, and without throwing money away, the more you know about the production processes that follow, the more effective will your designs be. Although each process has its limitations, which are frequently the subject of irate discussions between designers and printers, each process has its potential, which the many printers I have spoken to often believe to be unfulfilled by designers, simply because they are not always aware of all that the industry has to offer.

If there is a theme running through this book it is "talk to your printer first." Surprisingly, for a business whose main purpose is communication, the communication between printers and designers is not always as close as it should be and is often no more than minimal — until the problems start, that

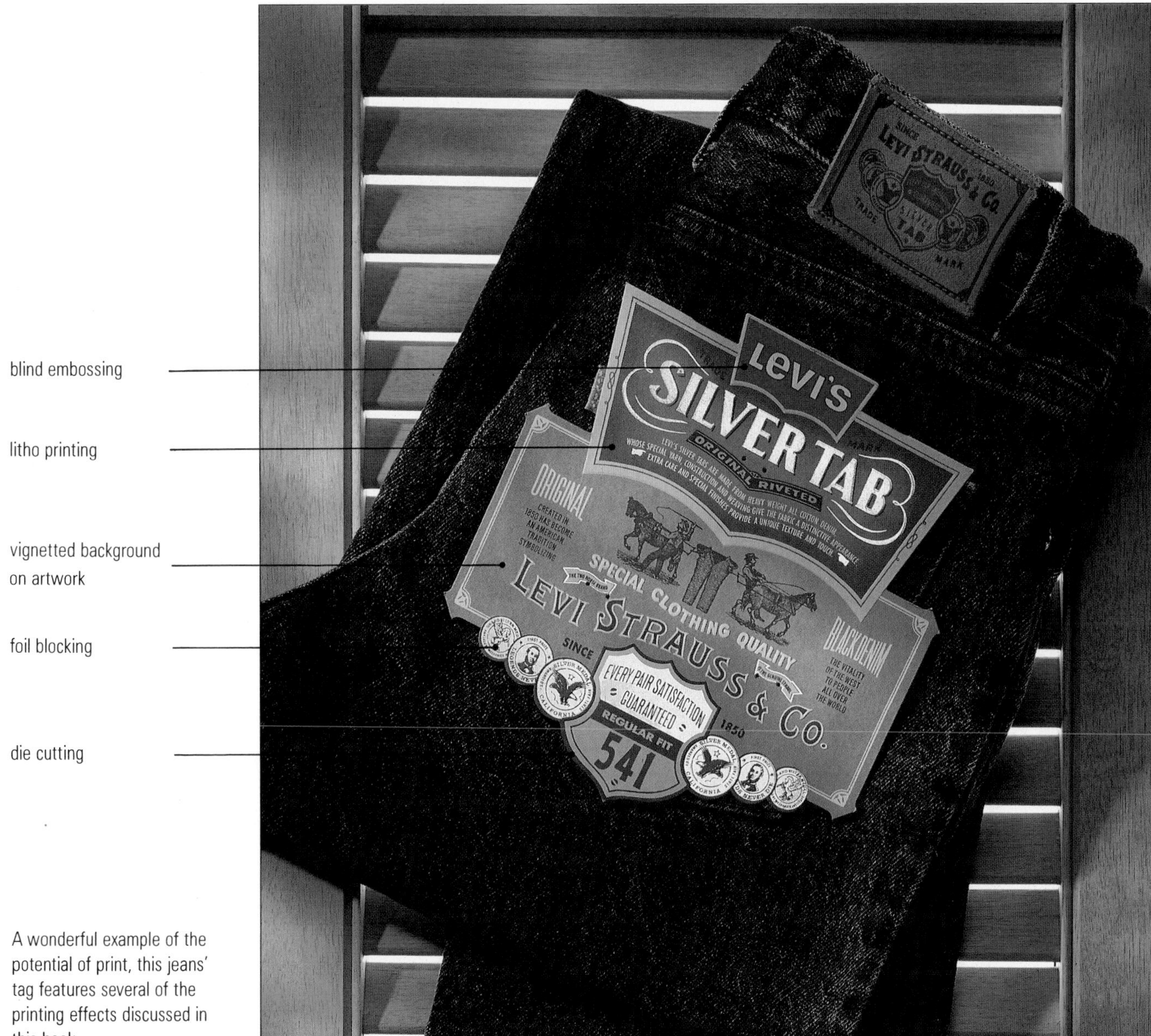

A wonderful example of the potential of print, this jeans' tag features several of the printing effects discussed in this book.

is. Printers tend to feel victimized by designers, while designers feel that printers are doing their utmost to wreck their designs. This should not be. It is axiomatic that noncommunication, in whatever sphere of life, causes problems, and this is especially true in print and design.

This book does not merely describe printing processes, however. It does, of course, explain each process and how the effects are achieved, but it also gives design guidelines for working within the different processes; it contains practical advice on scheduling times, the suitability of different substrates and which effects can be combined with which; and it includes information about other applications for the particular processes and their relative costs, often suggesting ways to keep cost down.

I hope that by using this book you will gain a greater understanding of the print processes available today, and then, by talking to your printer before you begin your design, that not only will you save time, money and, most likely, your sanity, but that you will also find new ways to create more outstanding products and to overcome problems that had in the past seemed insurmountable.

Print and design are wonderful and exciting industries, and it is not hard to be enthusiastic about them. I'm an enthusiast, and so, I can assure you, are the majority of printers. Let's talk to each other, and we are certain to see some extraordinary and exciting products.

Wayne Robinson

A
TECHNICAL
NIGHTMARE
BROUGHT TO YOU BY
LASER SCAN
SOCIETY
Yuppies
The Real Branding Opportunities
Ray-Ban
Quality Not Quantity
Data Com
Processor
Card
MARVEL COMICS
CAPTAIN AMERICA
1.00 US
$1.25 CAN
381
JAN
UK 60p
THIS GUN'S FOR HIRE!
PALADIN
IF YOU WON'T HELP ME NAIL THE SERPENT SOCIETY, CAP--I'LL FIND SOMEONE WHO WILL!
AHA! IT IS THE MAN WE'RE LOOKING FOR. WHAT'S THIS? LOOKS LIKE HE SET MOONSTONE FREE FOR AMOROUS REASONS!
PLEASE, LOVER -- THE MANACLES. I WANT TO CARESS YOU SO BADLY...!
ALL RIGHT, MOONY ...I'LL FREE YOUR ARMS.
WHAT CAN YOUR MOON-BEAMS DO TO AN INVULNERABLE MAN ANYWAY? BESIDES TICKLE, THAT IS.

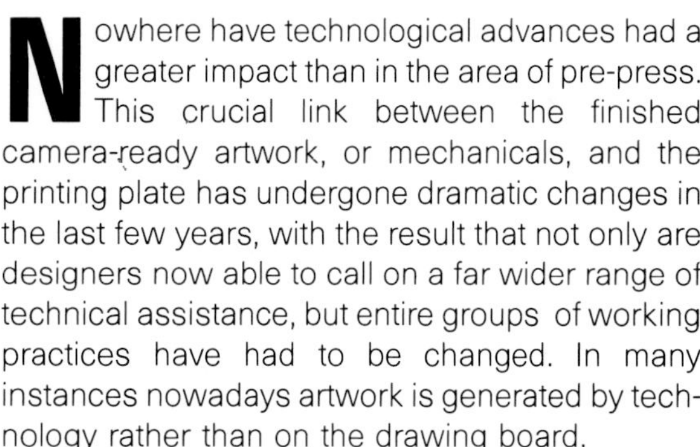

Pre-Press

SECTION ONE

Nowhere have technological advances had a greater impact than in the area of pre-press. This crucial link between the finished camera-ready artwork, or mechanicals, and the printing plate has undergone dramatic changes in the last few years, with the result that not only are designers now able to call on a far wider range of technical assistance, but entire groups of working practices have had to be changed. In many instances nowadays artwork is generated by technology rather than on the drawing board.

Designers can now produce work that they could previously only imagine. There is virtually nothing that cannot be achieved with a computer-generated graphics system; often, indeed, it is the designer's imagination that is the limiting factor. In addition, the introduction of desktop graphics programs on low-cost work-stations allows designers substantially to reduce their costs and time in pre-press production by completing the typesetting and page makeup themselves – which is more exciting than it sounds! More color is now available to more people than ever before thanks to low-and mid-cost repro systems, which can carry out much of the work previously only possible on the large, extremely expensive systems.

Today's designers must understand modern technology, even though the scope is, literally, breathtaking, both in terms of the creative potential and possible cost reductions. The pages that follow describe these modern pre-press technologies as they relate to you, the designer.

HOT METAL TYPESETTING PROMOTION

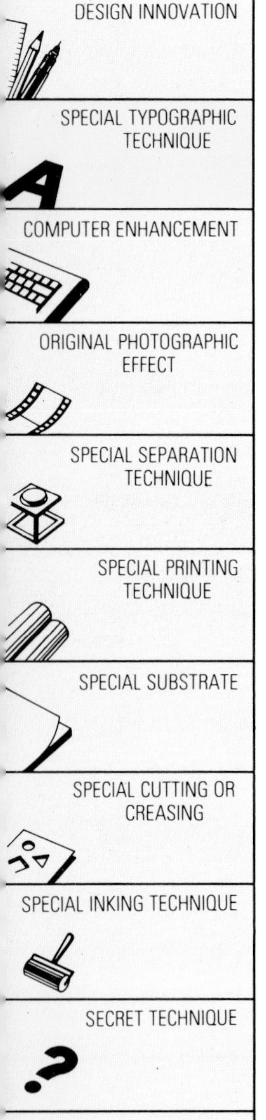

For almost 100 years hot metal was the principal method of setting type. Superseded by computerized typesetting in the last 20 years, the setting of type by hot metal has now almost ended in the developed world, although it is still widely practiced in some developing countries. Nonetheless, hot metal typesetting is still available, and it can be used by designers in conjunction with letterpress printing to achieve a variety of effects.

Hot metal type is literally that — a combination of lead, tin, and antimony is heated, and the characters are stamped into it by a brass matrix. It is set by a keyboard operation and is instantaneous.

Hot metal offers the designer high-quality type and extreme flexibility, for the text can be changed at the very last minute, even when it is on press. The type is of the highest quality because, apart from some very recent editions, fonts were originally designed for metal and have had to be modified in the transfer to computer, losing some of their subtlety in the process.

Hot metal type is a useful medium for bringing an old craft look and feel to products, although it has to be said that this is more discernible to those in the trade than to the general public, who may be aware of the effect only subconsciously.

Press runs using hot metal and letterpress can be very short, and an additional advantage is that there is very little waste of paper in making ready, which helps to bring the costs down. Type set by hot metal can be used to print onto almost all papers and boards and onto some plastics.

Other applications

Hot metal typesetting is useful for solid text in books, journals, and the like, and in addition, it is becoming increasingly popular for promotional work, where it can offer a "special" look that helps to set products apart.

Relative costs

Hot metal is not necessarily cheaper than cold computer type, particularly not the type from the new desktop systems. However, the quality is noticeably better. Platemaking is cheaper than for litho because there are no consumables such as films and plates involved, and the metal is simply remelted when it has been used and put back into the pot.

Hot metal type was originally set by hand before being superseded 100 years ago by machines such as the Linotpye which set whole lines. Setting by hand is still the best way to mix and match metal typefaces.

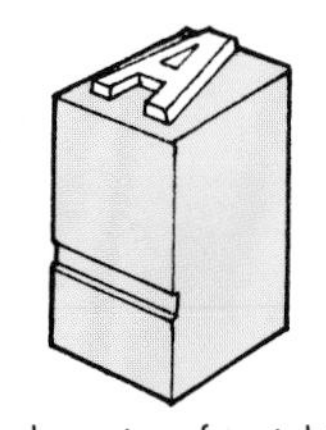

a character of metal type

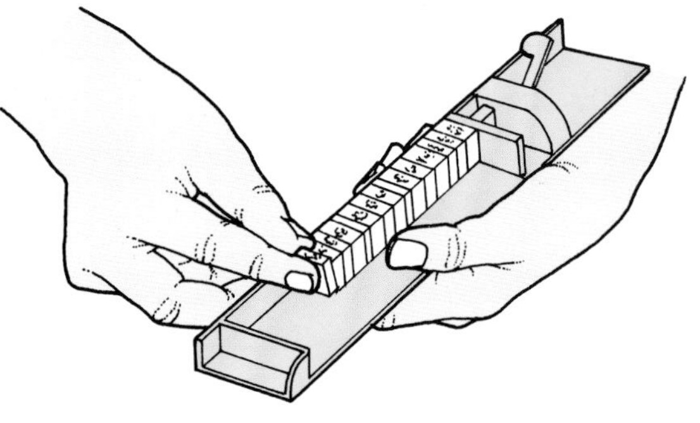

The majority of typefaces now in use were originally designed for hot metal. Advocates of the system claim that print produced by hot metal will always be aesthetically superior because photoset and digitized type have, inevitably, lost something of the beauty of the original faces in their translation to the new technologies.

PRE-PRESS

COMPUTERIZED TYPESETTING BROCHURE

Setting type in all of the thousands of fonts available is, for the most part, a fairly uncomplicated operation that can be carried out on dedicated typesetting systems or, increasingly, on DTP systems, which are much cheaper and easier for the layperson to use. However, the DTP system can lend itself to the creation of unsightly pages when people who have no typographic training operate it — so be careful!

Producing non-roman text such as mathematical and chemical symbols, and characters from the Cyrillic, Greek, Arabic, Hebrew, and Oriental alphabets is now relatively straightforward thanks to highly developed typesetting systems. There are hardly any letters that are not digitized now, although it is usual for these non-roman characters to be found only in specialist typesetting houses. In addition, some of the new desktop systems, including Apple Macintosh, can produce non-roman work, although in a more limited and slower form.

Computerized typesetting offers the designer greater opportunities to use non-roman letters and symbols, and because it is far easier to use a pre-digitized symbol or letter than to draw it by hand, such symbols and letters are used increasingly in creative work.

Decision-making made easy

Computerization can also take away much of the hard work by making decisions about pagination, and it offers the potential of automatic sorting for dictionaries, directories, and the like, thus saving time, money, and space. Designers can avoid much laborious work if they make full use of the available programs. For example, it is possible to instruct the computer to make the first occurrence of a new letter throughout a directory a drop capital. Leaders and folios can be similarly taken care of. Automatic restyling makes the task of designing directories with the brief to save as much paper as possible immeasurably easier.

Non-roman typesetting takes approximately two or three times longer than normal work; for example, if a straightforward 256-page book takes three or four weeks to typeset in roman characters, the same size non-roman book should take between 10 and 12 weeks.

This 16-page circular brochure for a New York design group was typeset on a Macintosh system. The grid was designed on paper and then fed into the Mac. Text was set on the Mac and fed onto the grid in the system. The positions of the graphics and linebreaks were roughly worked out on paper, then the graphics were laser scanned into the system in low-resolution format so that the text could be run around them — although that makes the whole process sound a lot simpler than it was! The whole job took a month of intensive work from start to finish, with the editor working in-house alongside the designer. Nonetheless, the cost savings were tremendous. The designer says the total typesetting bill was around $1,000, a fraction of the minimum $15,000 she would have expected to pay for conventional typesetting. Only one face was used in the main body of the magazine; the page titles on the top left were hand-drawn as artwork and added to the bromides.

Other applications

Non-roman characters are used in scientific books and journals, and for typesetting many foreign languages, including those of Eastern Europe, the Middle East, and the Far East. Theological journals and books also often require non-roman lettering. Creative work in such areas as packaging and advertising is increasingly using computer-set symbols, usually following the trend of whatever is fashionable at the time. The automatic sorting facilities available are used in dictionaries, directories, and catalogs.

Relative costs

Non-roman setting is up to three times more expensive than roman setting because of the time needed to set the type and the cost of the initial fonts. Although using Apple Macintosh computers slashes the costs, the quality is not as high and the time taken is longer.

COMPUTERIZED TYPEFACE DESIGN DIRECTORY

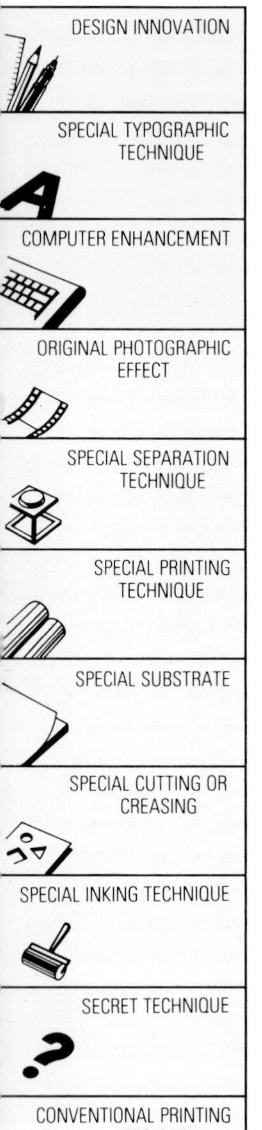

DTP systems, such as Apple Macintosh now enable designers to create their own typefaces quickly and inexpensively. There are two levels of operation. The first, and by far the cheapest and quickest, is to work from an existing PostScript font using one of a number of software type-manipulation programs. These programs enable designers to manipulate the letters to suit the requirements of a job, stretching, bending, elongating, shrinking, compressing, and cutting, and performing a host of other techniques to alter the letters. Once one letter has been manipulated and the desired effect achieved, the programs match the rest of the alphabet to suit.

System's drawbacks

One of the drawbacks of this approach is that, once it has been created, the type can be output only in PostScript, which limits the potential of the design — it could not, for example, be used to create the vinyl letters on the sides of aircraft or vans. In addition, manipulating fonts in this way has to be done with extreme care from an aesthetic point of view: the potential for disaster is huge.

The major advantages of the process are cost — the programs are cheap — and time — an entire typeface font may take only a day to create.

The second kind of operation, the creation of completely new typefaces, and typefaces for output through non-PostScript language typesetters — those using Cora and Densy, for example — which tend to be top of the line, can also be accomplished on Macintoshes, and indeed Macintoshes have made the creation of new typefaces much more economic. However, only one or two programs are available — the Ikarus M from URW in Germany, for example — and the work requires a specialist. Moreover, while specialists will be more than happy to create new faces, they will not create a design for you that is based upon an existing typeface.

The main benefits of using type designers are the quality of work produced and the fact that the typeface can be output through any typesetter or imagesetter. The drawback is the cost: a designer will take about 150 hours to produce a new alphabet.

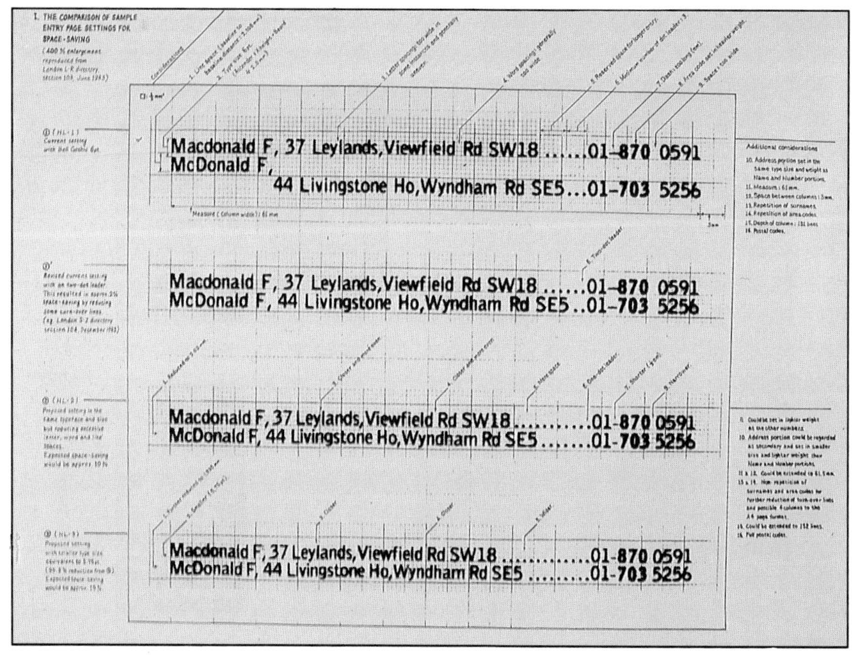

Type designing has many applications, not only in promotional work but also, as in this case, in the highly functional task of saving space in telephone directories. By designing a new typeface dedicated to this solution the agency was also able to provide the phone company with a substantial paper saving, since the new face meant more telephone numbers per page. The two lines of type at the top of the sheet are in the original face with the revised and condensed face below. The space saving meant that fewer lines turned.

jkI N65fg

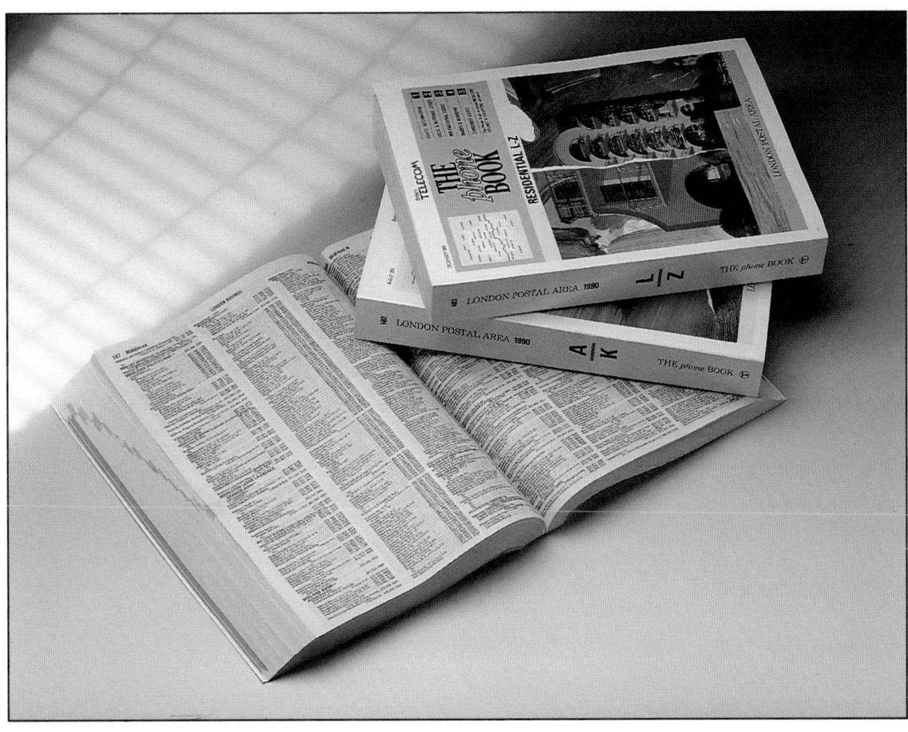

The refining of an early stage letter (**above**), done by hand, and (**top**) the final letter design, which allowed for more telephone numbers per page.

The finished result (**far right**) shows how in the residential listings the new pages have four columns instead of the original three (**right**) and more numbers per column. The net gain to this phone company was that for the London area it now only had to produce three phone books instead of four. Among the factors that had to be taken into account when designing the new face was the need to have different weightings in the business listings (**above right**).

270 Gold L — LONDON POSTAL AREA — Goldberger M 270

415 Price A — LONDON RESIDENTIAL — Price L 415

A finished piece from a book of sheet music (**above**).

Music typesetting can be produced using a computer (**right**). The advantages over conventional hand-setting are many: computer setting is quick and flexible; mistakes can be easily rectified; and any alterations carried out quickly.

COMPUTERIZED MUSIC SETTING
SCORES

Setting music, whether creatively for promotional work or for actual musical scores, is a complicated business and an area in which rules are difficult to find, because they are often broken as soon as they are made.

Music setting can be carried out by computer, and the new Macintosh-type units have programs that are quite capable of producing the annotations. It can also be set by hand, which is the traditional but dying method, or by transferring preprinted images, which is commonplace in the Far East. You could also, of course, create the music as a piece of artwork, although this would be a time-consuming process, and the result is unlikely to be accurate. Specialist music setters would generally be the best people to turn to, but many competent typesetters have some sort of music-setting facility on their systems, so if you need only a line or two for a creative piece, it is worth asking them first.

Font and "type" size

There is no limit to the size of type that can be used, although there is a standard size for musical scores. For creative work, however, any size is possible. There are three or four fonts that can be used. With computer-set music, which is now the primary production method, the Qwerty keyboard simply translates to musical symbols, so that the lowercase Q is a quarter note, the lowercase B is a flat note, and so on. The computer program will create the template, produce and position the notes and symbols automatically, and allow the lyrics to be input. Computer setting has great advantages over hand-setting: it is quick and flexible, mistakes can be easily corrected, and alterations can be carried out in no time. Corrections and alterations to hand-drawn music will usually mean starting all over again. Hand-drawn music does, however, have an individuality and offers more variety of style than the computer-set version, and this may be your best approach.

Scheduling time for music setting varies tremendously. If you want a single line for, say, an advertisement, you should be able to find someone who will produce it for you the same day on a computer or within a week by hand – if you are prepared to pay. Alterations and corrections will take as long. It might take up to 12 weeks to have an entire musical score set, although this could come down to a month during a slow period for the setter.

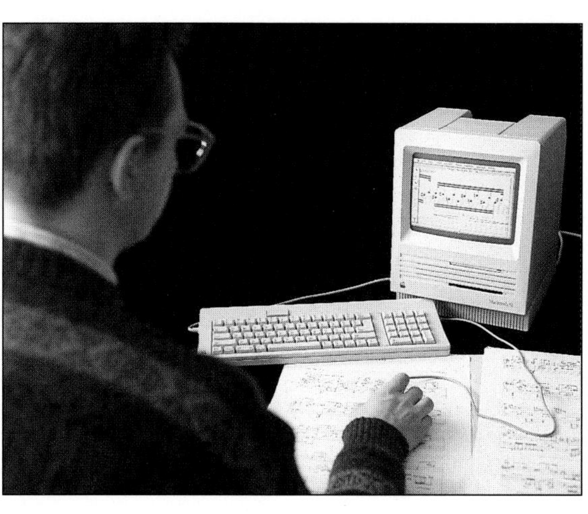

Other applications

Musical annotation is commonly used creatively in all sorts of promotional work, including advertisements, point-of-sale displays, book covers, posters, and packaging.

Relative costs

Using a music setter with a Macintosh-type computer will be cheaper than using a hand craftsperson. If your own typesetter has musical type on disk, this would be cheaper still, but accuracy may be a problem. Drawing music yourself as a piece of artwork is likely to take time and be more expensive in the long run, but if you are short of work for a day or two, it might prove to be an interesting project!

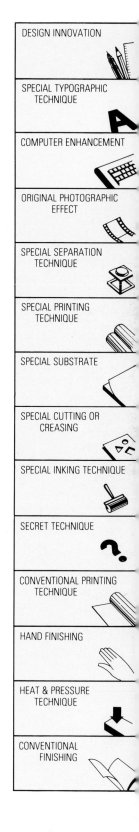

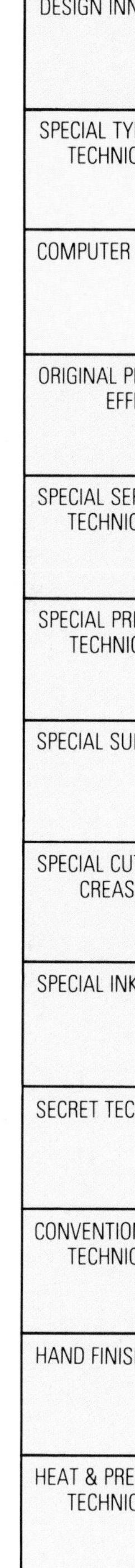

PRE-PRESS

IMAGESETTING PROMOTION

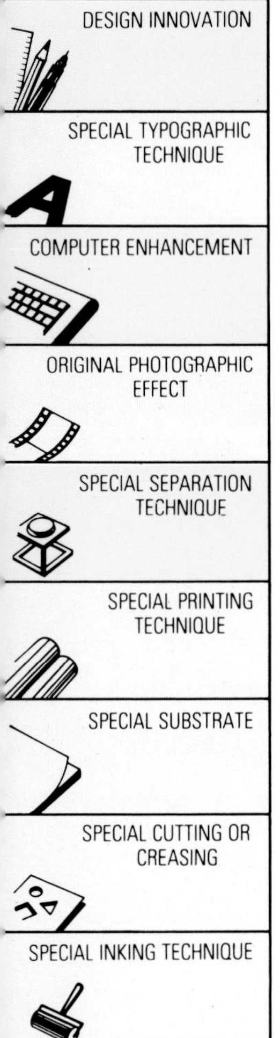

For many years the preserve of the scanner companies, electronic page composition (EPC) has now become available through the major typesetting vendors, and at a cheaper price. The systems are able to take in images through scanners and text through any wordprocessor, and manipulate the two, generally in DTP software packages. Imagesetting color systems may work in the primary colors, red, green, and blue, rather than the secondary printing colors, cyan, yellow, and magenta, although the digital information is converted to CYMK for output. (CYMK stands for cyan, yellow, magenta, and black.) Once manipulated, the color-separated films are output through the imagesetter. Proofing is by means of Cromalins or a direct thermal printer.

For the designer the advent of imagesetting color basically means cost savings on conventional EPC systems, and so provides opportunities to use color in areas where clients previously may have held back because of budget constraints. As well as handling the mechanical features of page composition, all the systems available can provide some sort of color retouching, masking, and cropping, produce tints and gradations, and color in their own text and tint areas. In addition, because the systems are open to many of the DTP graphics packages, their proponents claim that the potential for graphics is extremely high. At present the major drawback is that imagesetter systems do not pro-

Other applications

Imagesetting color still has some way to go before it will be used for the front page of *Vogue*, but for much brochure, pamphlet, and magazine work imageset color is satisfactory.

Relative costs

Cost is where imagesetting color scores. You should pay at most 50 percent of the comparable cost of using an EPC system, and possibly much less. This is entirely due to the fact that equipment is relatively inexpensive.

3 LETTERBOX 7 · MICKEY TAKES A BOW...

The seventh issue of Letterbox provided an ideal design and production problem for a test run on the LinoColor System. By its very nature, the magazine would stretch the system to the limits of its capabilities. The proof of the pudding lies within these pages and for those who wish to move into the next exciting stage of DTP we detail here the various stages of production.

• The Brief

Right from the start it was decided that the design of this issue should be approached from the standpoint of using the LinoColor System for the production of four-colour process work within the framework of desk top publishing.

The design had to reflect the problems of producing high quality process separations in conjunction with carefully considered typography to achieve a high standard of professionalism.

This meant incorporating as much colour work as possible along with vignetting, rotation, artwork scanning and to a lesser degree image manipulation.

• The Method

Page layouts and type specifications were produced and illustrative material prepared using Adobe Illustrator, Adobe Streamline and QuarkXPress. Illustrations varied from line art to 35mm and large format colour transparencies.

Working from the designer's layout and specifications the colour images were scanned in and manipulated as required, these files were then saved as TIFF for storage and EPS 5 for separation. The line art images were created in Illustrator or scanned in and converted from TIFF images into PostScript images using Streamline. All the elements were then placed into QuarkXPress and the page was built with text and images in place, initial proofs to the designer were produced using the ColorPrinter 30. Output was then produced on film positives from QuarkXPress through the Linotronic 330 using RIP 30. The films were then proofed and sent to the printers.

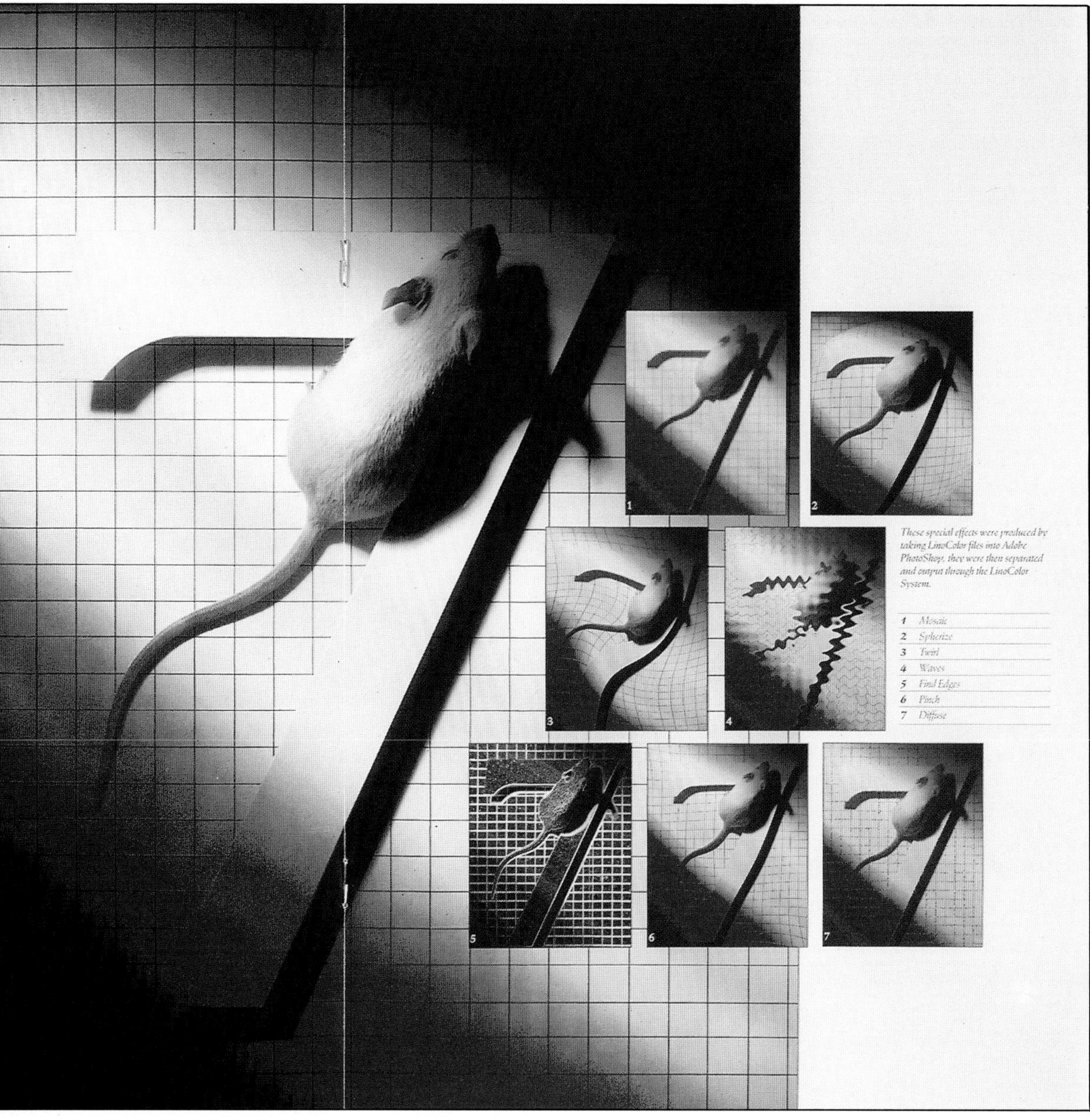

This promotional piece was produced at very low cost on DTP software, and output on an imagesetter. It includes vignettes and rotation and image manipulation, and the illustrations were input from scanned line art and 35mm and large format transparencies. The text was typeset, and the pages were made up on the DTP system before being output through the imagesetter in the four film separations. This whole technique is dramatically different from traditional methods of producing color pages, and it should mean that designers have the opportunity of including more color pages for lower prices in their work.

duce color to the same extremely high quality as conventional systems.

Scheduling times should not differ too widely from those required by conventional EPC systems.

COMPUTER GRAPHICS POSTER

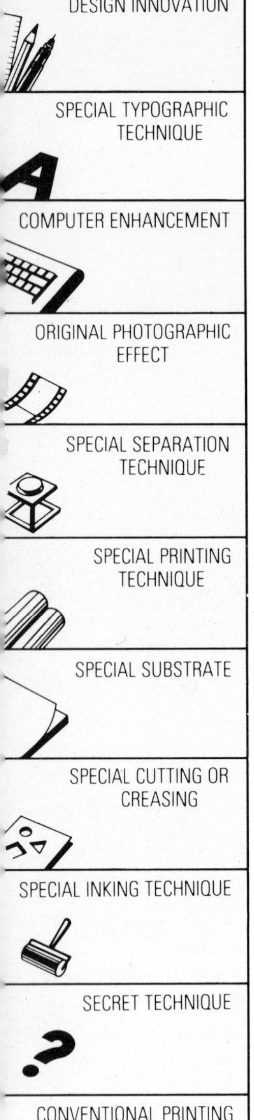

Graphics generated on a computer such as those produced by Quantel and Barco, give the designer an immensely powerful tool. In essence the systems are merely digitized tool-boxes, but they provide the designer with every possible creative tool, including airbrushing, paint, chalk, stencils, and cut-and-paste libraries. Not only can designers use them to create images from scratch, they can also introduce outside information, transparencies, and the like. Unlike EPC systems, which are mainly mechanical manipulation systems, computer graphics systems are largely creative, and they work in designers' terminology through the use of keypads, rolling switches, and pressure-sensitive pens. In addition, they work in real time, so when you command an instruction, it happens on screen.

Realizing the system's potential

The creative potential of computer graphics is enormous and virtually unlimited. It is true to say that there is nothing that cannot be produced on computers and much creative work that can be produced in no other way. It is possible to mix everything together, and complicated designs can be changed at the touch of a button; images can be merged together, and totally new images created out of unlikely materials.

Scheduling time is far shorter than with conventional creative work. A system should be able to produce a design in a fifth of the time needed for comparable conventional work. Beware, however, the creative potential of a computer graphics system. Because it operates in real time, the art director can sit beside the designer and consider work he had not previously thought possible, and that may take longer. Working with a system becomes addictive.

The unique advantages of computer graphics systems are the speed, the cost reductions, the real-time operation, the resolution, and the facility it offers to the designer to produce anything that exists within his or her imagination.

Other applications

Apart from advertising work, graphics computers are being used increasingly on such work as record album covers. In addition, they are able to preconstruct as yet uncompleted products — for example, automobile manufacturers may have a mock-up of their new model but are not in a position to photograph it in all its finished, gleaming splendor. A graphics computer can not only construct the final result but also go on to create a picture of someone driving it in an alpine forest.

Relative costs

Graphics systems bureaus are currently charging between $450 and $525 an hour. However, you can expect the design to be created in anything from a third to a tenth of the time it would take to produce conventionally.

This collage poster was designed for a color separation house to show the capabilities of its computerized graphics system. The machine-like image is of the printing process — from photographing the mechanical at the top, separating the colors, inking the printing rollers through funnels, to printing the (enlarged) dot at the bottom. All the imagery and lettering were generated on a computer, and the techniques involved included cloning, reflecting, ghosting, and washing with color.

Photography and Design: Thomas Wedell and Nancy Skolos, Skolos, Wedell + Raynor, Inc. 1988 · PaintBox Designer: Yu Ling Wang, Laserscan, Inc.

Left and **Below left** These slides were output on traditional slide-making equipment. The award-winning "user friendly" slide (**left**) was produced in three stages. First, image capture through a VHS video camera included the designer's hand, a VDU monitor, and a carefully lit wine glass. This took an hour. Then the separate images were manipulated together, the final design being made of five layers of images. The processes used included masking, airbrushing, brushing and blending, and the manipulation took around five hours. It took around 30 minutes to output the final result in vector file format. The slide (**below left**) was created mechanically through 15 multiple exposures, and it took eight hours of imaging on the fastest camera in Europe! It was designed for a software house in Texas.

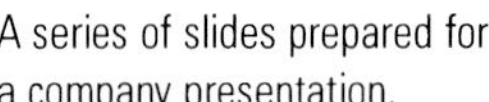

A series of slides prepared for a company presentation.

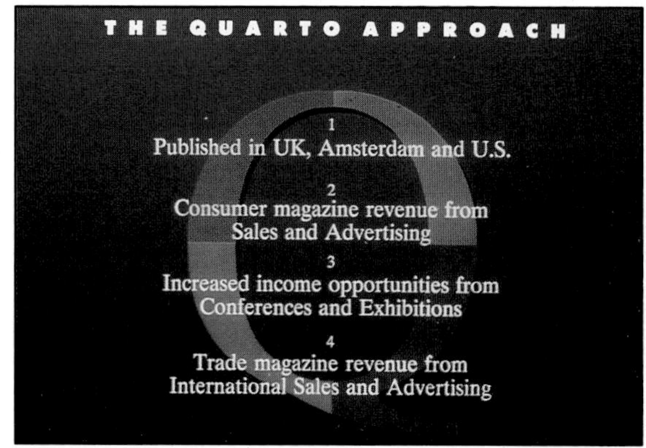

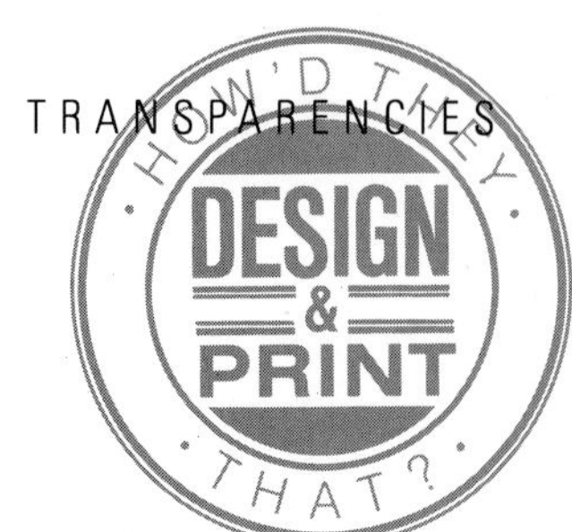

COMPUTERIZED TRANSPARENCIES
PRESENTATION

Until recently transparency slides had to be produced mechanically, by time-consuming hand and camera operations, or electronically, with slidemakers, which are extremely expensive. Now, however, transparency slides can be designed far more easily thanks to desktop computers, although it is important to realize that there are limits to what can be achieved.

The software programs available provide relatively easy and cheap design facilities, and a decent desktop package should be able to produce anything that more conventional systems can come up with. Once the design has been created on the computer, the slide can be produced either in-house or at a bureau on a slidewriter.

A 16.8-million-color palette

The best software programs give a palette of 16.8 million colors, and there are really no limitations on the creative potential of the new systems, so long, that is, as they use PostScript operating language. As well as allowing a wider package input, this also enables all the PostScript fonts to be used. Non-PostScript slide programs cannot handle PostScript fonts and will only output the three font families — Times, Helvetica, and Courier — built into the slidewriter.

Apart from the creative time that is spent on screen, the slidewriter takes between 5 and 15 minutes to output a slide, depending on its complexity. The output slidewriter is limited in that it can produce only 35mm slides, while traditional slide producers can be used to obtain slides of different sizes, including 5×4in (127×102mm). In addition, slidewriter resolution is 4000 lpi (lines per inch), compared to the 8000 lpi that can be achieved by the traditional systems. However, for the purpose of 35mm slides this makes no practicable difference, since 35mm slide film cannot support a resolution of much more than 4000 lpi.

Other applications

Applications for slidewriting are many and varied, the most popular being for business and organizational presentations and for marketing pitches. They can also be used for art exhibits and other circumstances where a more creative approach is needed.

Relative costs

Slides produced on a DTP/slidewriter system cost a fraction of those produced by the traditional methods, and although they are obviously more expensive than those produced by hand, the process is faster and offers more creative potential. If you are producing more than 20 or so slides each week, it would probably be worthwhile to bring the whole operation in-house, rather than to use a bureau for slidewriting. Using a non-PostScript program will save a considerable sum, as it obviates the need for an RIP interface, but the limitations are serious.

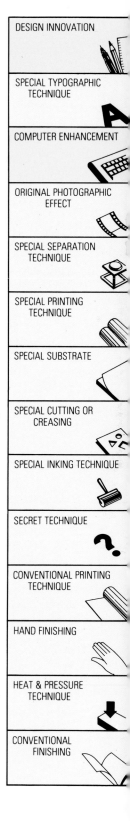

THE FUTURE
Quarto are committed to continued growth
through dynamic development of core
business and acquisition

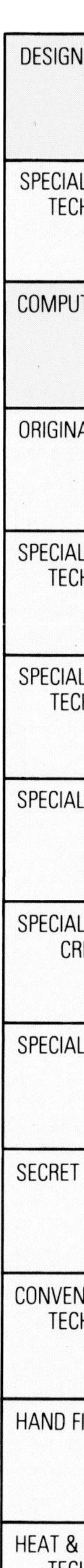

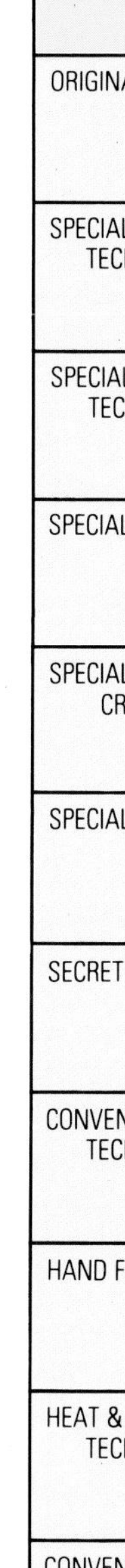

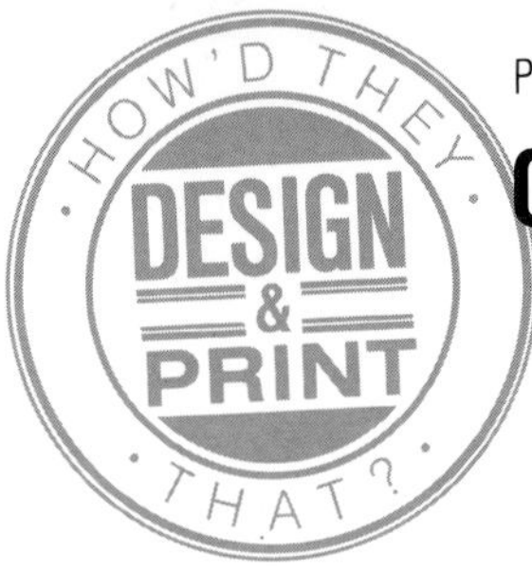

COMPUTERIZED DESIGN COMIC BOOK

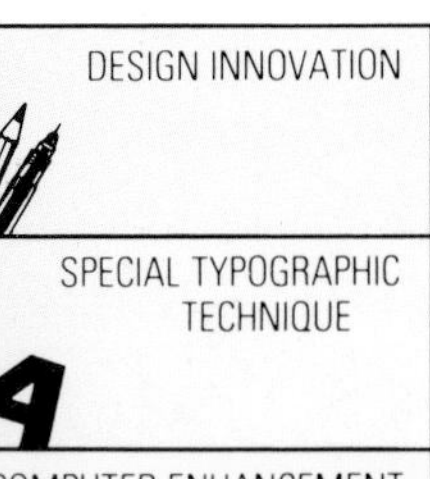

DESIGN INNOVATION

SPECIAL TYPOGRAPHIC TECHNIQUE

COMPUTER ENHANCEMENT

ORIGINAL PHOTOGRAPHIC EFFECT

SPECIAL SEPARATION TECHNIQUE

SPECIAL PRINTING TECHNIQUE

SPECIAL SUBSTRATE

SPECIAL CUTTING OR CREASING

SPECIAL INKING TECHNIQUE

SECRET TECHNIQUE

CONVENTIONAL PRINTING TECHNIQUE

HAND FINISHING

HEAT & PRESSURE TECHNIQUE

CONVENTIONAL FINISHING

The advent of computers has made designing comic books infinitely easier. Now, instead of hours of tedious coloring, computers can be programmed to fill in areas of color in an instant. The computers needed are not necessarily expensive, either.

Comic books are traditionally printed by letterpress, but this is dying out now; by flexography, which has come to dominate in recent years; or by web offset, either heat-set or cold-set. Flexography is the cheapest process, and it certainly gives good enough results. Cold-set offset is the next least expensive, and heat-set lithography is for really classy-looking comics. Sheet-fed lithography can also be used for short runs.

Coding for color

Comics are usually drawn at either 150 or 200 percent of the final printed size. The story is written, and outlines are pencil drawn and scanned into the computer. The colors are then determined, and each area of the comic is given a color code. As soon as the appropriate key is pressed, the area floods with the relevant color, along with all the other areas coded for the same color.

The skill in this process is getting the black outlines correct at the start. Unlike the colored areas, which can be changed ad infinitum, the outlines cannot be altered later. The colors used in comics tend to look very flat, partly because of the poor quality of paper used, and partly because of the

This comic was produced by a computer. The initial outlines were drawn by hand, then scanned into the computer, which colored in areas according to a number assigned by the designer. Captain America's gloves, for example, would be number 3, which is a particular shade of red. The time-saving potential is huge and is matched by the cost savings, added to which the equipment necessary is not overly expensive — and you thought it was the jokes that made comic publishers smile! When the design is finished, a thermal proof is taken of each page, although this is used only to check position, not as an accurate color guide. However, the front cover is treated differently. A better quality proof is required, and it is often printed by a different process, so that while the inner pages may be printed by flexography, the cover is often printed by litho. Flexography gives a much duller-looking print.

Other applications

Comic production processes are primarily used for children's and adult fantasy stories. Comics can also be useful tools for conveying information – from government health agencies to population groups with low literacy levels, for example. They can also be used successfully for promotional work.

Relative costs

Comics are relatively cheap to produce, mainly because of the low cost of the paper and the flexographic printing process.

flexographic printing process. Unless you are specifying a coated stock for heat-set lithography, you will do well to avoid aiming for bright images; concentrate instead on making the best of downbeat colors. If you are designing an advertisement for insertion in a comic, make sure you know which stock will be used with which printing process before you begin, and create your design accordingly. Whichever process is used, you should have six or eight colors at your disposal, and double that number if the press is run again, but that brings potential problems with register.

Scheduling time for a comic to print should only be a week or two, but allow a further three weeks to move from scratch to film for platemaking. The minimum run length varies according to the process – for flexography it will be around 20,000.

Holograms and foil blocking are perfectly acceptable in comic production, although laminating and varnishing are not really suitable for most comics, because the quality of paper used is not good enough to support either process. However, if a coated paper is used, laminating and varnishing are perfectly possible.

COMPUTERIZED FORM DESIGN STATIONERY

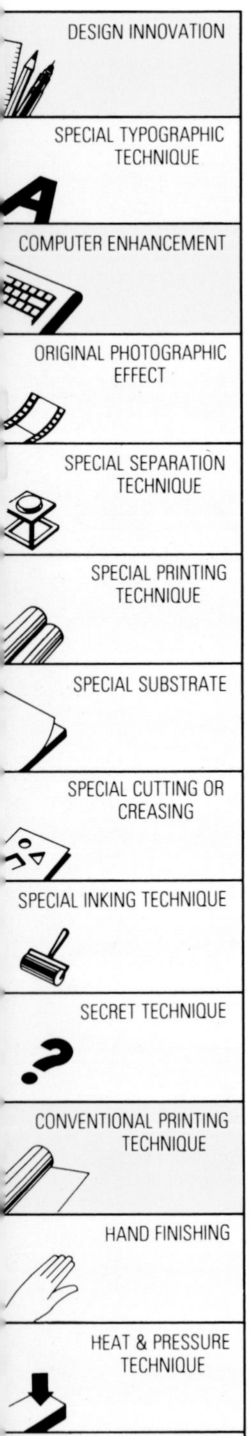

Designing business forms may not be the sexiest work in the world, but electronic design systems, such as those manufactured by Purup and Disc, offer tremendous opportunities for creativity. The systems are electronic work-stations with software specifically written for the design of business forms. Designs can be created, viewed, and changed quickly by using keypads and color monitors, and the systems work in both line art and process color. They enable designers to create work that would not be possible by other means.

Creative potential

The systems can be used to create designs from scratch, or they can receive digital data from almost anywhere. They can create text, and every imaginable tint and vignette in every percentage combination of screen rulings and screen angles. Facilities include mask cutting, electronic pasteup, zooming and cropping, and it is possible to draw freehand, trace, scan, color elements, distort, manipulate, bend, twist, and rotate. The package should also include a two-way dispro feature which counteracts the effects of artwork stretching when it is wrapped around a printing cylinder. A thermal proofer will generate proofs and, although it is not exactly color accurate, it does enable the designer to view different color combinations on hard copy.

Electronic systems should take around one tenth of the time needed for hand and camera production. Moreover, they give the option of changing a tint at the flick of a switch, while changing a tint under line art or text on a conventional business form would mean that everything had to be remade. In addition, one or two of the systems now offer direct-to-plate production, which cuts out the film stage altogether, thereby saving further time and money.

This business form for a German electronics company was generated entirely on computer. The recipient of the form is immediately aware of the nature of the company's business, through the company utilizing a space which is dead without some kind of design. The colors of the logo in the top right-hand corner are tremendously strong for this type of paper, and represent quite a breakthrough. However, the softer colors have been retained for the main part of the illustration, where type for each order or invoice will be overprinted.

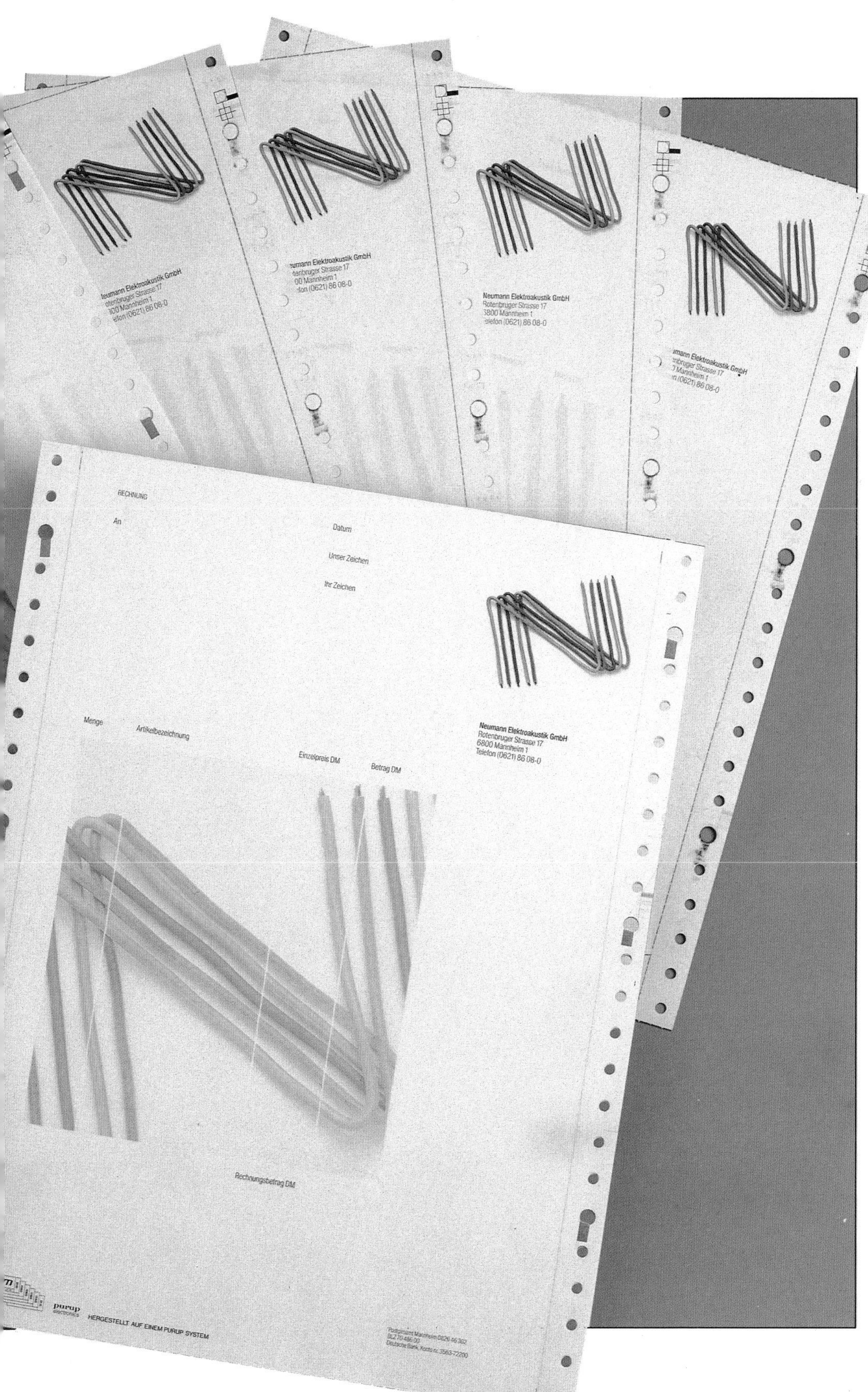

Other applications

Computerized business form systems can also be used to originate labels, packaging, cartons, metal decoration, and plastic credit cards, and also heat-fusible transfers for textile-printed silk screen, and check and security prints.

Relative costs

While a cutting knife, pen set, and camera are cheap in terms of capital outlay, electronic systems save around 90 percent of the time needed to create designs. In addition, they open up areas of design unavailable with conventional tools.

BICYCLES
CYCLES MOTOS TRICARS "GRIFFON"
The cult of the dream machine
The bicycle has developed to become an essential part of leisure, whether as the vehicle of romance ridden along country lanes, or the machine of sport, object of one of the most famous sporting events, the Tour de France. In today's green age, however, the bicycle is taking on a new significance: as a clean, cheap and efficient method of transport.
WRITTEN BY NICK SANDERS
UpDate
GREEN PAGES
Incorporating World's ecological pages with contributions from leading environment societies.
Earthwatch 89/91
Conservation Foundation 93
World Opinion 95
Fats waller in England
Tourist boycott to save the turtle
THEFT OF THE NIGHT
Hebridean galley sets sail from Galway
APRIL 1991
£2.00
WORLD
MAGAZINE
FIGHT FOR THE THRONE OF NEPAL
SHAKE UP AT THE NATURAL HISTORY MUSEUM
WALES AS IT ONCE WAS
NATIONAL PARKS OF SOUTH AFRICA
THE THREAT OF PLANT THIEVES
EARTHWATCH UPDATE AND CONSERVATION FOUNDATION
MIRROR OF INDIA
WORLD A BBC MAGAZINE
PEOPLE, PLACES, WILDLIFE, TRAVEL AND THE ENVIRONMENT

ELECTRONIC PAGE COMPOSITION
MAGAZINE

Electronic page composition (EPC) systems are the means by which most pages in magazines, brochures, and catalogs are produced. EPC systems are actually composed of several computers in a variety of configurations and levels, but there are always three basic units: an input scanner for digitizing artwork and photographs; a central work-station at which the images are manipulated and pages compiled; and an output recorder, which exposes the digital information in halftone form onto film for platemaking.

Systems' function

The two prime functions of EPC systems are electronic repro and page composition. Electronic repro is discussed elsewhere in this book. Electronic page composition includes the creation or, if appropriate, the retrieval of the page grid, the automatic dropping in of rules, borders, running heads or feet, and folios, and the creation and insertion of tints and vignettes. Retouched illustrations can be dropped into place, and the entire page can be output in its four process-color format, cyan, yellow, magenta, and black.

Electronic page composition can now be carried out extremely quickly because personal computers can be used to prepare the page makeup, which can be transmitted in digital form straight into the EPC system, where the pictures can be dropped in. In addition, if you output through an imagesetter, text and graphics can be produced together, which eliminates two stages of integration and reduces time and cost yet further. You should be able to ask for, and receive, 24-hour turnaround in most cities of the world. The use of an EPC system combined with a PC has dramatically reduced the lead time for some applications, including packaging, from six weeks to six days.

Relative Costs

Until comparatively recently EPC systems were extremely expensive. This was largely because using the same system to make up pages and to retouch illustrations meant that valuable time was spent on what is, essentially, a mundane task. Now, however, the advent of Macintosh- and PC-entry to the systems enables pages to be made on the low-level computer first, so that the EPC is used only for what it is best at, retouching. In addition, an entire new breed of EPC systems on off-the-shelf computers has recently been introduced, making the cost of the systems considerably cheaper.

Other applications

EPC systems are used to create pages in a host of areas, including magazines, brochures, and catalogs, as well as being used extensively for packaging.

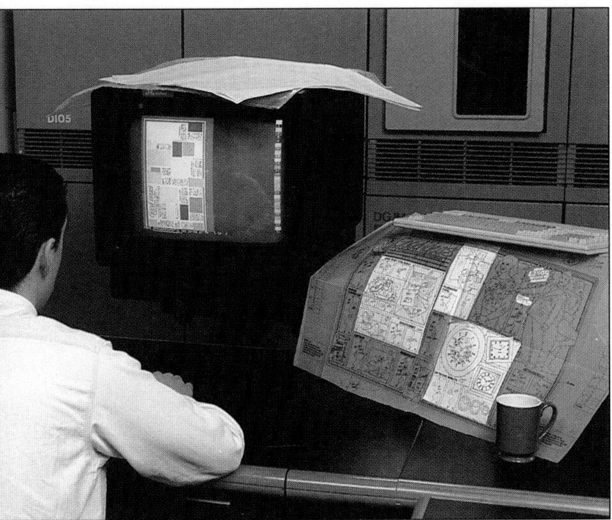

Pages and a cover from a high-quality magazine (**far right**) put together using an electronic page composition system. An EPC system in action (**right**). Such systems save time and money without compromising the look of the finished product.

DESIGN INNOVATION
SPECIAL TYPOGRAPHIC TECHNIQUE
COMPUTER ENHANCEMENT
ORIGINAL PHOTOGRAPHIC EFFECT

SPECIAL SEPARATION TECHNIQUE

SPECIAL PRINTING TECHNIQUE
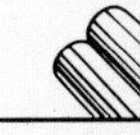
SPECIAL SUBSTRATE
SPECIAL CUTTING OR CREASING

SPECIAL INKING TECHNIQUE

SECRET TECHNIQUE

CONVENTIONAL PRINTING TECHNIQUE

HAND FINISHING

HEAT & PRESSURE TECHNIQUE

CONVENTIONAL FINISHING

PRE-PRESS

DESKTOP PAGE DESIGN
CORPORATE IDENTITY/PROMOTION

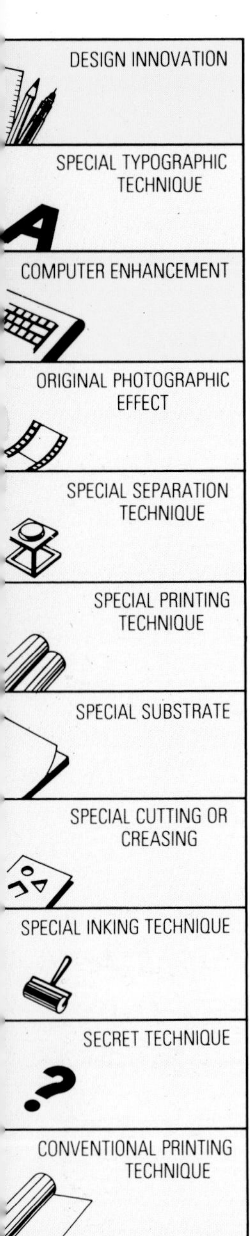

During the 1980s most color separation houses installed electronic page composition (EPC) systems. These are highly elaborate and technically brilliant pieces of equipment that cost a fortune and sent more than a few color separators to the wall trying to meet the repayments, but they did permit faster production and offer more creative design possibilities than the previous handcrafted methods of page composition.

Designers used to create artwork, send the finished artwork, sized transparencies, and page grids to the color separation house where it would all be compiled into one complete page, with the pictures and colors manipulated to a fantastic degree. The whole process was very time-consuming and expensive, with the designer to-ing and fro-ing between the studio and the color separation house to ensure that everything went according to plan. Then DTP systems came along, enabling designers to make up electronic pages so that they could send a print-out to the color separator. These electronic pages were in low resolution, but eventually someone had the bright idea of linking the two systems, and now each of the big four EPC manufacturers has a digital link between the designer's DTP system and the EPC system.

This means that the designer can create a page on the DTP system, working with transparencies that have either been input on low resolution into his DTP system or have come from the scanner by means of a high-to-low-resolution converter. These can be positioned and manipulated in low format resolution on screen, and a thermal proof obtained. Then, when the designer is satisfied, the whole file can be sent by modem or by disk to the color separator. The EPC system accepts all the digital information, automatically positions the high-resolution transparencies, and outputs onto film.

In addition to the terrific cost savings in all of this, there are also large time savings, since the to-ing and fro-ing between design agency and color separation house is eliminated because the data can be sent both ways — once the data is on the EPC system it can be sent back to the designer for viewing before being output. The DTP/EPC links allow the designer to create work on screen until he or she is perfectly satisfied, view a proof, and then rest easy — well, almost.

Relative costs

One of the great advantages of the DTP/EPC link is cost. It dramatically reduces expenditure and time on work already in hand, and using a low-cost DTP system, which in all probability costs one percent of the price the EPC system, gives greater potential for including color in future products.

The images on this spread show the flexibility and creative potential of DTP design, particularly in the area of type manipulation. The image below is for a company brochure; stationery for another company is shown right.

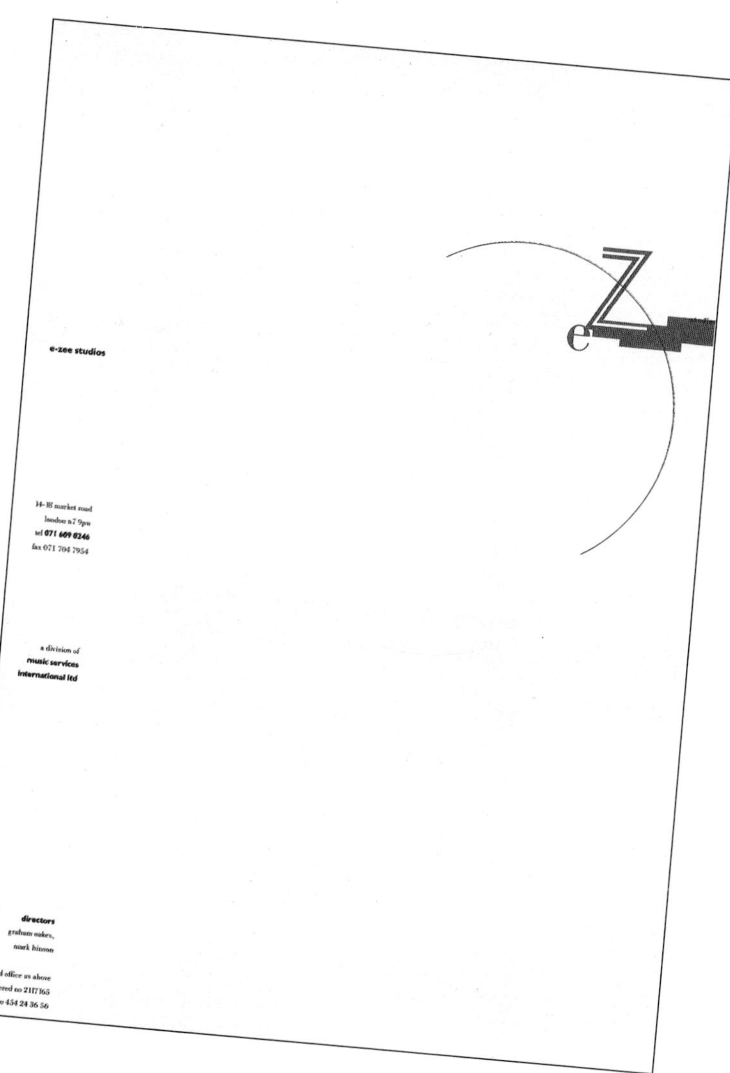
e-zee studios
14-18 market road
london n7 9pw
tel 071 609 0246
fax 071 704 7954
a division of
music services
international ltd
directors
graham oakes,
mark hinson
registered office as above
registered no 2117165
vat no 454 24 36 56

facilities
sound
excellence

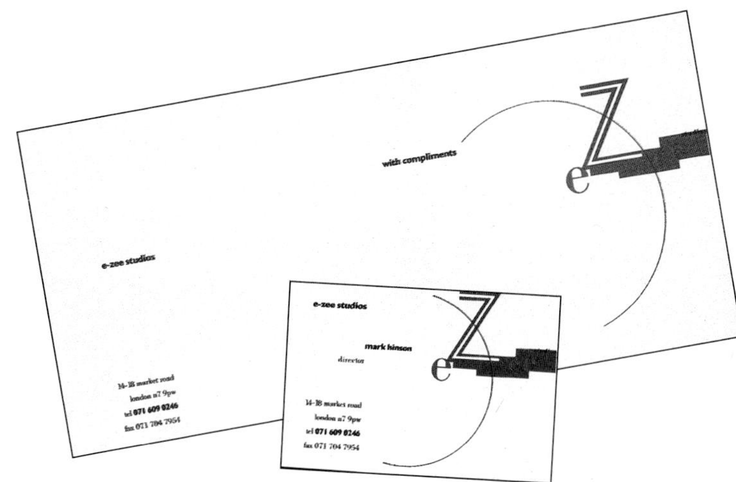
with compliments
e-zee studios
14-18 market road
london n7 9pw
tel 071 609 0246
fax 071 704 7954
mark hinson
director

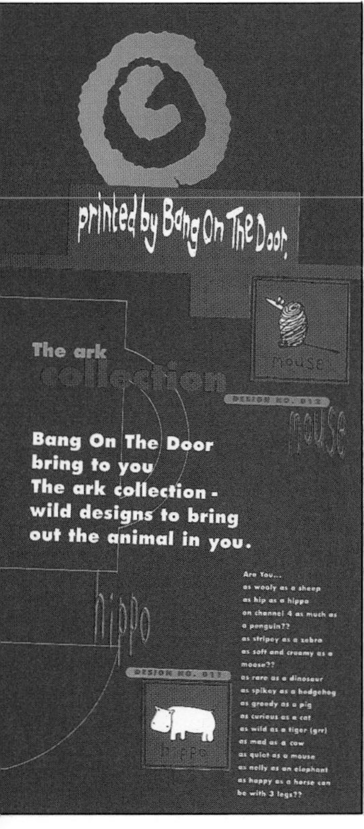
printed by Bang On The Door
The ark collection
mouse
Bang On The Door bring to you The ark collection - wild designs to bring out the animal in you.
hippo

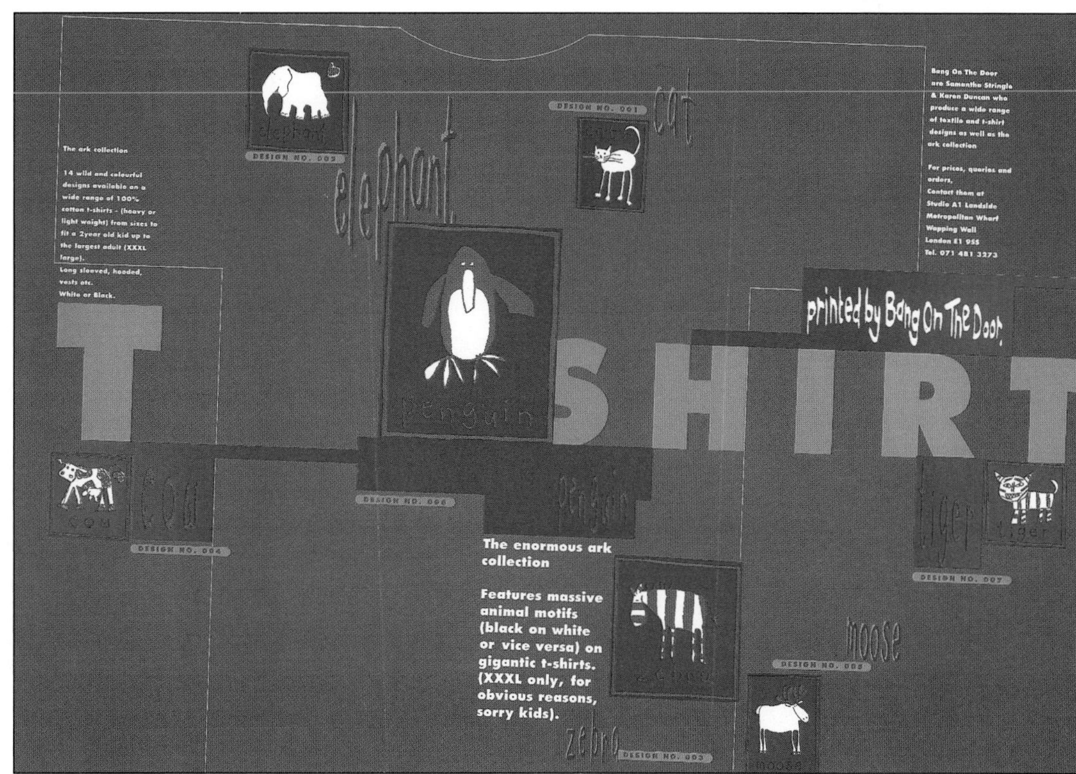
The ark collection
14 wild and colourful designs available on a wide range of 100% cotton t-shirts - (heavy or light weight) from sizes to fit a 2year old kid up to the largest adult (XXXL large).
Long sleeved, hooded, vests etc.
White or Black.
elephant
cat
penguin
T SHIRT
printed by Bang On The Door
The enormous ark collection
Features massive animal motifs (black on white or vice versa) on gigantic t-shirts. (XXXL only, for obvious reasons, sorry kids).
tiger
moose
zebra

SECTION TWO

On press

Putting ink on paper, board, or plastic is the crux of print production, and understanding the ways in which this apparently straightforward process can be achieved is a major factor in the success of most leading designers.

There are many different types of printing process, each of which has its own particular applications. Each, too, has its own peculiarities, which must be borne in mind while the design is planned and executed. If, as you work on a design, you are aware of the potential and limitations of print processes you will score in terms of both creativity and cost.

This section looks at all printing processes, ancient and modern, as well as considering some out-of-the-ordinary processes. Although the press itself has not changed as dramatically as pre-press equipment in the last few years, the quality that can be achieved and the quantities that can be successfully handled have increased steadily. If you read the pages that follow carefully, you will begin to appreciate the various printing processes and the particular applications of each.

RUPERT'S
SAINT·LOUIS
SPARKLING HERBAL MULTIVITAMIN DRINK
PURDEY'S
elixir vitæ
25cl
SPARKLING HERBAL MULTIVITAMIN DRINK
PURDEY'S
elixir vitæ
25cl
ADELE PALMER
National Gallery
TRAFALGAR SQU.
DUNCANN ST.
CHARING CROSS
cabcharge
ABC 5678
CHRISTMAS
CLOTHES SHOW
GREAT COATS & CATSUITS...
TARTANS & TRAINERS...
DRESSING HAIR...
JOHN BARNES & NELLIE BOSWELL...
WIN TWO CARS...
A FLAT STOMACH IN 15 DAYS!
FREE!
PRETTY POLLY STOCKINGS
WORTH £1.35

LETTERPRESS LABELS/PROMOTION/PACKAGING

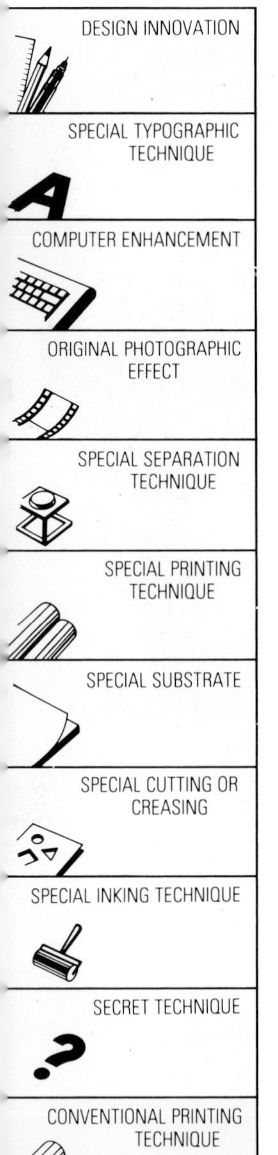

Until about 15 years ago letterpress was the printing process most widely used throughout the world. Although it has now been surpassed by lithography in most countries, letterpress is being used increasingly for the special effects it can produce and its inherent flexibility.

To print traditional letterpress, lines of type produced by hot metal are placed in a chase, or page format, and laid on a press. Ink is applied to the surface, the excess wiped off and the substrate passed over the raised type, with the ink being transferred from the type to the substrate.

Letterpress offers typography of a quality that many would argue is not available with computerized typesetting and lithography. This is because typefaces were initially designed for letterpress printing, and as they have been transferred to computer setting there have had to be some modifications to their appearance. As a general rule, type printed by letterpress is quite distinctive to the trained eye: it is sharper and more solid looking than litho-produced work. In addition, line work printed by letterpress is claimed to look better than when it is reproduced by litho because the ink is pushed gently onto the substrate, it spreads a little when the impression is made, and there is usually a thicker film of ink. However, it is not usually possible to reproduce halftones to the same degree of quality as those printed by litho.

Another advantage of letterpress is that it offers the facility for very late changes to the text; a line of type can be taken out of the chase and replaced with another line while it is on press. With lithography, the whole platemaking process has to be repeated.

The pre-press production time is around the same as for lithography, but the traditional presses are far slower, producing only a fifth or a sixth of the amount of work in the same time. The minimum press run is one; the maximum can be hundreds of thousands. It is possible to print letterpress onto any paper or board and, with care, onto some plastics. Any post-printing operation — varnishing, laminating, or foil blocking, for example — can be carried out on letterpress printed work.

Letterpress is also widely used now for the production of labels for bottles and cartons. In this case the plate is not the traditional metal but a synthetic substance. The great advantage of printing labels by letterpress is that the printed labels all wind around in a roll, which lends itself to final application processes.

The labels used on this award-winning range of packaging were printed by letterpress **(left)**. The background was printed in Pantone yellow; process magenta was printed on top of the yellow to create the red type, and process cyan was overprinted to create the green. The illustrations were printed solid to fit. The four packages at the front were printed by lithography, and the effects achieved by the two processes had to match as closely as possible.

This promotional item (**right**), which was designed for a craft organization, was printed from both metal and wood type in Gill. It took seven printings to achieve the final result.

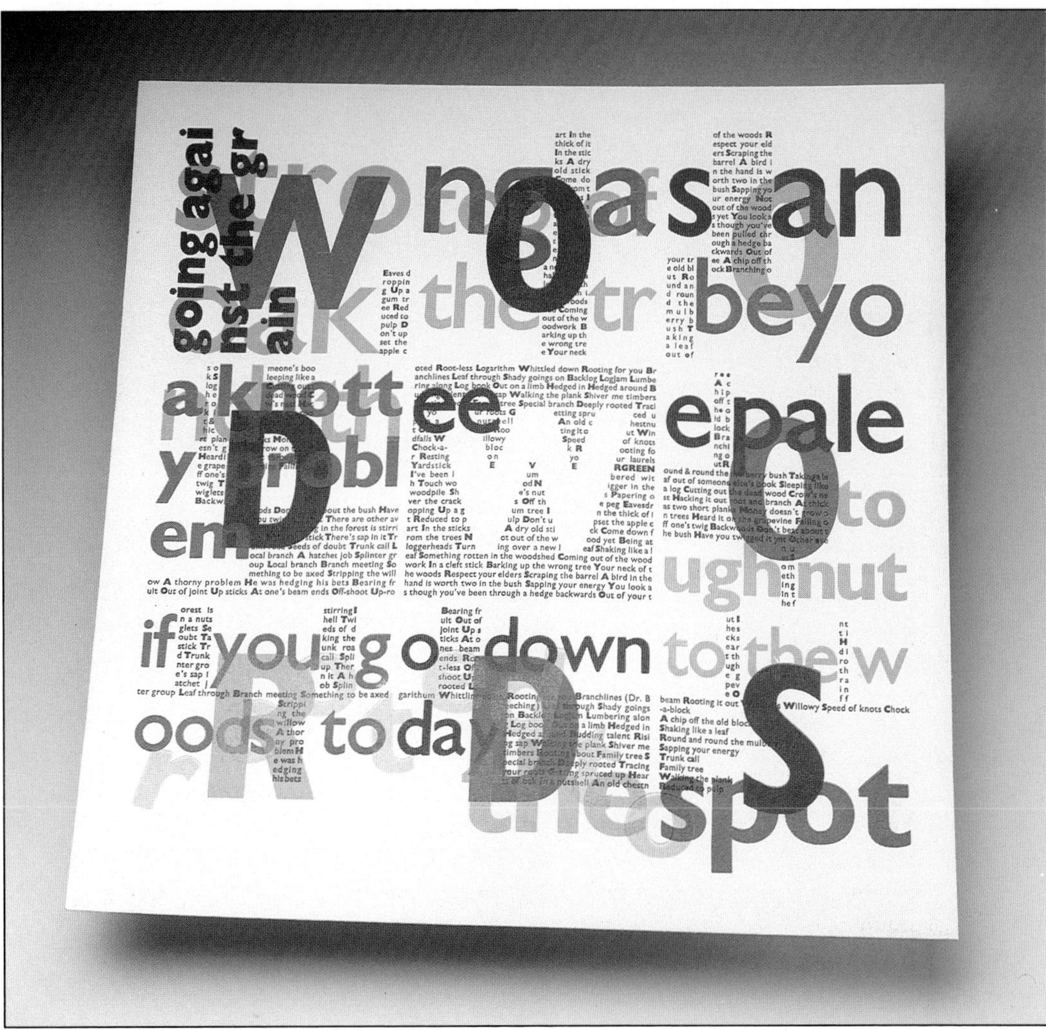

Specifying letterpress means that, with a few modern exceptions, you will be using the typefaces in the format for which they were originally designed. This tends to give a better quality appearance to the type than can be achieved with computerized typesetting, which uses digitized faces that have, inevitably, lost something of the original in translation. The quality of the printed letters of this Creed (**below**), for example, will have type purists drooling. It was printed by letterpress in two colors with wood and hand-set metal type. The Creed was actually designed to wrap around church candles, and it was printed on glassine, a glossy, transparent substrate.

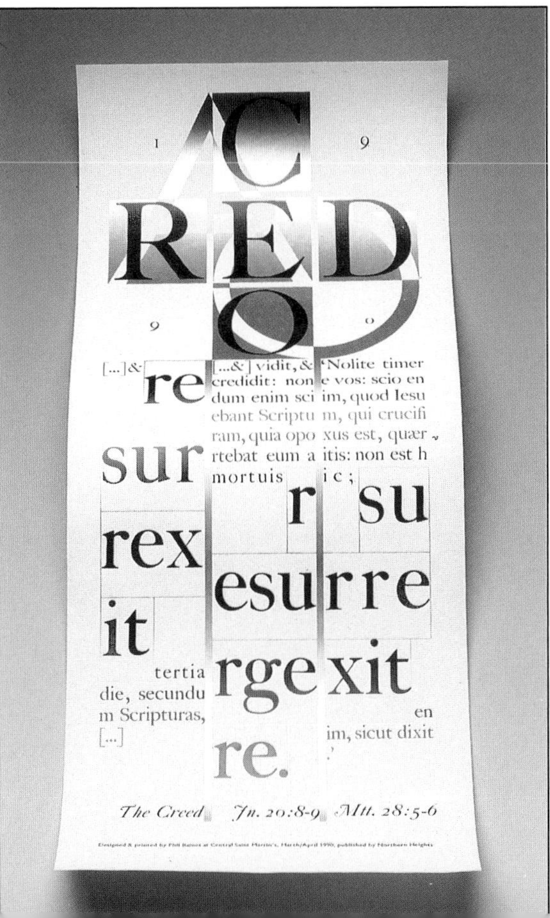

Other applications

Letterpress is especially suitable for producing work with large amounts of text, such as books and journals. It is also invaluable for brochures and booklets such as those produced by enthusiasts and societies where the aim is to achieve a "craft" feel, and to get away from a mass-produced effect. Promotional material is also given a quality feel by the use of letterpress, although it is not, of course, suitable for color work.

Relative costs

The production costs of letterpress printing vary, and the same product may cost more or less than litho. In the main, letterpress printing is now only carried out by small printing companies that are enthusiastic about their craft, and not all are prepared to take outside designs. However, it is unlikely that costs will be a stumbling block.

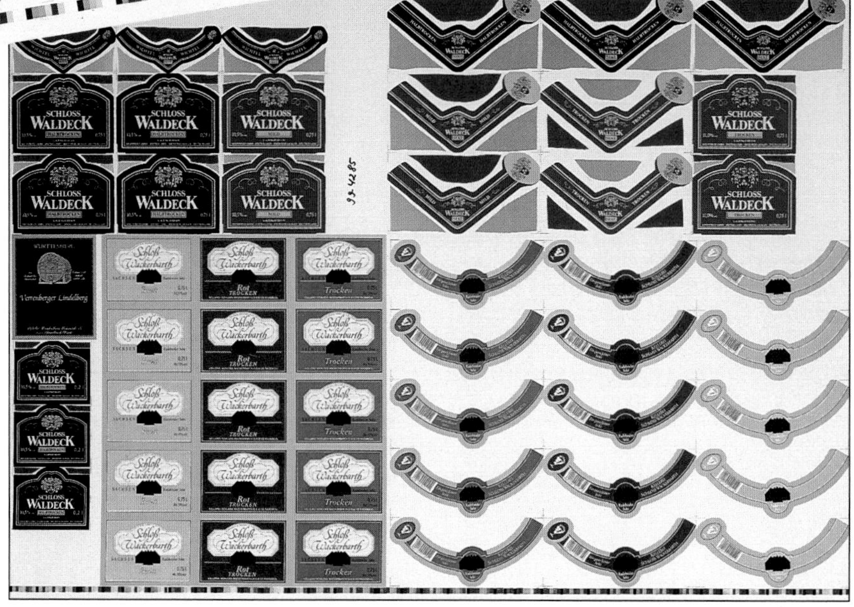

These running sheets of labels have been printed using sheet-fed gravure. The results are an excellent demonstration of the advantages of sheet-fed gravure, which allows for intricate designs using impressive effects such as pearlescent, gold, silver, and metallic inks.

SHEET-FED GRAVURE LABELS

Using sheet-fed gravure enables the designer to create a host of impressive looking finishes by adding special effects including golds, silvers, pearlescents, and metallic inks. In addition, new materials are regularly being introduced, including the Iriodins, which overprint inks and give such effects as gold and metal lusters, silver white pigments, and interference – that is, the ink looks a different color depending on the angle from which it is viewed.

Adding high-quality finishes

Adding high-quality finishes through sheet-fed gravure printing was not fully viable for many years because of the high cost of the gravure cylinder that carries the printed image. However, a breakthrough by a printing–plate manufacturer now allows synthetic wrap-around plates to be used to carry the ink, and these make the process efficient.

Until now the alternatives to sheet-fed gravure were bronzing for gold and silver, and silk-screen printing for pearlescents and metallic inks. Bronzing is not a particularly accurate method; it is very messy, and it is also more expensive, while silk screening is slow and can be inconsistent.

Sheet-fed gravure, on the other hand, gives a totally consistent effect over the whole run length. It is fast in production, it enables the most intricate designs to be used, and it is probably the most inexpensive way of putting special finishes on a product, depending, of course, on the run length. The maximum print run is claimed to be more than one million, while the minimum depends on how much you want to pay per unit; for runs of less than 500 it may well be prudent to use silk screen. A sheet-fed gravure finish can be added to virtually any other piece of print, although there may be a few problems printing on to screen-printed stock.

The scheduling time for sheet-fed gravure is similar to that required for offset litho. Once the artwork has left the designer it is simply a matter of making a negative, exposing it on to the plate, and wrapping the plate around the cylinder.

Sheet-fed gravure can be used on a range of surfaces, and it should also be able to print on to plastics, although this is more difficult and depends on the solvents in the ink, because the wrong type would destroy the plastic.

Other applications

The added-value finishes available through the use of sheet-fed gravure can be used for a wide range of applications, generally in areas where the packaging needs to be impressive and expensive looking. Among the most obvious areas are cigarette packs, drinks labels, candy boxes, cosmetic containers, promotional packages such as those used at Christmas, and even the highest quality stationery for both business or personal use.

Relative costs

Sheet-fed gravure is a relatively inexpensive method of adding special finishes: in 1990 a plate cost around $525. Although silk screen may be selected for reasons of cost for very short runs, the process has drawbacks. From the point of view of the designer, and certainly for a run of anything over a few hundred, sheet-fed gravure is the more cost-efficient process.

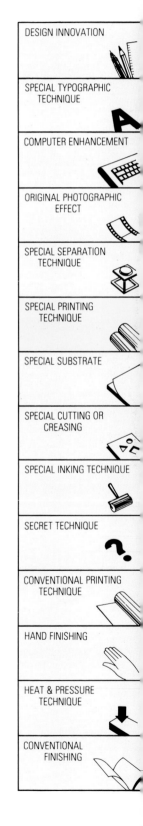

ROTARY GRAVURE PACKAGING/MAGAZINE

Rotary gravure is the printing process that gives the highest quality print and the greatest level of consistency across a print run. However, the costs of the process mean that it is not viable for anything less than long runs.

Until recently, artwork that was to be printed by gravure was scanned, and an electronic engraving machine translated the scan and engraved cells into a cylinder, according to the image. Just being developed, however, are interfaces between electronic graphic design stations and the engraving machines, which means that hard copy artwork will no longer be necessary.

Once the cylinder is on the press, the cells are filled with ink, and the ink is deposited on the substrate. The high degree of consistency that can be achieved with gravure is possible because the cylinder does not wear and there is no ink/water relationship as in lithography, while the high quality derives from the fact that the density of ink deposited is greater than in any other process apart from screen printing. In addition, there is little dot gain, and the printing machine ensures that register is kept almost totally accurate. Rotary gravure presses are web-fed.

The process's potential

When designing for gravure printing it is advisable to work with the substrate in mind: plastics will have different characteristics from low-grade board, which will have different characteristics from high-grade gloss art paper. Low-grade paper, for example, will require high-density inks. Gravure will print very fine type extremely well, which is particularly useful for packaging on which technical information may have to be incorporated by law. There is no limit to the number of colors you can use, the newest machines can print eight colors in one pass. Metallic inks print very well with gravure, because of the weight that can be achieved, and golds and silvers are also well suited to the process. Gravure will, in fact, reproduce any design extremely well.

Gravure printing requires a long schedule, although the difference between gravure and web-fed litho is not as great as it used to be, and many Sunday newspaper supplements are printed by gravure, so printers can achieve a fast turnaround. In addition, reprinting an item such as packaging will be much quicker the second time around because the cylinder will already be engraved. The minimum cost-effective press run is around 400,000 copies; the maximum run is unlimited.

Gravure can print on to low- or high-quality paper and board, unsupported foil from 7 microns thick, tissue paper, PVC, polythenes, and almost all flexible packaging materials. It is easy to laminate or varnish onto gravure, and it is, in fact, often done on the press, with one of the printing units converted to a coater for the run.

Printing by gravure will always give excellent results, even on low-grade paper like that used by Britain's *Sunday Times* for its magazine. The sharpness of dot and fidelity of reproduction that can be achieved are second to none, which is, of course, crucially important in long-run work. This magazine, for example, has a press run of more than a million, and the advertisers who pay for it want to see their products looking as wonderful in the millionth copy as in the first. Notice how well the hair is reproduced, and the very clean reverses.

As well as printing long-run magazines, gravure's other main strength lies in printing flexible packaging (**left**), where it again scores in terms of the sharpness of dot, quality of reproduction, and consistency over long runs. These cookies, for example, are sold by the million every week, and the consumer has to know that it is the same product this week as last. The image is, in fact, printed on silver foil — just one of the many flexible substances for which gravure is ideally suited.

Other applications

There are two distinct uses for gravure printing: for publications and for packaging. When gravure is used for publications, it is usually for long run work and work that has to be totally color accurate. Mail order fashion catalogs are one of the main examples of this kind of work — the color in every single copy the catalog must be exactly the same as the article of clothing that arrives through the customers' doors. Brochures and newspaper supplements are also printed by gravure. On the packaging side, gravure is used for long-run, high-quality work on flexible materials. It has faced increasing competition from flexography in recent years, but it is still ahead of that process in terms of quality and consistency, although flexography scores on short run and price.

Relative costs

Rotary gravure is the most expensive printing process, although it becomes increasingly competitive with web offset for runs between 500,000 and 2 million. It is more expensive than flexography for packaging, although the print is of superior quality.

SHEET-FED LITHOGRAPHY PACKAGING

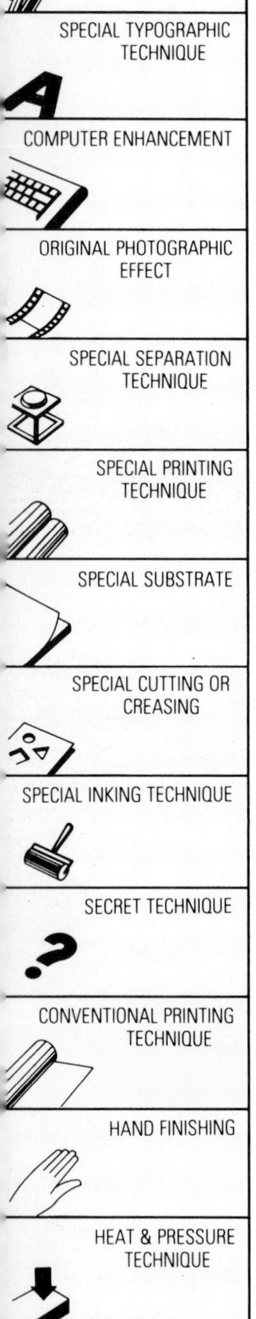

Sheet-fed lithography is the most widely used of all printing processes, having eclipsed letterpress some 15 or 20 years ago. It gives excellent quality print, particularly for color work, and the sharpness of the image should satisfy even the most demanding of clients. It is used for most everyday commercial printing, and although the process cannot reproduce the full tonal range, good litho printers should be able to achieve every gradation between 3 and 98 percent. A litho press usually prints up to a maximum of six colors in one pass, and one of these can be used for on-line varnishing.

Offset lithography works by means of a combination of ink and water on the printing plate, and it is the relationship between the two that is crucial to the success of the print. This is why lithography is not generally as consistent as gravure; maintaining exactly the same balance throughout a run is virtually impossible. However, as in all printing processes, the introduction of modern technology is continually minimizing variations in quality.

There are practically no images that cannot be reproduced by lithography, so long as they are printed on paper or board. Rigid plastics can be used, but they create extra problems as they tend to mark as they pass through the press. Plastics also take longer to print. You can print by lithography on top of screenprinted bases, but this can be difficult if the screen ink has been deposited too heavily. The range of inks that can be used for lithography includes conventional types as well as metallic, fluorescent, and other formulations.

Overnight production is a realistic proposition in many parts of the world, and lithography is certainly the quickest and most flexible process. Varnishing, laminating, foil blocking, adding holograms, embossing, and die stamping are among the countless effects that can be included on litho-printed products. However, if you want to add spot ultraviolet varnish over a matte-laminated litho-print, you will have to be careful, for the materials are not the most compatible of bedfellows.

The minimum press run will depend on the type of work. For a single-color letterhead, 100 copies would be an economical number, but for a four-color process job, the run will be much greater. There is no maximum, and although the plates will wear out after 250,000 copies or so, a new set should be a totally accurate rendition of the first.

Other applications

Sheet-fed lithography is used for a huge range of printed products, including books, magazines, brochures, leaflets, cartons, corrugated cases, letterheads and business stationery, cards, posters, and mailshots. It is also used to print on metals and plastics.

Relative costs

The longer the run, the cheaper the unit cost. With paper color printing, however, there is a point — at around 10,000 to 20,000 sheets — at which a move to web-fed rather than sheet-fed lithography becomes more cost effective.

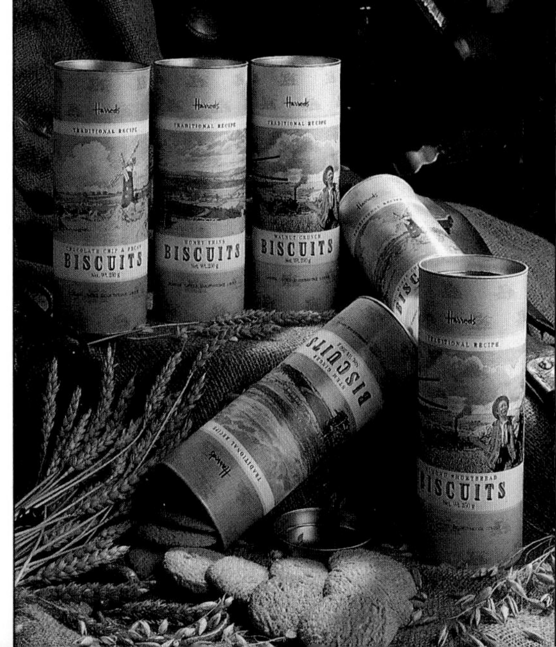

These illustrations were produced from the four printing colors — cyan, yellow, magenta, and black. All litho color work is produced from these four process colors. You can specify Pantone or house colors instead of, or as well as, the process colors. The cookie labels demonstrate the beautiful way in which litho can reproduce subtle blends of colors. The compact disc covers were originated on a variety of media.

Rachmaninov
Piano Concerto No.2 in C minor, Op.18
Mussorgsky (orch. Ravel)
Pictures at an Exhibition
CLASSICAL COLLECTION
TOTAL TIME 65:28
DDD

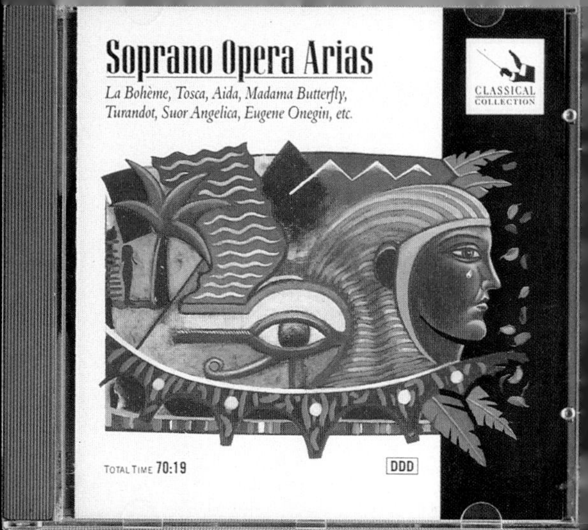
Soprano Opera Arias
La Bohème, Tosca, Aida, Madama Butterfly,
Turandot, Suor Angelica, Eugene Onegin, etc.
CLASSICAL COLLECTION
TOTAL TIME 70:19
DDD

Mozart
String Quintet in C, K.515
String Quintet in G, K.516
CLASSICAL COLLECTION
TOTAL TIME 64:42
DDD

Elgar
Cello Concerto
Enigma Variations
Alexander Baillie, cello
BBC Philharmonic Orchestra
Conducted by Edward Downes
CLASSICAL COLLECTION
TOTAL TIME 60:55
DDD

The Elizabethan Collection
Music for lute and viols from
the time of Queen Elizabeth I
CLASSICAL COLLECTION
TOTAL TIME 65:26
DDD

Mozart
Eine kleine Nachtmusik, K.525
Serenata Notturna, K.239
Divertimento in D, K.136
Divertimento in D, K.137
Adagio & Fugue, K.546
CLASSICAL COLLECTION
TOTAL TIME 61:00
DDD

WEB-FED HEAT-SET LITHOGRAPHY MAGAZINE

- DESIGN INNOVATION
- SPECIAL TYPOGRAPHIC TECHNIQUE
- COMPUTER ENHANCEMENT
- ORIGINAL PHOTOGRAPHIC EFFECT
- SPECIAL SEPARATION TECHNIQUE
- SPECIAL PRINTING TECHNIQUE
- SPECIAL SUBSTRATE
- SPECIAL CUTTING OR CREASING
- SPECIAL INKING TECHNIQUE
- SECRET TECHNIQUE
- CONVENTIONAL PRINTING TECHNIQUE
- HAND FINISHING
- HEAT & PRESSURE TECHNIQUE
- CONVENTIONAL FINISHING

Web-fed heat-set offset lithography is used to print high-quality color work on papers and lightweight boards. The paper is fed in from a roll, printed in up to eight colors on both sides at once, dried by heat — usually in a gas-fired oven — as it passes off the end of the press, and then folded into signatures normally of 16 or 32 pages, although any multiple of 4 is acceptable.

Proponents of web-fed heat-set lithography claim that the quality of print matches that of gravure, although it is commonly acknowledged that gravure gives a greater depth of color and greater fidelity to the original, which is why only gravure would ever be used for the fashion sections of mail order catalogs. The great advantage of web offset, however, is in the press run — much shorter runs are possible than with gravure. Runs of as little as 10,000 are cost effective, and half that number can be efficiently produced on what is known as a mini-web — that is, a half-width press. For runs of between 10,000 and 500,000 copies, web offset really has no competition; for runs below that, sheet-fed offset is usually a better bet, and for longer runs gravure is sure to be worth considering. In addition, on many web presses it is now possible to change one of the plates during the run to allow variable information to be included — for example, a page of regional addresses. Heat-set web offset is ideal for high quality color production, and most presses will allow you to use the four process colors along with a couple of others in one pass.

Most consumer magazines and brochures are produced by heat-set web-fed lithography, an extremely fast and accurate process. Lead times are low, and you can print the four process colors plus up to four other colors on both sides of the sheet in one pass. This magazine is typical of the work that can be produced by heat-set web offset — the colors are bright, the register is tight, and there are some black-only pages. Bleeding the title in this way means that the guillotine operator must be highly skilled.

Golden rules for design

Using heat-set web offset will enable you to print virtually anything that you can design. However, there are a couple of golden rules to observe. First, try to keep your design away from the edges of the page and the fold. No machine folder will work to more than 0.03937in (1mm) accuracy, and if you are designing right into the gutter the result will be unpredictable. Printers suggest that you keep at least ¼in (5mm) away from the trim. Second, if you are planning to use box rules, keep them well away from the edges. Tolerances both on press and particularly in the bindery are not zero, and pages are often not perfectly square, so that it is easy to spot if a box rule near to the edge of page is slightly out of line. Either move the box in from the edge, or, if it has to be at the trim, tilt it.

Scheduling time for web offset presses is less than for gravure. Platemaking is straightforward, and the presses run extremely fast — up to 60,000 spreads per hour.

The papers that can be used range from 30lb bible paper to 150lb paper of the kind used for magazine covers. Laminates and varnishes can be applied, although this is usually done to the cover off-line, once it has been printed. Ultraviolet varnishes can be applied directly on the press, but they have to be used with ultraviolet inks. Printing with this combination gives a glossy effect.

Other applications

The majority of consumer magazines are printed by web-fed heat-set offset, as are brochures and annual reports and accounts with a circulation of more than about 15,000. Leaflets, advertising literature, and anything that needs to be printed by the tens or hundreds of thousands is ideal for web offset.

Relative costs

Web-fed heat-set offset is economic within its range from 10,000-15,000 through 400,000-500,000. For runs of more than 500,000 gravure is a serious contender, although web-fed lithography has advantages when it comes to scheduling times.

WEDNESDAY, NOVEMBER 28, 1990
Today
FOR A BRIGHTER TOMORROW
25p
WIN £000's
STILL TIME TO GET YOUR CARD
PAGE 29
Today CHRISTMAS Gold Card
YOUR LETTERS
John Roy Major, youngest Premier since 1894
MAN OF
PENNY WARK and PAUL WILENIUS
FRIDAY, NOVEMBER 23, 1990
Today
FOR A BRIGHTER TOMORROW
25p
Souvenir Edition
INCLUDING 12 PAGE PULL-OUT
THE
goes out
with
TUESDAY FEBRUARY 26, 1991
Today
25p
FREE WEEKENDS
PAGE 23
for all readers
FIREBALL OF DEATH: An Egyptian tank leading a convoy explodes in flames after driving over Iraqi mine yesterday
RETREAT
Saddam orders beaten Iraqi troops to quit Kuwait as the Desert Rats go in
ROUTED AND HUMILIATED: Page 2 RATS ADVANCE: Page 2 MISSILE SLAUGHTER: Pages 4 & 5

WEB-FED COLD-SET LITHOGRAPHY
NEWSPAPER

Web-fed cold-set lithography is a fast and cheap method of printing for long run work on lower quality paper. The term cold-set means that there are no drying facilities on the press. In consequence the ink on the product never really dries, which is why you often find a deposit of black ink on your hands after reading a newspaper. A roll of paper is fed into the press at one end, is litho printed in two blacks if it is a monochrome publication (one for the type and one for the photographs), or in five colors if it is a color publication (two blacks, cyan, magenta, and yellow). The press then cuts and folds the product into its final form — a 64-page tabloid newspaper, for example.

Design for web-fed cold-set lithography needs to take account of the fact that the paper used is often of very poor quality; it is uncoated and usually between 25lb and, for the better quality papers, 40lb, which is not only thicker but will give greater brightness.

The screen rulings possible on cold-set lithography have improved of late, but they still lag behind heat-set work; between 65lpi and 100lpi is customary for cold-set printing. This means that fine detail is lost. In addition, because the paper is so rough, the plate may not always reach the bottom of the deepest troughs on the paper surface, which may result in the white showing through. Dot gain — that is, the increase in size of the dot from film to paper — is also noticeable, so anything more than a 70 percent screen is likely to appear solid. If, therefore, you have designed an advertisement for a magazine that is printed by gravure or by heat-set lithography, where the quality is high, it will be in your interests to modify it if it is also to appear in a newspaper.

Scheduling time

Scheduling time on cold-set presses is incredibly short; they can run at a rate of up to 70,000 copies an hour, and they are made-ready very quickly. The minimum press run is not much less than 40,000, and the maximum is in the millions.

The golden rule for work printed by cold-set lithography is to keep the design open. High contrast images will always reproduce well, whereas images with fine tonal gradations may just appear gray. You would not use other effects — laminating or varnishing, for example — on cold-set printed work because they would take far too much time and would not, in any case, work well.

This newspaper is typical of the work that is produced by cold-set web-fed presses. From a distance, the quality of print looks reasonable, but close up you can tell it is not in the same league as heat-set printing. However, if you keep your designs open, use plenty of contrast, and avoid fine detail, you will make the best of the limitations imposed by the cold-set web-fed process.

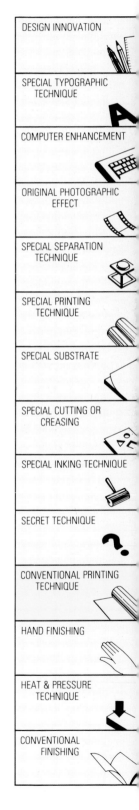

Other applications

Cold-set web printing is used primarily for newspapers, for which quality is of secondary importance to time and cost. Other newspaper-type journals, supplements, and some magazines are also printed by cold-set lithography.

Relative costs

Although cold-set lithography is the cheapest form of web printing, it gives the poorest quality. As many cold-set presses are used for printing newspapers overnight, it may be possible to negotiate a reasonable price for using a press during the day, when it is normally idle — that is, if you are prepared to accept the quality.

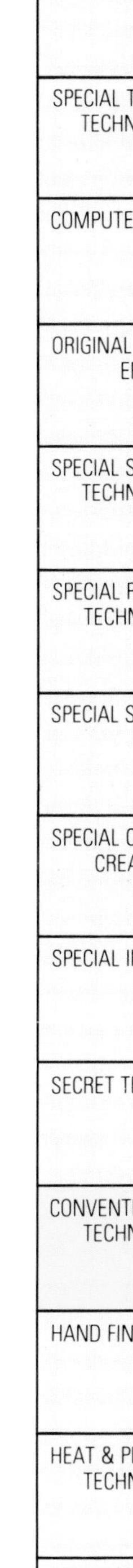

ON PRESS

SELF-ADHESIVE LABELS FOOD PACKAGING

Most self-adhesive labels are printed by flexography or by letterpress, although screen, gravure, and litho processes can all be used. Gravure, which gives the highest quality, has the highest origination costs. Screen printing lays down around five times as much ink as the other processes, giving high opacity and durability, so it is useful for specialist labels, including those that will be exposed to inclement weather, such as those used on expeditions. In addition, screen printing may be useful if you are looking for extremely bold, bright colors, or if you need a label on which the image can be felt. However, if you are planning more than a short run, screen printing will take considerably longer than flexography or letterpress. Wet-glue labels, which are declining in popularity, are also printed by lithography.

Letterpress and flexography

Of the two main processes for producing self-adhesive labels, letterpress will give the higher quality. Flexography can match letterpress only if every aspect of the process is used to its optimum level, and there is no leeway for tolerance. Flexography is, however, somewhat cheaper than letterpress. While both processes are excellent for printing linework and solids, printing halftone highlight dots needs to be undertaken with care. Designs incorporating vignettes and suchlike are always liable to suffer in the lighter areas. If you can, keep these to a minimum. Letterpress will be better than flexography. Letterpress will also handle small type better than flexography, which can tend to squash it, producing an outer ring around the character, and you should take extra care if you opt for a face with fine serifs.

Modern label presses can print up to nine colors in one pass, and they also include in-line laminating, perforating, and numbering. It is also possible to incorporate hot foil blocking and smell encapsulation into labels.

The scheduling time for printing self-adhesive labels can be just a few days if necessary, although a couple of weeks is more likely in the normal course of events.

Self-adhesive labels can be printed on papers, boards, laminates, gold and silver foils, acetates, fabrics, tags, indestructible papers, vinyls, and polyethylenes. Wet-glue labels are generally printed on paper.

Other applications

Self-adhesive labels can be used on a huge variety of products, ranging from the consumer goods found in supermarkets to industrial products and products for the chemical, agricultural, and pharmaceutical industries. Designing for pharmaceutical applications requires an extra degree of care since there has to be some device to ensure that labels are not mistakenly applied to the wrong bottles. Wet-glue labels have a similar range of applications.

Using a self-adhesive label with a clear plastic package is one of the cheapest and most attractive forms of packaging — as long as the product inside looks good! These labels combine a four-color halftone illustration with text, and a house color has been used to illustrate the weight and cost of the product.

Relative costs

Wet-glue labels are the cheapest to print, although the post-printing processes are labor-intensive and more costly than for self-adhesive labels. Flexography is the least expensive way of printing self-adhesive labels, but quality may not be all you would want it to be. Gravure, on the other hand, has extremely high quality but a price to match, and it is uneconomic for all but the longest runs. Letterpress costs more than flexography but less than gravure.

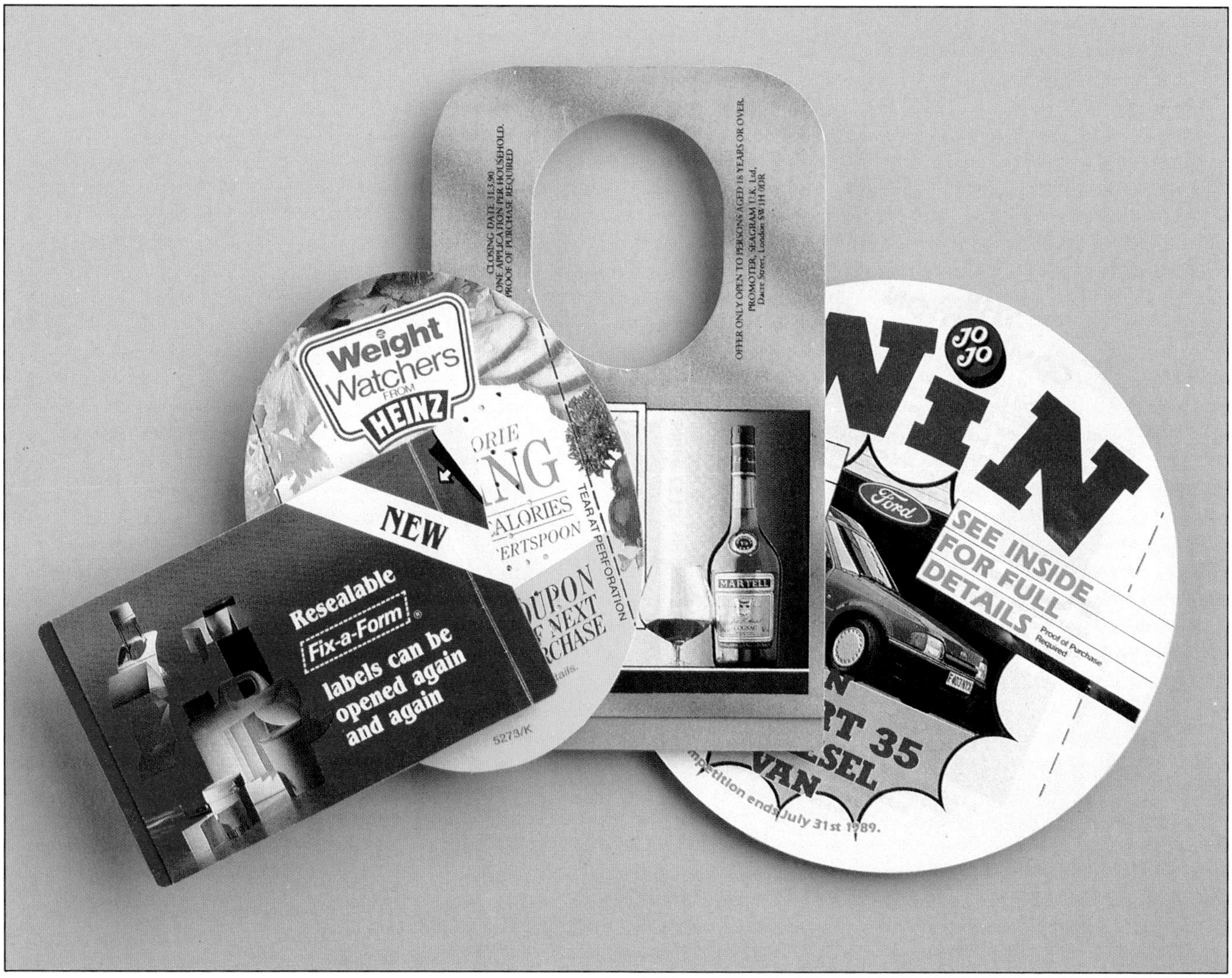

CLOSING DATE 31.3.90
ONE APPLICATION PER HOUSEHOLD.
PROOF OF PURCHASE REQUIRED
OFFER ONLY OPEN TO PERSONS AGED 18 YEARS OR OVER.
PROMOTER, SEAGRAM U.K. Ltd,
Dacre Street, London SW1H 0DR
Weight Watchers FROM HEINZ
NEW
Resealable
Fix-a-Form®
labels can be opened again and again
TEAR AT PERFORATION
5273/K
MARTELL
JO JO
Ford
SEE INSIDE FOR FULL DETAILS
Proof of Purchase Required

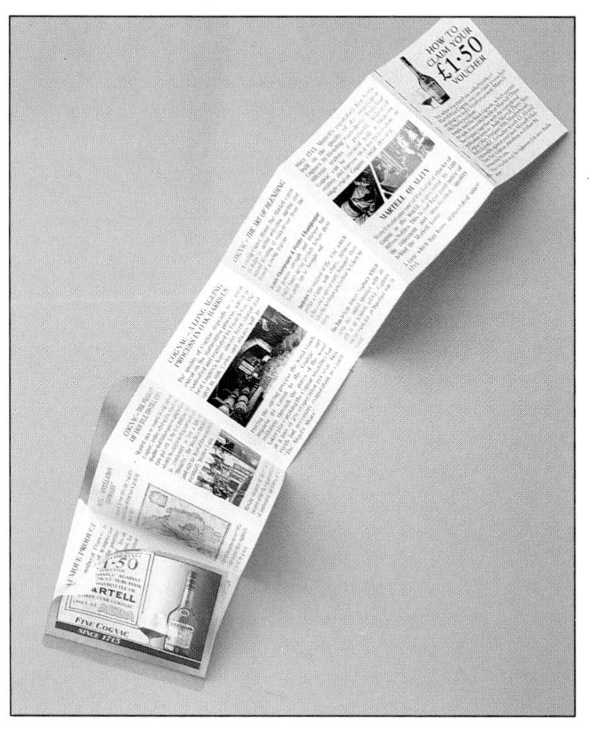
HOW TO CLAIM YOUR £1·50 VOUCHER
FINE COGNAC
SINCE 1715

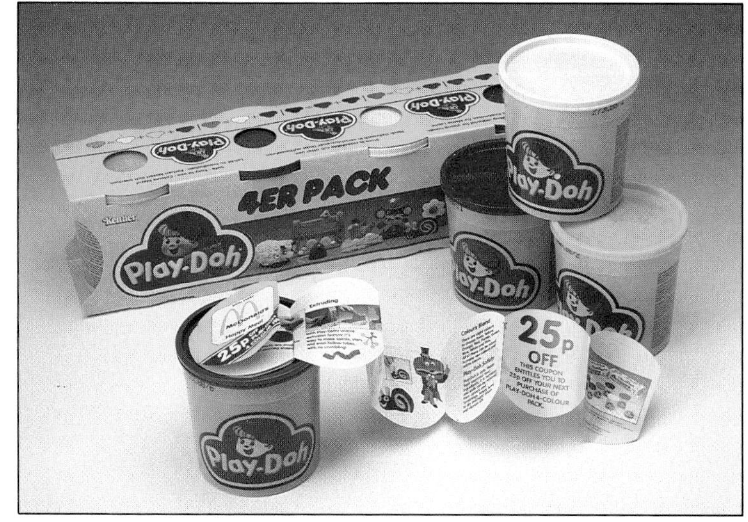
4ER PACK
Play-Doh
25p OFF

MULTIPLE LABELS AND FORMS
PROMOTION

The use of multiple labels, basically those that peel away from the front of a product, has developed rapidly in the last few years. One label on a product can carry only limited information, but if the client needs to convey additional details — for promotional, legal or purely information reasons — multiple labels provide a low-cost alternative to putting the package in a box and inserting a leaflet.

The labels are generally printed either by letterpress, which may limit the potential for using halftones, or by a combination of letterpress and lithography, which gives more flexibility. It has been known for multiple labels to be printed in as many as 16 colors, although six or eight are more usual. There are no problems with using small typefaces.

Scheduling the job

Producing multiple labels and forms obviously takes longer than printing regular self-adhesive labels or single forms, although in theory it should be possible to achieve a 24-hour turnaround. However, the scheduling really depends on the printer having the capacity, and you should normally allow between four and six days for the pre-press activities and a similar amount of time for printing.

The minimum press run will depend on how much the client wants to pay. If you are designing for a container carrying an expensive chemical, a press run as low as 5,000 may well be viable. However, if you are designing for a low-priced item, such as a honey jar, then the minimum print run will need to be far higher so that the cost of the labels can be borne by the product.

Although multiple labels and forms can be printed onto any substrate that will bend, the thinner the paper the easier it is. Perceived quality, however, may mean that a slightly thicker substrate is used, and coated papers obviously give a higher quality feel than uncoated stock.

Other applications

As well as being used for promotional work on supermarket products, multiple labels are used in a wide variety of applications, including areas where legislation requires a substantial amount of information to be given with the product. These uses include such items as agro-chemical and pharmaceutical products. Multiple forms are used when several different pieces of information have to be contained within the same package, and applications include parking tickets and customs and courier forms.

Relative costs

Producing multiple labels is obviously more expensive than printing single labels, although you do get more than a commensurate amount of additional information space for your money. It is also cheaper to print these labels than to have to produce a box for the product and print a leaflet to insert in that.

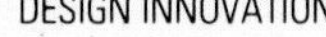
DESIGN INNOVATION

SPECIAL TYPOGRAPHIC TECHNIQUE

COMPUTER ENHANCEMENT

ORIGINAL PHOTOGRAPHIC EFFECT

SPECIAL SEPARATION TECHNIQUE

SPECIAL PRINTING TECHNIQUE

SPECIAL SUBSTRATE

SPECIAL CUTTING OR CREASING

SPECIAL INKING TECHNIQUE

SECRET TECHNIQUE

CONVENTIONAL PRINTING TECHNIQUE

HAND FINISHING
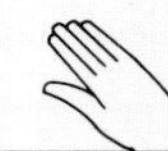
HEAT & PRESSURE TECHNIQUE
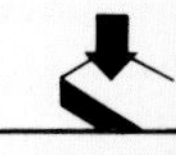
CONVENTIONAL FINISHING

A range of multiple labels and forms; these provide a cheaper alternative to having to put the product in a box and inserting a leaflet.

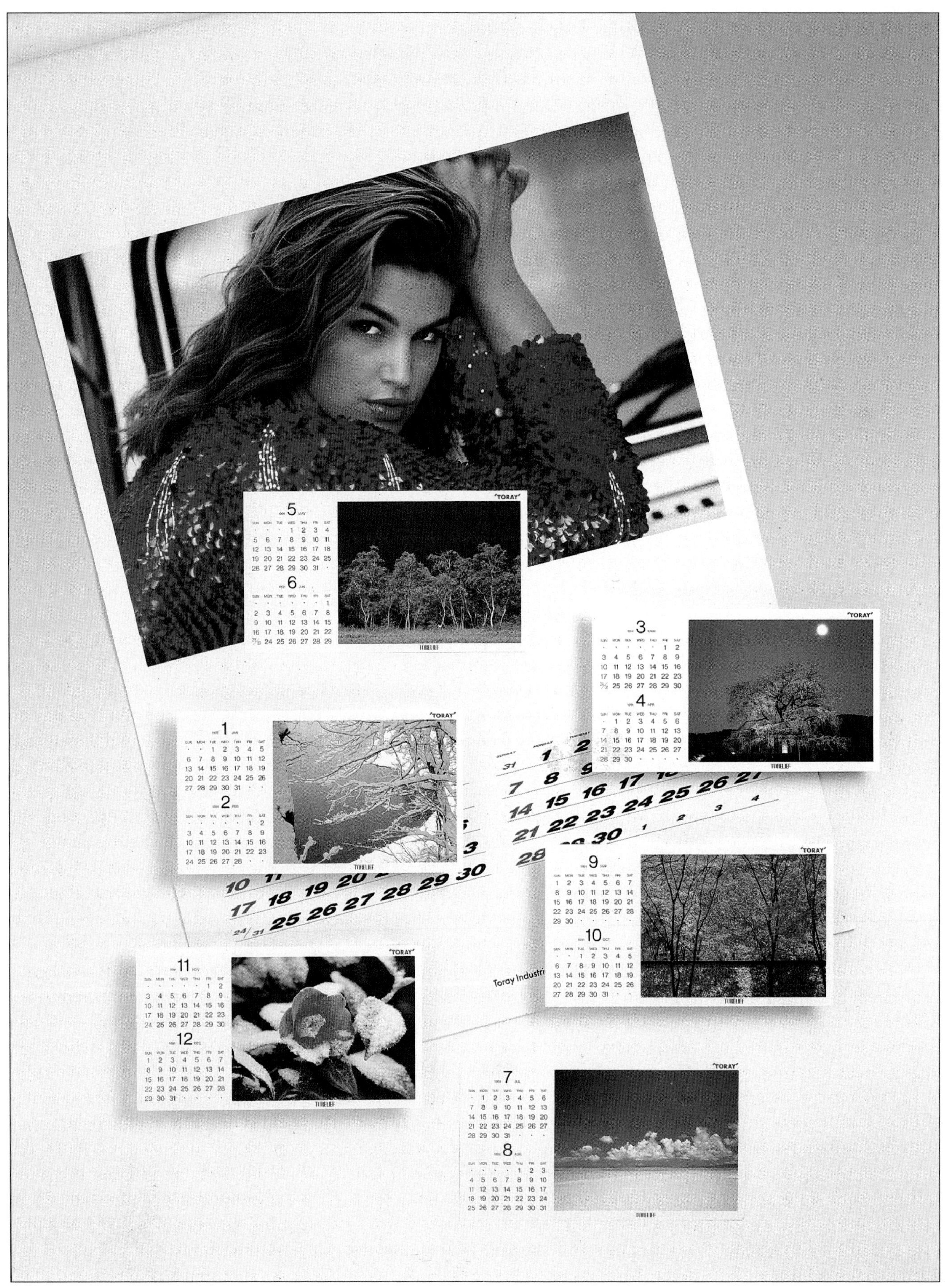
"TORAY"
TORELIEF
Toray Industri

WATERLESS/DRY OFFSET CALENDAR

Waterless offset is rapidly increasing in popularity, particularly in the Far East, because of its ability to produce extremely high quality printed work. It is best suited to fine screen work, such as fine art prints and some calendars — anything, in fact, that needs to be of the highest possible quality.

Unlike conventional lithography, the printing plate for waterless offset has a silicone layer that rejects the ink in the non-image area, while the imaged area is ink attractive. The absence of water from the final printing process offers several advantages, and from the designer's point of view means that designs will reproduce far better in terms of color brightness, detail, and fidelity. The main drawback is that printing machines have to be adjusted to print by this method, and controlling the ink temperature, for example, is crucial. The process, therefore, costs more.

Stronger colors

Printing by waterless litho gives a better dot, which means that colors are stronger, there is more accurate and consistent registration, less change in color throughout the length of the run and better drying. It also results in less dot gain, which means that the reproducible tonal range is extended. This is particularly noticeable in fine screen work, the area for which it tends to be specified.

Scheduling time is the same as for conventional litho, but the actual printing time is, if anything, quicker and there is less waste.

In addition to printing on paper and board, waterless offset is well suited to printing on plastic and other non-permeable substrates, which has always been difficult with conventional litho.

Other applications

For work that has to stand out from the crowd — a piece of packaging, for example — it may be worth considering printing by waterless litho. The process was developed primarily for fine art reproduction, so it will enhance any printed product, although the cost constraints may prove too great.

Relative costs

Waterless lithography is substantially more costly than the conventional kind. The costs of the plates and inks alone are likely to increase the unit price of each product by 30 percent. In addition, the specialist nature of the process may allow printers to charge a premium.

Superb quality print can be achieved with waterless lithography — the colors are stronger and the images sharper than is possible with conventional litho. These four-color promotional calendars from the manufacturers of waterless plates are marvelous examples, but something of their quality has been lost in the printing of this book, which is by conventional lithography.

DESIGN INNOVATION

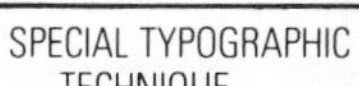

SPECIAL TYPOGRAPHIC TECHNIQUE

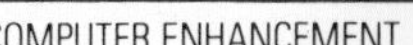

COMPUTER ENHANCEMENT

ORIGINAL PHOTOGRAPHIC EFFECT

SPECIAL SEPARATION TECHNIQUE

SPECIAL PRINTING TECHNIQUE

SPECIAL SUBSTRATE

SPECIAL CUTTING OR CREASING

SPECIAL INKING TECHNIQUE

SECRET TECHNIQUE

CONVENTIONAL PRINTING TECHNIQUE

HAND FINISHING

HEAT & PRESSURE TECHNIQUE

CONVENTIONAL FINISHING

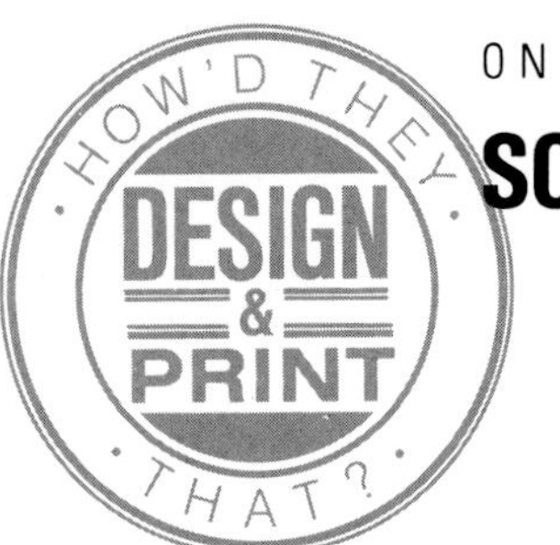

SCREENLESS LITHOGRAPHY MAP

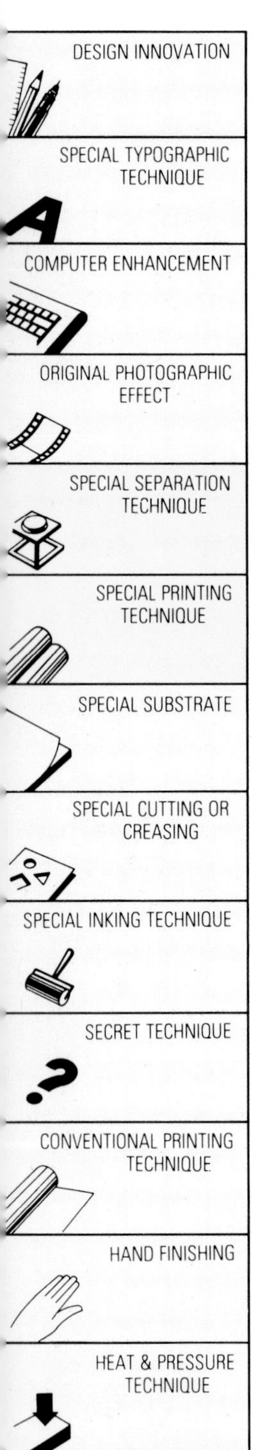

As its name suggests, screenless litho is a method of producing litho plates without the screens normally used to break up the image into the halftone dots present on conventional litho. Instead of being scanned into its four process colors with electronically generated dots, the image is separated using filters on a camera to give continuous tone images. Special plates are needed to print the images because ordinary plates would fill in. Producing screenless litho is a highly skilled operation, and there are very few printers who are prepared to print by the process.

Why screenless lithography?

The main reason for using screenless lithography is that everything that is seen on the original is printed. Conventional screened lithography misses out the image at either end of the density scale, the extreme highlight and shadow areas. Because it is not reproducing dots, screenless litho can accommodate the entire density range, and nothing is missed out. It is ideal, therefore, for the reproduction of ancient manuscripts, such as the Domesday Book, because all the stains and background dirt are reproduced, and give an authentic appearance.

The scheduling time required for screenless lithography can be far longer than for conventional litho. Not only does the reproduction using cameras and filters instead of cameras take longer, but the press makeready can take far longer because there are no color bars or dot-to-dot register points to work from. As with conventional litho work, there are no limits on the minimum or maximum run lengths, although the longer the better, since the majority of the costs are incurred in repro and press makeready.

Although screenless litho can, in theory, be printed onto any paper substrate, in practice uncoated stock is the most suitable, both from a practical printing point of view and because the original document is likely to have been printed on an uncoated paper, if you are trying to emulate a historical document.

Other applications

Apart from reproducing historical documents, screenless lithography can be used for extremely high quality work of any nature.

Relative costs

Printing by screenless lithography is very expensive. The repro will cost between 8 and 10 times that of conventional litho, and press costs will be two or three times as much, since the makeready takes so much longer.

This map has been printed by screenless lithography — that is, without any dots. This enables a complete tonal range of from 0 to 100 percent to be reproduced, rather than a range of from 3-5 to 95-97 percent as in conventional litho. The great advantage of the process is the quality that can be achieved. This map, which was printed in four colors on drawing paper, appears in the equivalent of 600 lines to one inch, which is three times the resolution of conventional high-quality printing.

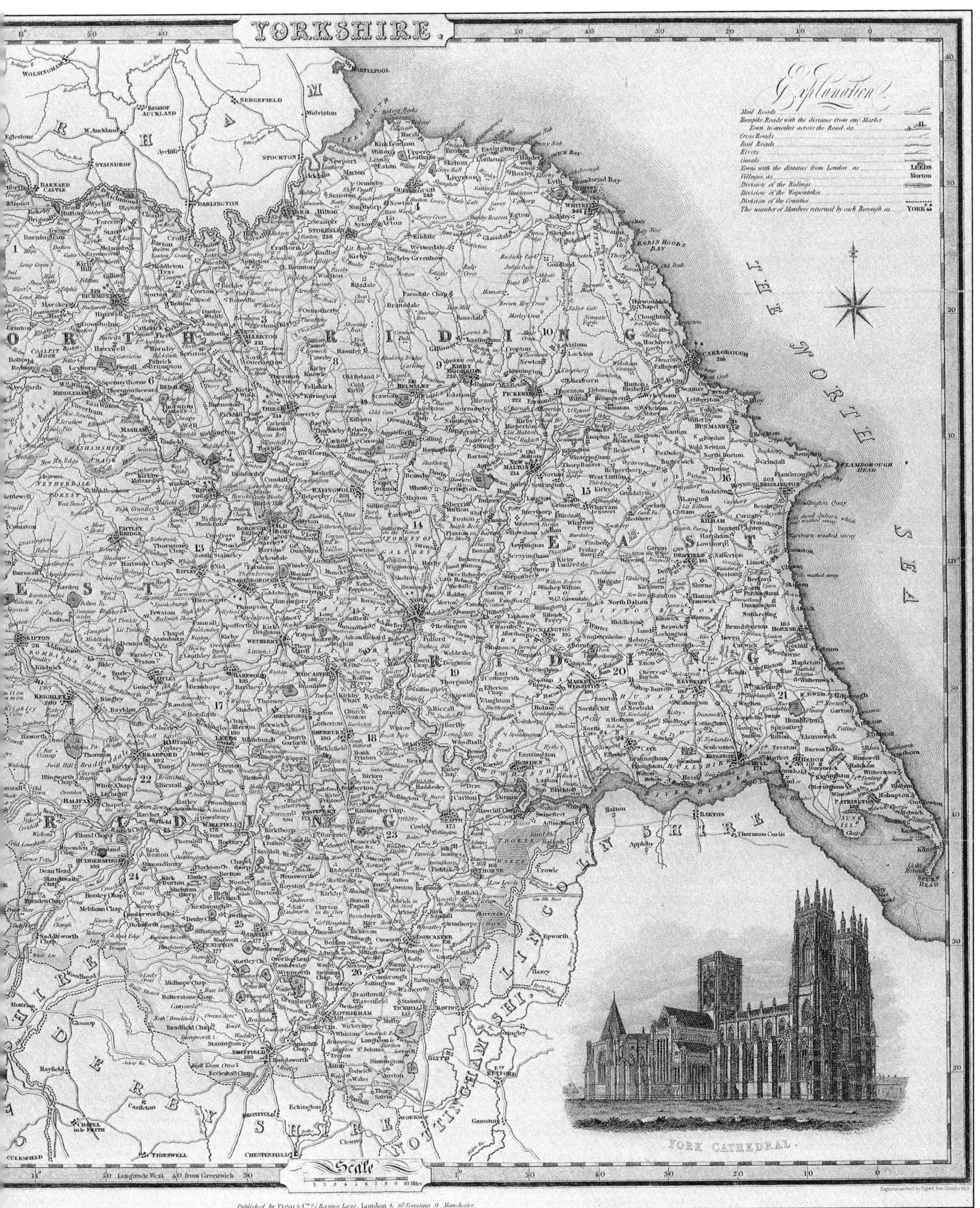

YORK CATHEDRAL.

ACETATE AND POLYESTER PRINTING
PROMOTION/BOOK

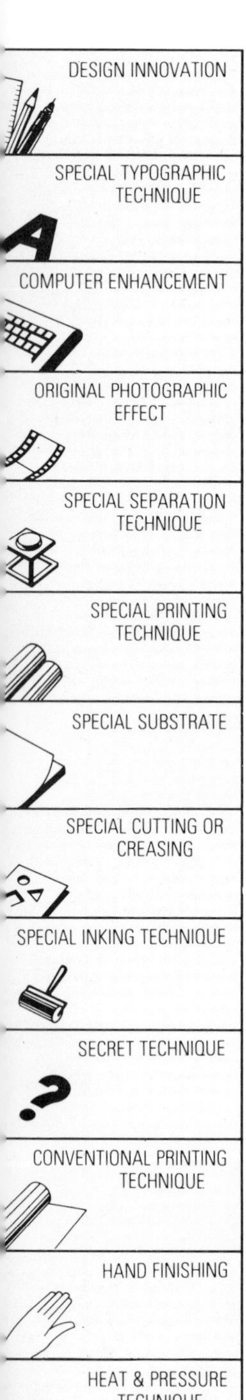

Offset lithographic printing on polyester or acetate sheets is a relatively new process but one that is sure to increase in popularity because it can give a higher color density than printing on paper. The brightness of color that can be achieved on polyesters is astounding. In addition, polyester and acetate substrates have the advantages of greater longevity and, in most cases, greater durability than paper.

Acetate can be printed either by offset lithography or by screen printing, although screen printing does impose production and definition limitations. Until recently, of course, any plastic-based material was printed by gravure, with its high start-up costs, or by flexography, with its relatively poor quality. The real breakthrough has come in the potential to print these substrates by offset lithography. Now, manufacturers in Japan, the United States, and Europe have produced materials that are capable of taking an image from an offset press, and this means that extremely high quality is possible at reasonable cost for both short and medium-length runs.

All the new materials can accept ultraviolet inks, and one or two can even accept conventional litho inks, although non-UV inks will take at least 12 hours to dry. There should be no problems with register, and halftone work can be as fine as on conventional offset litho paper. When designing work that is to be printed on a transparent acetate of some kind, the golden rule, of course, is to ensure that a white background is printed first or that the sheets are interleaved with a white substrate. Some of the new acetates and polyester-based products are available with an opaque white base. The material itself is available in weights ranging from 203 to 1016 ppi (pages per inch).

Although these new materials have made the use of offset lithography possible, you must ensure that your printer knows exactly what is involved, because just about every aspect of printing on acetate or polyester is more difficult on conventional stock. For example, the material is particularly susceptible to scratching if it is not handled carefully. You would be well advised to look very closely at every sheet that you have had printed — not just the top one.

Finishing processes can be a problem too, but, in general as long as the operation is carried out carefully and slowly, it will be successful. It is important to bear in mind that different types of material have different characteristics: some, for example, can be folded as often as you wish; others have to be perforated before they can be folded. Stitching and hot-melt binding are also possible, as is guillotining, but always check with the printer before specifying a particular process.

Printing on polyester or acetate takes longer than conventional lithographic printing on paper, simply because of the care that has to be taken of the substrate. If you allow double the production time of a conventional litho print job, you should not be far off in your schedule.

Applications

Polyester should be selected whenever you want to achieve the highest possible quality. It is widely used for such products as catalogs, calendars, posters, back-lit signs, point-of-sale displays, promotional print work — anything, in fact, that is likely to be displayed outdoors or to be handled by many people over a long period of time.

Relative costs

Printing on polyester or acetate is more expensive than printing on paper or board. First, the material itself is more costly; second, ultraviolet inks, which are more suitable, cost two or three times as much as conventional inks; and third, the printer will charge more for the extra time that the careful handling of the material requires.

A spread from a book which reconstructs ancient sites, showing how they look now and how they looked in their heyday (**above and right**).

A demonstration piece shows the potential of acetate overlays (**below** and **below right**). Here three different overlays reveal the cutaway interior of La Scala theater in Milan. The end result is a fascinating visual guide to the interior makeup of the building.

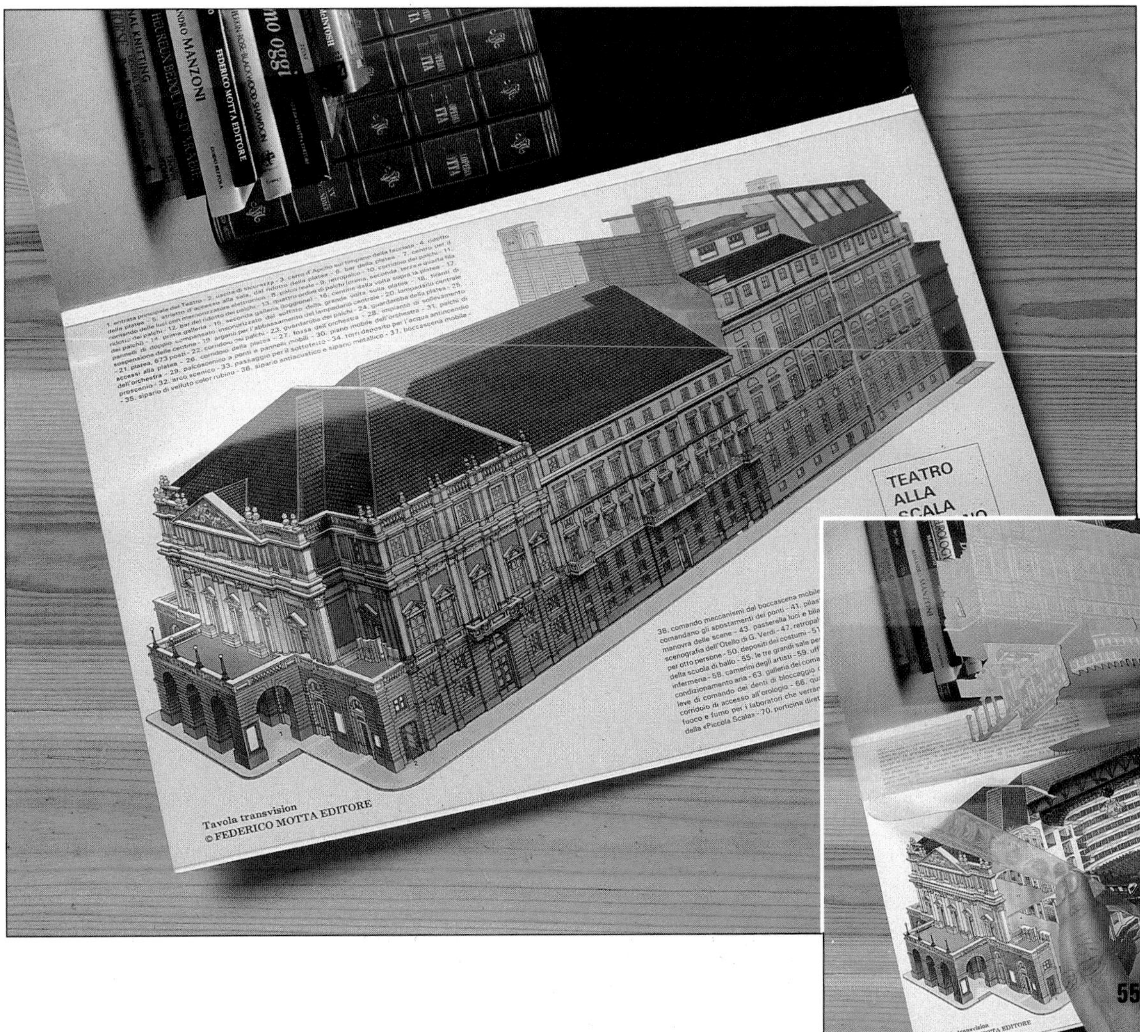

FLEXOGRAPHY PACKAGING

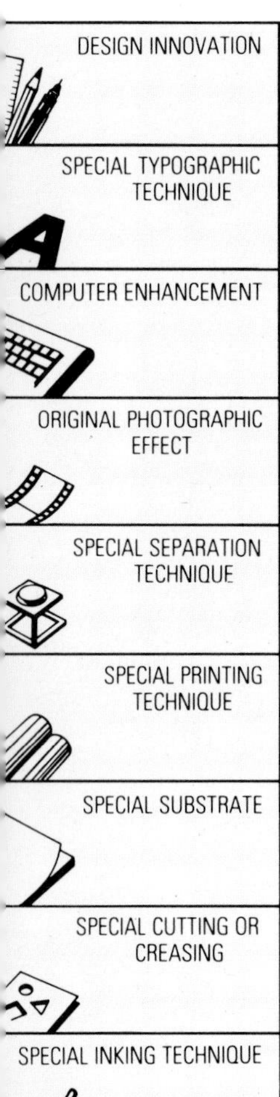

Flexography can be used to print well onto flexible packaging, carton board and, in fact, almost anything that comes in roll form. It is a web process, with a polyester relief plate receiving liquid ink which is deposited on the substrate. Up to eight colors can be printed at once. It offers serious competition to the gravure process in many areas in terms of quality, and it has advantages when it comes to costs, short run lengths, flexibility, and turnaround time.

Although once regarded as the poor relation of printing processes, flexography is now capable of printing high quality line and process work. It can be used for solids and reversed images, and some presses can print down to a 7-thou line. Almost all modern presses can print 120 lpi (lines per inch), and many of the higher specified machines up to 180 lpi, and even this has been exceeded. However, it has to be borne in mind that the screen ruling is restrictive, and although some very impressive designs have been printed by flexography, most printers are not likely to reproduce fine work too well. If it is not carefully controlled, the process tends to lead to excessive squashing of the dot. Similarly, very small type should be avoided and reverses, while possible, also have to be handled with care.

Scheduling time is much shorter than for gravure. A good trade separation house should be able to produce a set of six or eight plates in 24 hours; producing the same number of gravure cylinders will generally take several days. Printing speed for halftone work is around 590-656ft (180-200m) a minute, for line work around 980ft (300m) a minute. Minimum run lengths will depend on the number of colors: it should be possible to find someone to print over 16,000ft (5,000m) of single color, but multicolor printing would have a significantly higher minimum. Maximum run lengths are in millions of yards.

Flexography presses often include coating units for varnishing and spot varnishing immediately after printing.

Flexography can be used to print on paper, films, polypropylene, polyester, nylons, surlyns, polythene, corrugated board, hessian sacks, multiwall paper sacks, and envelopes.

Other applications

Flexography is the ideal process for printing on frozen-food packaging, multicolor corrugated point-of-sale display, bread bags, diaper (nappy) packaging, multiwall pet food bags — anything, in fact, that needs to be printed on flexible packaging.

Relative costs

Flexography compares very well to gravure with regard to costs, although much more care is necessary to attain the same quality. A set of plates should cost no more than 50 percent of the price of a set of gravure cylinders, and as flexo presses are cheaper than gravure and need less labor to operate them, the process itself is cheaper.

Flexography is an inexpensive method of printing on flexible packaging materials, whether they are plastics, foils or, as illustrated on these two pages carton board. As long as you avoid very fine halftones, it is possible to achieve perfectly acceptable quality with the process. This line art illustration for an ice-cream carton is printed in three colors.

SCREEN PRINTING
PROMOTION/POSTER/CALENDAR

The quality of screen printing has improved dramatically over the last 10 years, and it is now commercially acceptable. It is still the simplest printing process of all. Basically, ink is pulled over a mesh that is supporting a photo-stencil. The positive image areas let the ink through to be deposited on the substrate, while the non-image areas do not. Many of the presses in operation can print up to 5,000 images an hour and achieve a high level of accuracy in register.

Screen printing is the one process that can print on virtually any material and on any shape. It can produce fantastically bright colors, printing up to 14 colors in one pass, although most screen printers have machines with a maximum of six, eight, or ten colors.

The disadvantages of the process are that detailed work does not come out well. Even the modern, sophisticated machines still produce a coarse effect compared to the results of litho or gravure printing. Four-color process work has to be handled with the greatest of care, and you should try to find a printer who can give you more than 100 lpi (lines per inch); in most cases it will be 70 lpi. If possible, you should produce designs that work with line and solid color. Screen printing reproduces fine lines very poorly; they appear jagged and have pieces missing. Type does not reproduce well either, with serifs especially affected and, if they are fine, often not appearing at all.

Fluorescent, metallic, day-glo, and glitter inks work well with screen printing.

Scheduling times for screen printing are relatively fast, depending, of course, on the complexity of the job — one color on a sheet of paper will be printed far more quickly than eight colors on an irregular object. One of the major benefits of screen printing is that it works well for short runs, because it is relatively cheap to make-ready — the minimum print run is, literally, one. It is possible to foil block, laminate, varnish, and litho overprint onto screen-printed material, although there are potential problems in all these processes, which are more apparent if the ink deposit is especially heavy.

One of the main attractions of screen printing is the fact that it can be used on practically any material — paper, board, plastics, PVC, vinyls, acetates, wood, metal, glass, and textiles. In addition, the process is used for much three-dimensional work.

Screen printing is ideal when the print run is very short or when the substrate will not readily travel through a litho press, as is the case with plastics, woods, and metals. This promotional figure (**left**), which stands 8ft (2.4m) tall, was screen printed in a single color on recycled stock, which was then laminated to chipboard. Although it is often thought that silk screening should be used only when fine detail and high quality are not needed, this is not strictly true. The illustration (**below**), for example, is for part of the Chaps range by Ralph Lauren, and it was used to promote the highest quality product.

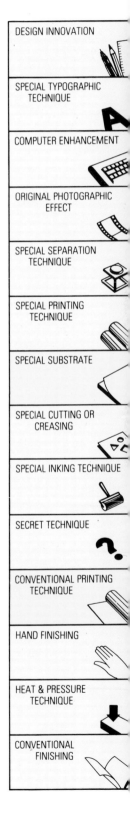

- DESIGN INNOVATION
- SPECIAL TYPOGRAPHIC TECHNIQUE
- COMPUTER ENHANCEMENT

- ORIGINAL PHOTOGRAPHIC EFFECT

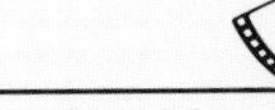

- SPECIAL SEPARATION TECHNIQUE

- SPECIAL PRINTING TECHNIQUE

- SPECIAL SUBSTRATE

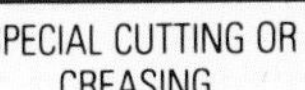

- SPECIAL CUTTING OR CREASING

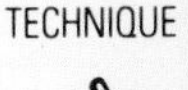

- SPECIAL INKING TECHNIQUE

- SECRET TECHNIQUE

- CONVENTIONAL PRINTING TECHNIQUE
- HAND FINISHING

- HEAT & PRESSURE TECHNIQUE

- CONVENTIONAL FINISHING

Screen printing is ideal for promotional work. This Australian-designed image was produced for external use on European poster columns (**left**). Screen printing gives a durable image, and the colors have a high level of brightness because of the amount of ink that is deposited, which is far greater than in any other print process. Another application for the process is printing on plastic materials such as this shopping bag (**right**).

These are probably the world's most expensive calendars! (**below** and **below right**). Only 500 were produced for a UK brewery, but each page was screenprinted in four to six Pantone colors. The whole calendar had more than 50 different colors in it. The ink was laid onto white art board, and type sizes were as small as 9pt. The cover page tells how the calendar came about and who commissioned whom, and it includes each firm's logo again printed in Pantone process ink. Each of the inside pages depicts a UK pub sign, with the Pantone system used to guarantee fidelity of color reproduction.

Other applications

Screen printing is used for products with short print runs and for which the graphics need to be particularly striking; for example, it is often used for point-of-sale material, posters, and plastic and metal sign work. A large proportion of packaging for electrical products is screenprinted. In addition, many products that are an irregular shape are screenprinted; this is sometimes achieved by direct printing and sometimes by printing a transparent film transfer and applying the transfer to the product. Fashion and promotional clothes are screenprinted, and the process can also be used to apply varnishes, particularly spot varnish, to pre-printed lithographed work.

Relative costs

The costs depend on the job. For short run work, screen printing is the cheapest process, but even though great progress has been made in recent years, it is still comparatively unsophisticated, and the costs are never likely to be as high as those of other processes.

THERMOGRAPHY LABELS/STATIONERY

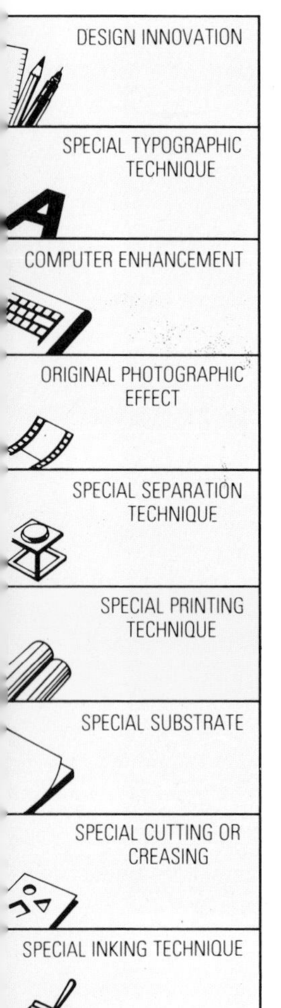

Thermography is a relatively inexpensive method of giving a prestigious look and feel to printed matter. The process gives a raised inked image, which is achieved by spraying the still-wet litho-printed ink with a thermographic powder, which is then heat-fused to the ink. Its main drawback is that most thermographic systems cater only for $8\frac{1}{2}\times11$ size stock.

Incorporating a thermographic image into a design offers much potential, and most thermographic printers believe the process to be under-used by designers.

Adding thermography to a design will increase the production time, but not substantially. The minimum print run will be determined by how much the client is willing to pay, since all the costs are in setup: the longer the run, the cheaper the unit price.

Thermography can be incorporated into designs that are going to be printed on paper between 30lb and 80lb, and on cardboard between 135lb and 270lb. However, the designer needs to beware of porous papers and cardboards, which are not suitable at all. Other substrates to be avoided are carbonless and heat-sensitive papers, and plastics. Combining fine and coarse images on the same design may cause problems, since different types of powders are produced for different types of work, and a fine powder will not give a good result on a large image, and vice versa. Trying to thermograph type that is smaller than 6pt should be avoided. One further danger with thermography is when the paper or board will be used through a laser printer, when the heat may cause the powder to melt. It is also important to remember that you cannot varnish over thermography.

A thermographic image is produced by inking the required area and then spraying thermographic powder over the sheet. The powder adheres to the ink and is sealed in place by heat. Finally, the sheet is cooled. If your design is to be produced by thermography, you should bear in mind that the neutral powder tends to lighten the image, so you may want to specify a slightly darker tone of ink to compensate.

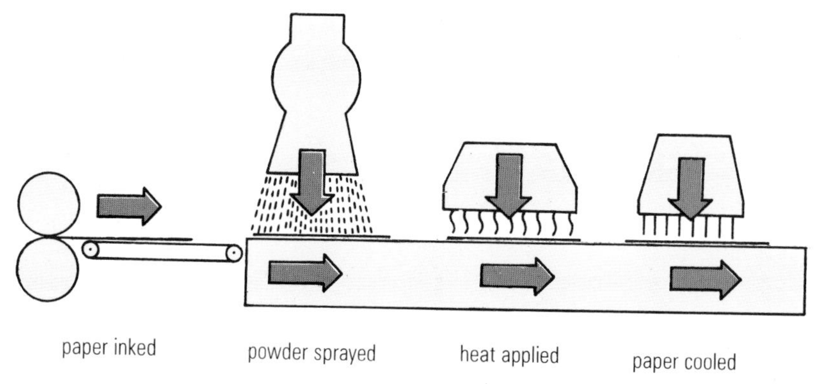

YOUR GOOD TASTE SHOWS ON WARREN LUSTRO GLOSS ▪ YOU'LL SOON BE RECEIVING COPIES OF OUR LATEST LUSTRO GLOSS BROCHURE, FOOD FOR THOUGHT ▪ PACKED WITH MOUTH-WATERING 4-COLOR FOOD PHOTOGRAPHY, IT'S AN IMPRESSIVE DEMONSTRATION OF WHAT CAN BE DONE ON THE EVER-POPULAR LUSTRO STOCK ▪ WE'RE SURE YOU'LL PUT IT TO GOOD USE ▪ SO TUCK IN YOUR NAPKIN AND GET READY TO EAT UP THE COMPETITION ▪ ▪ ▪ ▪ ▪ ▪ ▪ ▪ ▪ ▪ ▪ ▪ ▪ ▪

Thermography combines well with other techniques, as can be seen from these labels for pasta sauce. The labels were printed in six colors on recycled paper, and line work was printed by thermography, which is very unusual for labels. The type on the paper merchant's promotional brochure was thermographed in two colors. Note how the designer has avoided using a typeface with fine serifs in anticipation of potential problems.

Other applications

Apart from promotional work, which is where the designer can use the process most creatively, thermography is mainly used in stationery, letterheads, business cards, envelopes, and compliment slips. In addition, greetings cards can be enhanced by thermography.

Relative costs

Thermography will probably add between one fifth and one third to the unit cost of each product; the longer the run, the cheaper it will become.

SELF-ADHESIVE VINYLS VEHICLE SIGNAGE

DESIGN INNOVATION
SPECIAL TYPOGRAPHIC TECHNIQUE
COMPUTER ENHANCEMENT
ORIGINAL PHOTOGRAPHIC EFFECT
SPECIAL SEPARATION TECHNIQUE
SPECIAL PRINTING TECHNIQUE
SPECIAL SUBSTRATE
SPECIAL CUTTING OR CREASING
SPECIAL INKING TECHNIQUE
SECRET TECHNIQUE
CONVENTIONAL PRINTING TECHNIQUE
HAND FINISHING
HEAT & PRESSURE TECHNIQUE
CONVENTIONAL FINISHING

Designing for the transportation industry has changed rapidly over recent years with the advent of self-adhesive vinyls. Formerly, the majority of work was produced by signwriters, who often took a day or more working on the side of a truck. Now, however, self-adhesive vinyls can be produced for a whole fleet in the same amount of time, and they give the designer far greater potential.

The lettering or designs can be cut either by a traditional die or by a computer plotter. There is now an enormous range of colors for the vinyls, and you should be able to specify virtually anyhue. In many cases this can obviate the need for printing.

If illustrations are needed, they are printed almost exclusively by screen process, since it is difficult to print onto the non-absorbent surface by lithography. The screen process enables bold colors to be printed, but fine detail should be avoided. Up to 20 colors at a time can be printed by screen, and although this is too much for most work, insignia and coats of arms, for example, can contain as many as 13 or 14 colors.

Specifying vinyls

It is important when specifying self-adhesive vinyls to ensure the correct vinyl is being used. For example, if a truck is going to be driven from the frozen wastes of Alaska down through the deserts of Arizona and on into the jungles of central America, no one can cut corners. Many a design has come unstuck, literally, because the wrong, usually cheaper, vinyl was used.

Traditional dies are faster and more economical for large quantities, but shorter runs are best produced on a laser plotter straight from the computer. Once the die is made, which can take up to a week, it will produce the cut vinyl design at the rate of several a minute.

It is possible to laminate or varnish on top of vinyl, although in most cases laminating will not add anything except a little extra protection.

Vinyls can adhere to virtually any type of vehicle side, whether it be metal, the glass-reinforced plastic used by cold storage wagons, or the PVC used for curtain sides on some trucks.

A witty design shows a fridge door opened to reveal the contents within (**right**). The bold colours of the halftone mean the image can be read while the van is in motion.

Fine detail does not normally lend itself to large-scale applications, however it works very well in this example (**below**).

Other applications

Vinyls can be used for a host of transportation purposes, although it is essential to specify the right one for the right application. Although they are now able to cope with the wildly varying climatic conditions experienced by aircraft, not everything is achievable: Concorde, for example, expands by 14in (36cm) during flight, which rules out the use of vinyls. They can, however, be used on ships and yachts, even though they are exposed to inclement weather conditions.

Relative costs

For anything but one-of-a-kind, self-adhesive vinyls are less expensive than signwriting and last longer. Computer-cut lettering is less expensive for short runs, but for any substantial amount a die should be cut.

FLEXIBLE/CARTON PACKAGING FROZEN FOOD

DESIGN INNOVATION
SPECIAL TYPOGRAPHIC TECHNIQUE
COMPUTER ENHANCEMENT
ORIGINAL PHOTOGRAPHIC EFFECT
SPECIAL SEPARATION TECHNIQUE
SPECIAL PRINTING TECHNIQUE
SPECIAL SUBSTRATE
SPECIAL CUTTING OR CREASING
SPECIAL INKING TECHNIQUE
SECRET TECHNIQUE
CONVENTIONAL PRINTING TECHNIQUE
HAND FINISHING
HEAT & PRESSURE TECHNIQUE
CONVENTIONAL FINISHING

Frozen food packaging is of two kinds: the flexible, plastic packaging in which vegetables and the like are usually presented, and the carton packages in which pizzas, pies, and cakes are sold. The whole range of printing processes is used — gravure, flexography, lithography, and screen printing — and the only technical provisos are that the inks have to be taint-free and grease-resistant to be used on packages for such products as fish sticks and ice cream, and that they must be able to retain their structure at temperatures of -22°F (-30°C). You should bear in mind that such inks may not always permit the same levels of glossiness that are possible with conventional inks.

Within these parameters, your design need not differ from work for conventional flexible and non-corrugated cartons. Flexible packaging will look better if gravure is used, and it is possible to achieve greater fineness of detail with that process. However, gravure is more expensive and can be used only on long runs. Flexography is likely to give squash, which will manifest itself in the smaller detail areas — the type, for example, may have a halo around it.

Carton board has to be sealed, usually by applying a varnish, to make it moisture-proof, otherwise it would disintegrate. An ultraviolet varnish will give a higher degree of gloss, and if you can stand the expense, use ultraviolet inks also. Foil blocking is another option, but remember to foil before applying the sealant. However, foil blocking is not particularly effective in these circumstances and slows down the process considerably. You would be better advised to use a metalized material or a metallic ink from which you can get quite good results and not slow down the process or increase the costs to any significant extent.

Potential pitfalls

Having said all of this, there is a multitude of complexities to take into account. You should discuss the potential pitfalls with your printer. The conditions that have to be met are demanding because the legal restrictions on food packaging are many and wide-ranging.

Using flexography to print the packaging will give a far shorter scheduling time than gravure because of the origination process associated with that process. Flexography also has a much lower minimum press run, while gravure is not economical for anything less than hundreds of thousands. Producing the cartons is very fast, and minimum run lengths can be as low as a few thousand.

This package for ice creams was printed in the four process colors by offset lithography. A sealant varnish was laid over the top to help prevent the packages from disintegrating in the freezer.

This illustration of frozen vegetables was printed on a heat-sealed, metalized substrate, which was, in fact, used as part of the graphic presentation. The cartons were printed by photogravure, which gives the highest possible quality in commercial printing.

Relative costs

Flexography is considerably cheaper than gravure printing for flexible packaging, and the quality differential is not always so great that gravure is the only option. The use of inks and ultraviolet varnish will push the cost of cartons up, but not to a great degree.

REGISTERED
OBAN
1794
WEST HIGHLAND MALT

OBAN
'Little Bay of Caves'

OBAN
'Little Bay of Caves'
Along the shores of Lorn lies a record of man far more ancient than that of any city in the land. The first settlers arrived on the mainland in 5,000 BC and sheltered in the natural caves of the land then known as 'an Ob'. The 'Distillery Cave' was one such shelter hidden in the Creag a' Bharrain cliffs which rise dramatically above the
'OBAN DISTILLERY'
Producers of a Delicate
SINGLE MALT
WEST Highland MALT
SCOTCH WHISKY

TUBE ROLLS BOTTLE PACKAGING

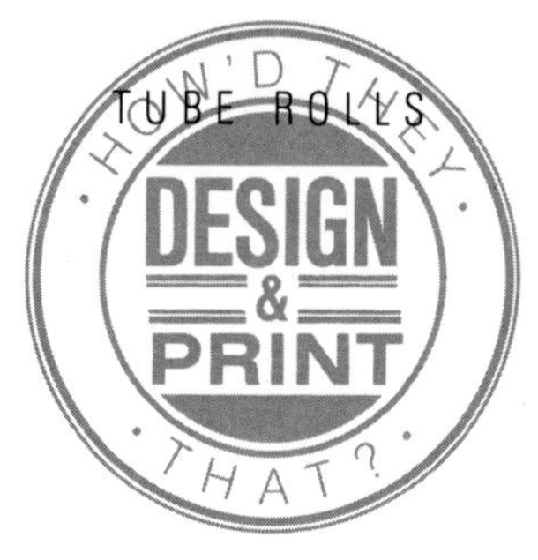

Designing for print on a spiral-bound tube roll poses some unique problems. Spiral-bound tubes get their name from the fact that they start life as flat board, which is wound around a tool to form the tube. Any print that is added is almost always produced by printing onto paper by lithography or gravure and then pasting the paper around the tube.

When you are designing an image for a tube, it is important to appreciate how difficult it is, given commercial production parameters, to make both edges of the printed sheet meet each other perfectly when they have been wrapped around the tube. You should therefore always steer clear of horizontal lines in your design; they are unlikely ever to meet up at the join. In fact, if you can create a design that has at least ½in (1cm) of white space along either edge of the join, you will avoid considerable aggravation.

Embossing the design

If you are planning to emboss the design, make every effort to consult the printer and try to confine the embossing to small areas. When the sheet is being stuck to the tube, pressure is applied to make it adhere, and if the wheels used to apply the pressure run over an embossed area, which is probable if it is a large part of the design, they are likely to crush it. If you know where the wheels are going to run, you can plan your design around their path.

There are also several ways of designing for tubes to save on costs. If you can run a color off the base and top of the design, there will be no problems with register when it comes to fitting it around the tube. If, however, the base and top of your design finish in horizontal lines before the end of the tube, you will create serious problems for the printer and some financial woes for yourself as the printer tries to align the sheets perfectly. If you can bleed off the top and bottom in the same color, you will reduce costs still further because the printer will produce the sheets with the head of one next to the base of the other, saving up to 50 percent of production time, with the associated savings.

It is also worth talking to your printer about the size of the tube. Tubes generally come in standard diameters, and if you want a non-standard size a tool has to be specially made, which will increase both the cost and the scheduling time. Using a standard-sized tube will achieve considerable cost savings.

Scheduling time for tube roll production is around 12 weeks, although it is perfectly feasible to reduce this by half. The minimum run is quite low, since the most expensive part of the process is the tube itself.

Both varnishing and laminating are possible on tube rolls, and so is embossing.

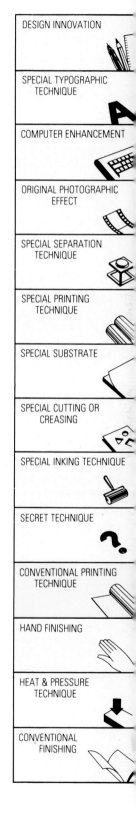

The crucial aspect of tube roll printing is to ensure that you cannot tell whether the design is slightly off-center or not, since the tolerances allowed in commercial production may not always guarantee perfectly straight alignment when a flat sheet is wrapped around a cylindrical object. By avoiding horizontal lines and using non-defined top and bottom edges, this design precludes any problems of this kind.

Other applications

Tube rolls are used for a wide range of packaging applications as well as for promotional work.

Relative costs

Tubes are considerably more expensive than conventional square cartons.

DESIGN INNOVATION

SPECIAL TYPOGRAPHIC TECHNIQUE

COMPUTER ENHANCEMENT

ORIGINAL PHOTOGRAPHIC EFFECT

SPECIAL SEPARATION TECHNIQUE

SPECIAL PRINTING TECHNIQUE

SPECIAL SUBSTRATE

SPECIAL CUTTING OR CREASING

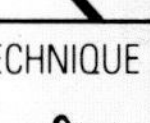

SPECIAL INKING TECHNIQUE

SECRET TECHNIQUE

CONVENTIONAL PRINTING TECHNIQUE

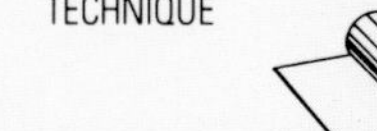

HAND FINISHING

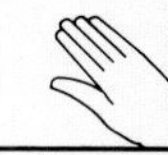

HEAT & PRESSURE TECHNIQUE

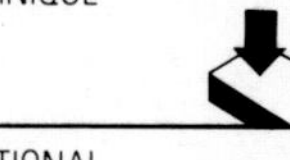

CONVENTIONAL FINISHING

PRINTING ON METAL CANNED FOOD

Decorating metal – that is, printing on tin (or, increasingly now, tin substitutes) – is achieved in various ways. The metal can either be printed as flat sheets and then formed into shaped cans, or the final, shaped containers can be printed. For the huge runs of well-known beverage cans, for example, it is likely that the manufacturers will have their own custom-built, hugely expensive can-production line both to manufacture and print the cans in one pass. However, for printing shorter run lengths, specialist printing presses print onto flat sheets, which are then converted into the appropriate shape. The processes used are either conventional lithography or dry lithography. Alternatively, screen printing may be used if fine detail is not important. A further method is to print onto a transparent transfer film, which, once printed, is adhered to the can.

Results to expect

The quality achievable by straight lithographic printing on tin should surpass that of conventional lithography on paper and board. Dry lithography does guarantee consistency throughout the length of a run, unlike conventional lithography, in which the consistency will vary. This is particularly useful because the majority of can-printing machines in use around the world are not new.

The use of translucent and transparent inks, varnishes, and coatings will considerably enhance the appearance of the can. The range of finishes is unlimited, and you can litho print in both process color and specified colors.

Scheduling time is virtually the same as for conventional lithographic printing on paper, and the minimum print run will depend on how much the client is prepared to pay, since much of the cost lies in plate preparation and press makeready. You can varnish on cans, but holograms tend to degrade. There is of course, no need to foil block since the substrate itself can be used as a foil.

The metal used for decorating has, historically, been tin, but as the price of tin has risen, various substitutes have been used, including aluminum, a tin-aluminum combination, tin-free steel, and tin-plated metal. It is possible to print on all these and achieve virtually the same degree of quality as on tin itself.

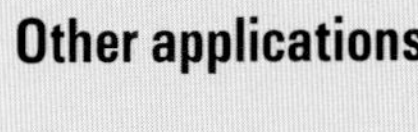

Other applications

In addition to food and beverage cans, decorated metal can be used for aerosols, trays, cookie and candy containers, cans for lubricants, bottle tops, and even promotional products such as album covers.

Relative costs

Because the substrate costs far more than paper or board, printing onto metal is expensive. Specialist equipment and labor also contribute to higher prices.

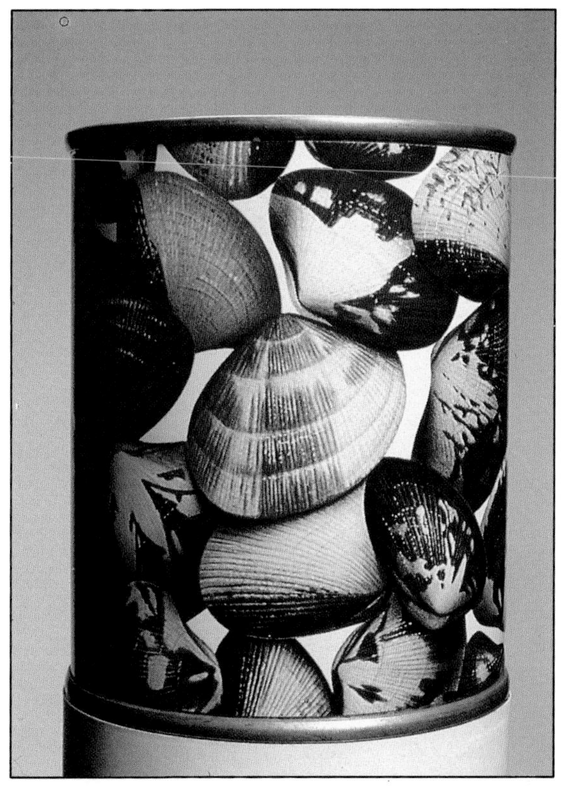

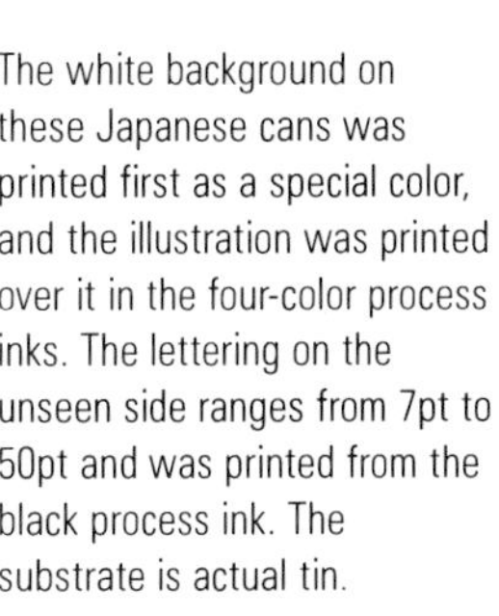

The white background on these Japanese cans was printed first as a special color, and the illustration was printed over it in the four-color process inks. The lettering on the unseen side ranges from 7pt to 50pt and was printed from the black process ink. The substrate is actual tin.

HOW'D THEY DESIGN & PRINT THAT?

NON-CORRUGATED CARTONS PACKAGING

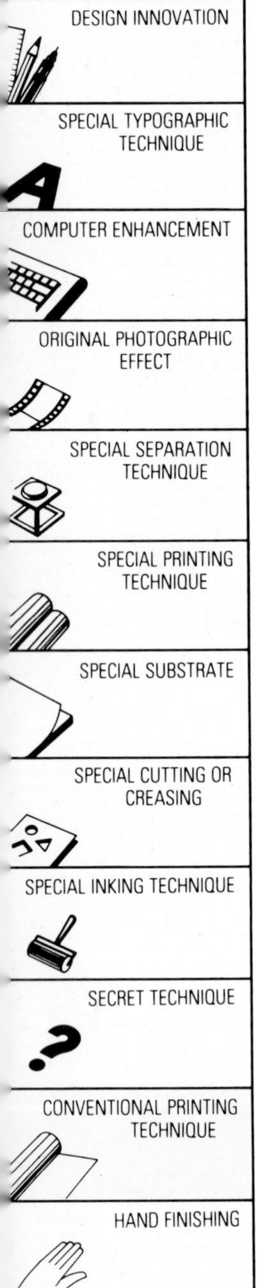

Many cartons are made out of non-corrugated board – that is, cardboard without any corrugated flutes between the two sides. Non-corrugated cartons can be standard rectangular boxes or irregular shapes, and either of these may include a plastic film window through which the product inside can be seen. Non-corrugated cardboard is normally printed by sheet-fed lithography although gravure may be used, especially for very long runs when the highest possible quality is required – cigarette packs are a typical example. With sheet-fed work, the carton shape is actually cut on a separate machine after printing; with gravure this operation will probably be carried out on the end of the press.

Designing for cartons is now extensively carried out on electronic systems, which can take into account the irregularities of shape and provide fast proofs by means of thermal printers and sample plotters, so that you can see roughly how your design is actually going to look on the three-dimensional carton. Any alterations can be carried out quickly and at no great expense.

Designing for irregularly shaped cartons

When you design an irregularly shaped carton it is crucial that you talk to the printer first. You need to know how the carton will be made up before you design for it, or you may find, for example, that part of your design is over a glue flap. Give the printer a line drawing of the proposed box before you design for it. There are 101 pitfalls to take into account, and talking to the carton-maker will help you to avoid them. Since cartons are printed by lithography or gravure, there is no limit to the number of colors that can be used. However, as most presses print six colors, with a few printing eight, it is best to keep to this number to print in one pass through the press. This reduces costs and ensures a good register. Some colors – lime green and orange, for example – are extremely hard to attain through the process mix, so try to keep special colors to the minimum.

If you are planning to emboss, die stamp, or foil-block the carton, make sure that these effects are at least ⅛in (3mm) away from each crease, otherwise you may crush the crease and provide an edge where the effect may be degraded.

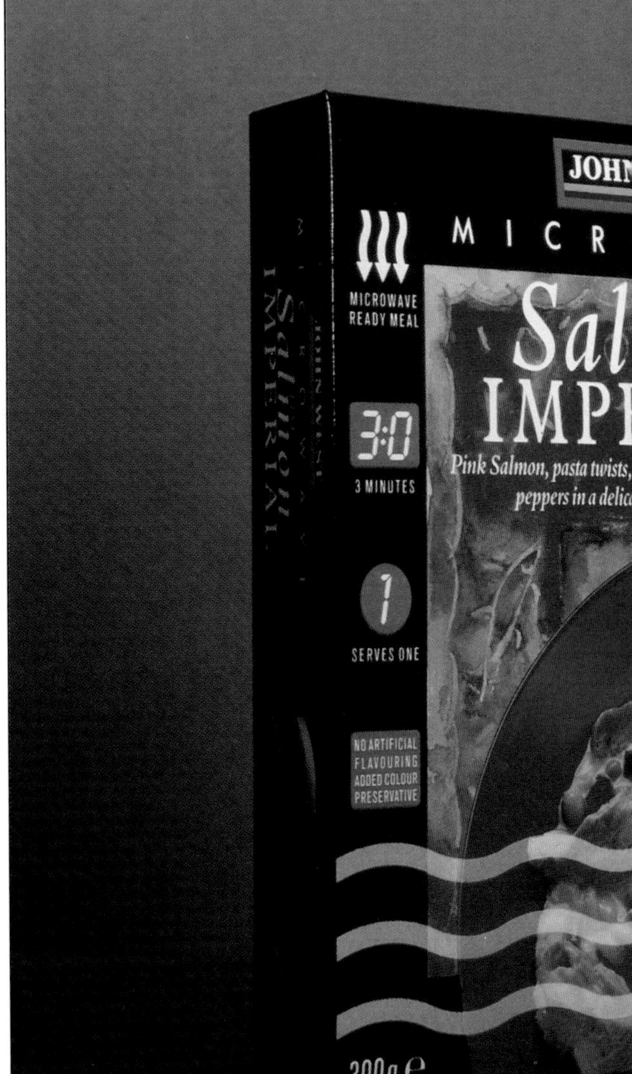

Non-corrugated cartons can carry the most intricate designs, as long as a decent cardboard is used. A fine degree of reversal is possible The appearance of the whole product is enhanced by varnish.

Other applications

Non-corrugated cartons are used for many supermarket products, with irregular shapes particularly in demand for candy and cosmetics. Liquor bottles are often packaged in non-corrugated cartons.

Relative costs

Sheet-fed lithography is much less expensive than gravure for all but very long runs. The varying prices of the different kinds of carton board affect the overall production price only to a small degree, apart from foil-covered board which costs 60 percent more than conventional board, and whose inks will add another 20 percent to material costs.

Non-corrugated cartons are printed either on regular carton board or on foil-covered board. Both vary between 135lb and 675lb. Printing on the foil will usually necessitate the use of ultraviolet ink, because the foil is non-porous and the only way to dry it is to expose it to ultraviolet light. Non-corrugated cartons are prime products to be varnished.

Scheduling time for cartons varies enormously. A simple rectangular box can be produced within a matter of days, while an irregular shape with a film window may take several weeks. In general, allow between five and six weeks from delivery of artwork.

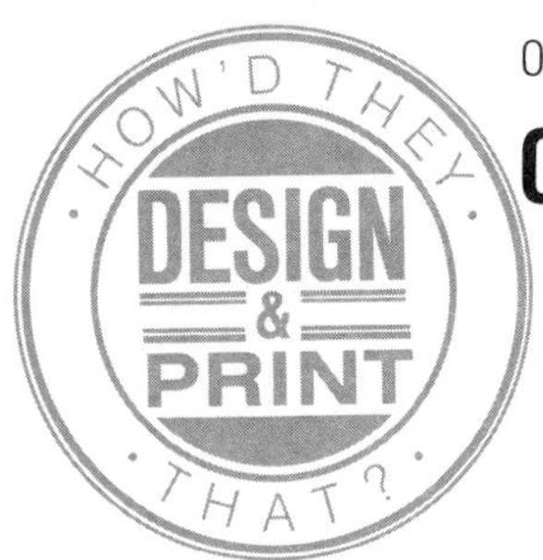

CORRUGATED CARTONS PACKAGING

Corrugated cartons are those that are strengthened by having a corrugated arrangement between the inside and outside faces of the board. These corrugations are called "flutes." The cartons are printed either directly by flexography, which is known as post-printing, or indirectly by litho printing onto paper and then attaching the paper to the carton; this method is known as pre-printing.

Pre-printing

Pre-printing offers a far greater degree of quality, for whatever you can print in a magazine you can print on the paper to glue to the carton. High-quality photographs and illustrations can be successfully used, as can fine line work, solid colors, and small type. With post-printing, in which the design is printed directly onto the carton, the choice is limited however. Carton board has a rough surface, and flexography is not the finest of printing processes. The solids are liable to demonstrate show-through, where the ink has not reached the bottom of the deepest troughs in the cardboard; fine serifs will be lost and delicate line work will probably suffer. The better the quality of the board, the better the print will be. You usually find, for example, that the board used for whiskey bottle cartons gives far better results than the board used for packaging cookies.

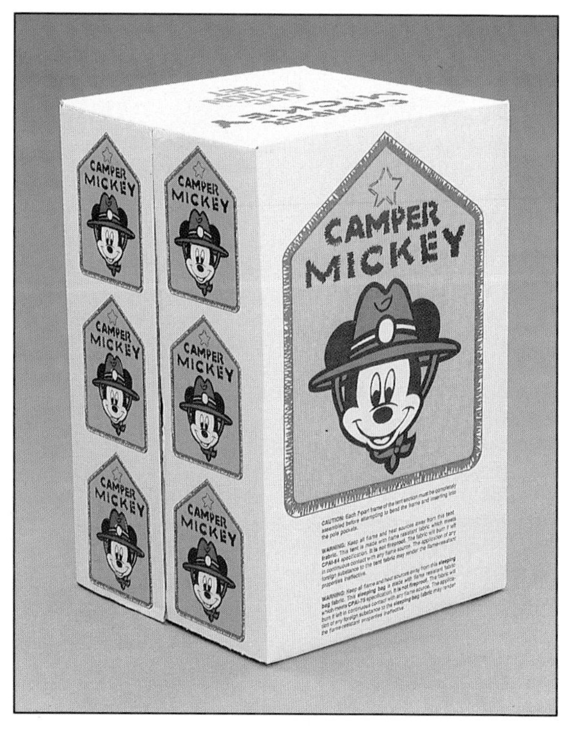

A selection of corrugated cartons using the post-printing technique.

Post-printing

If you are using post-print, you should utilize as few colors as possible, and try to stick to line art rather than using halftones. Pre-printing, of course, will allow you to use as many colors as you like, although in practice if you limit your design to the four process colors and one or two house colors you will see the best results.

Post-printing obviously has a faster scheduling time since only one process is necessary. Pre-printing involves the initial print and then attaching the paper to the carton. However, neither process will keep you waiting for long — a week should be plenty of time from delivery of artwork.

The major advantage of post-printing is that smaller print runs, even down to 500 or 1,000, should be financially practicable. Pre-printing demands a far higher minimum quantity level, as the setup and origination costs are considerably more. You may be looking at a minimum of 10,000 cartons before pre-print becomes viable. You can varnish corrugated carton board, but it would be sensible to steer clear of laminating.

There are three basic types of corrugated board — the coarse C-flute, which is ⅙in (4mm) thick, fine flute, which is ⅛in (3mm) thick, and double flute, which is ¼in (7mm) thick. Fine flute has more flutes. This means there is a better surface for printing on with flexography. Of course, with pre-print this makes no difference. Double carton board is a combination of fine flute and C-flute and is used when the cartons are going to be stacked, since it has additional strength.

Other applications

Corrugated carton board is used to package a huge variety of products, ranging from household appliances such as washing machines and refrigerators to music systems. It is also used for many homecare items, bottles and food, and most industrial packaging.

Relative costs

Post-printing is considerably less expensive than pre-printing, but you have to take the process into account when you are designing, for there is no way you can achieve high-quality halftone graphics on post-printing. However, with the sensitive use of line art, there is no reason why you cannot produce some very attractive color packaging with post-print.

ON PRESS

DIE STAMPING PACKAGING/BOOKLET

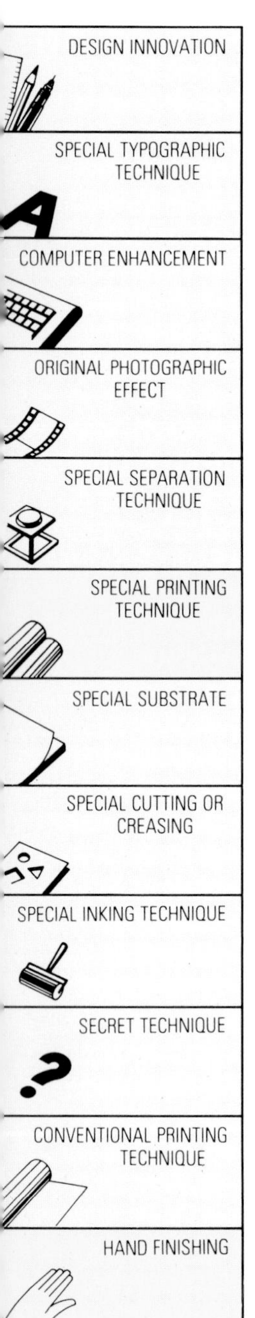

Die stamping is a well-established technology that gives high quality, raised printed images, and a finer print than lithography. A metal die is engraved, either by hand or photographically or both, inked, and forced onto a substrate, often in a male-female combination. The substrate then complies with the pressure and changes its dimension from a flat sheet into the relief image, receiving the ink at the same time. Theoretically there is no limit to the number of colors that can be printed on the same sheet by die stamping.

Product enhancement

Die stamping enhances any product to which it is applied and provides the potential for very fine design. For example, an elaborate coat of arms, or the "By Royal (or "Presidential") Appointment" insignia are ideal types of work for die stamping. The process can also be used in association with highly polished metallic colors to give an extremely glossy raised area. It is particularly suited to giving an old-fashioned look to a design.

It is possible to die stamp work that has already been printed by lithography or another process. A word of warning, however: register is crucial on such fine work, and there must be consultation between the designer, printer, and die stamper. In addition, there are limitations in the positioning of the die stamp.

Allow at least two weeks for production, more if it is a complicated job. As hand engraving is still necessary in many areas, the dies themselves can take up to a week to produce; the printing will take a similar length of time. Die stamping is also quite slow in production, even for simple, single color letterheads.

Die stamping can be combined with foil blocking, but extra care is necessary if the same sheet is to be laminated or varnished, and it is easier to specify die stamping after varnishing or laminating.

Almost any paper or board, from lightweight airmail to strong board, can be die stamped.

Die stamping is achieved by a male and a female die. The male die is inked and the substrate is passed between the two, when the male die is closed on the female. The dimensions of the substrate change to comply with the shape of the die, and the substrate receives its image.

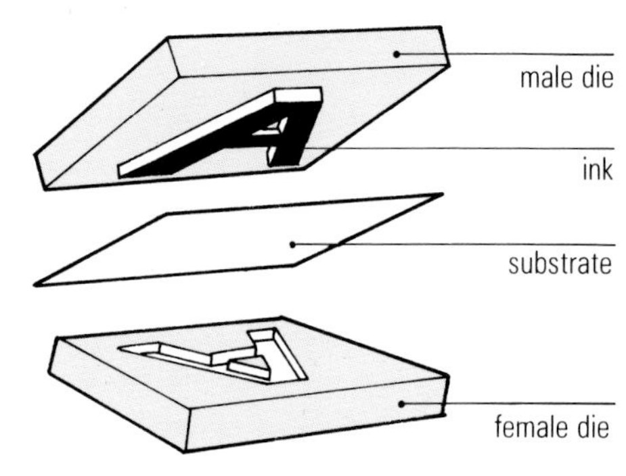

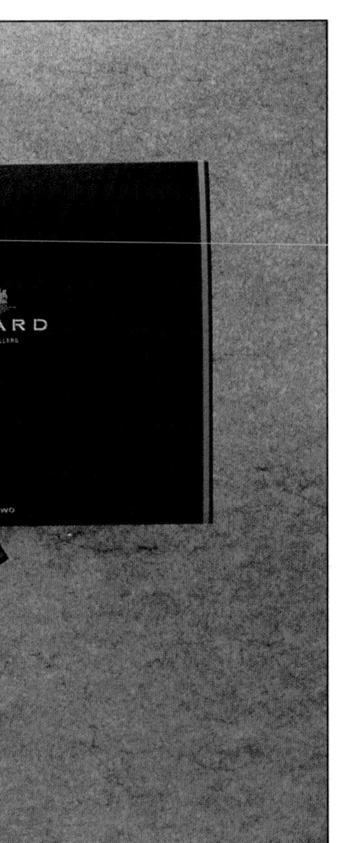

Other applications

Die stamping is well suited to any type of work that needs to look and feel prestigious. Packaging for items such as cosmetics, tobacco, alcohol, and candy is ideal for die stamping, if the cost of the product inside the box leaves room for the additional production costs. The process is also used for stationery for such professional groups as lawyers and financiers, and for high-class retail outlets. Promotional work can also be enhanced by die stamping.

Relative costs

Die stamping is not a cheap process, mainly because it is labor intensive. The die itself is generally hand-engraved. You will probably pay three or four times the price of having the same product thermographed, but the finished article will be in a different league.

This jacket for a promotional catalog of jewelry has been die stamped in gold leaf. The catalog was specifically aimed at rich people, and it was, needless to say, a very expensive affair. In fact, only a limited number were die stamped in gold leaf — the rest were printed in plain gold ink. Die stamping still takes a long time. It will probably take four weeks to get your own die designed, and the process itself is still mostly a hand operation. Do not specify die stamping if you are designing for a long run that needs to be out in an hurry.

SECURITY PRINTING BANK NOTES

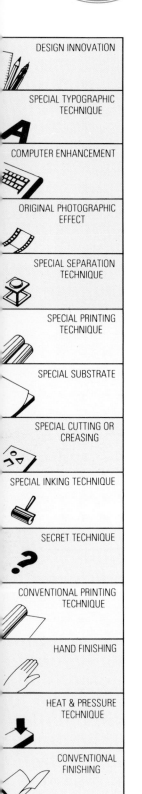

Printing currency involves a combination of lithography, intaglio, and letterpress. Lithography is used to print the background, by means of either the conventional or waterless process, conventional being cheaper and easier to print although waterless gives greater detail. Intaglio is used to print the detailed portrait, and letterpress to apply the numbering.

Designing for the lithographed background is a complex business. The register is absolutely critical since the best backgrounds from the point of view of security are composed of a mass of lozenge or diamond shapes, which, to the human eye, create a series of white lines. In addition, the background is usually printed from a rainbow, or split, duct, in which different inks are placed in each side of the same ink duct. You may, for example, decide to place red and blue in the duct, and in the middle the colors will merge. The effect is a whole range of colors, which is extremely difficult to counterfeit accurately.

Designing security devices

A host of security features needs to be designed into bank notes. The security devices are necessary on two levels — first, to convince the public that the notes are valid, and second, to permit official confirmation. Official security measures include the use of visible fluorescent inks, invisible ultraviolet inks and metallic inks, which change color according to the light source (when viewed under a neon light or in daylight, for example).

Do not use black ink when you design bank notes: it is far too easy to copy. The most difficult inks to reproduce are pastel shades — the more delicate the colors, the more difficult they are. You should avoid primary colors. Remember to keep the area around the watermark clear.

Intaglio printing

The second stage in the production of bank notes is the intaglio printing. This is usually how the image of the head of state, founder of the country, or other well-known person is printed on the note. Intaglio uses a hand-engraving process in which it can take up to three months to produce a single image for printing. It is similar to gravure in that the ink cells are recessed into the printing cylinder, but it goes one stage further in that the cells are of varying depth as well as of varying diameter. The result is to give a wide range of tonal change within one color, which may appear as three or four subtle shades. This technique is particularly difficult to forge.

Intaglio can also be recognized by touch, for the ink can be up to 150 microns off the surface of the paper. Complex intaglio designs may also incorporate tilt shadow patterns, by which different images appear depending on which way the note is viewed. Intaglio permits the reproduction of incredibly fine detail.

Finally, the numbers are applied to the notes by

Bank notes are often examples of the finest quality print of any kind. These Dutch bank notes incorporate a huge variety of printing effects within their design, including rainbow ducting, by which different colors are put in the same ink duct on the press. Note the absence of black ink from these and, in fact, from virtually all bank notes — it is too easy to copy.

letterpress. The latest security feature is to use numbering barrels of different sizes on the same number, so that individual digits look as if they have been misprinted. It is extremely difficult to reproduce this effect.

When you are designing bank notes it is obviously important to try to get a national flavor, and then try to adapt that to the general security principles. Many African countries, for example, favor geometric shapes with bold colors, which you would need to tone down; Arabic nations, on the other hand, tend to prefer soft, flowing designs, perhaps reflecting the desert landscape.

Scheduling time for producing bank notes, from the initial brief to delivery of the notes, is going to be a minimum of six months, and it may even be up to two years. However, once the design is agreed and the intaglio cylinder is made, it should be possible for the notes themselves to be printed relatively quickly. Printers capable of producing bank notes are rarely found in developing nations. The minimum print run will be no less than a million, and it is more likely to be 50 million. The paper is almost always specified by the country's central bank; it is usually between 55lb and 70lb and made from cotton rag. You can varnish notes, although this should be avoided in currency produced for developing countries, where the notes are often subjected to considerable wear and tear, which causes them to crack when varnished.

Other applications

In addition to bank notes, other documents that incorporate some or all of the same features include bonds, travelers' checks, the inside pages of passports, some vouchers — pan-continental travel vouchers, for example — stocks or share certificates, some visas, and some special-issue stamps.

Relative costs

Bank notes are necessarily expensive to produce because of all the security features that have to be incorporated. The fewer features you have, the more you can reduce the cost, but the greater risk you run of successful counterfeiting. A bank note has an expected life cycle of between six and nine months, although notes are kept in circulation for far longer in the non-Western world.

Due to currency regulations these bank notes have not been printed in their original colours or shown to their original size.

SECURITY PRINTING CHECKS

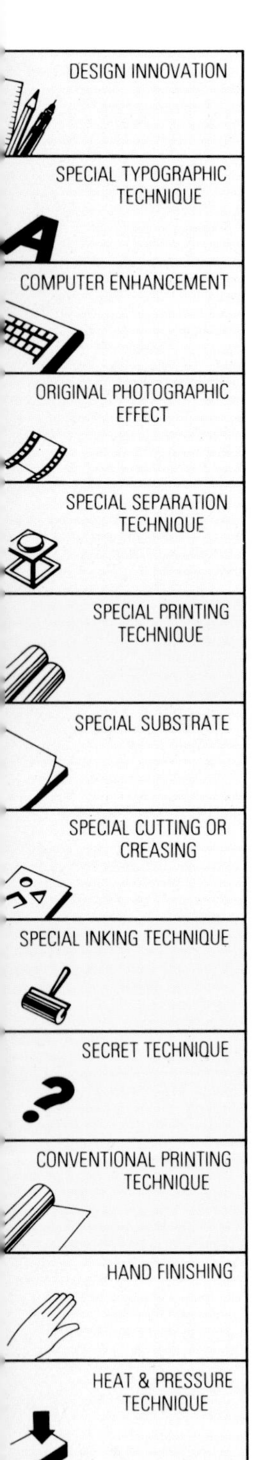

Checks are usually printed by conventional offset lithography, although a multitude of conventional and hybrid print processes may be used for the background printing, which has to incorporate a number of security features.

Standardized paper and design

In most countries the paper used for checks is specified by the government bank, and it is usually standardized. The basic design is also standardized to a certain extent, and the central banks insist on several specific items of information being in certain places. Inks, too, may be specified; for example, most countries insist that the background ink is water-soluble so that if someone tries to rub out a signature, the check itself will become defaced and thus rendered useless. However, if you are designing checks that will be used in the tropics, there is little point in using water-soluble inks because the humidity will adversely affect all the checks. In these circumstances, inks need to be solvent-soluble. Checks are often printed with special inks. Inks that cannot be photocopied are frequently used, and erasable inks are also common, since they rub off when a potential cheat tries to efface some other piece of information.

In the US and UK the numbers have to be in MICR; in most of Europe, however, numbers are in CMC7. In other countries that use the Roman system of numerals, the style of numbering will depend on who sold the country its banking system. In general, numbering has to be either by electrical or mechanical devices and with a once-only ribbon; very few countries permit the use of ink-jet or ion deposition.

If your design brief is to incorporate a company's logo into its checks, you must remember that colors will not reproduce as strongly on check paper as on conventional papers because it is not possible to attain the same density levels in printing with water-soluble inks, and the printed image tends to have a pastel effect. There is no limit to the number of colors you can use.

The scheduling time for check books can be up to three months, depending on the security features that have to be incorporated. However, if it is a simple job and a short run, it can be much less. Short runs can be 20 books if the customer is prepared to pay for them. Banks, of course, order checkbooks by the million, but most companies that want to use their own books will order in the hundreds.

It is usually either impracticable or too expensive to add special effects to checks themselves, although gold blocking, varnishing, and laminating can all be incorporated into the cover design.

The designs for these checks from a UK bank followed the American idea of having an illustration as part of the background. Both the illustration and the rest of the design have to be kept faint so that the main function of the document — to record a transaction — is not compromised. These checks were printed in the four-color process inks on a synthetic letterpress plate. For security reasons the inks are a special fugitive kind, so that if any attempt is made to interfere fraudulently with the check the inks will migrate across the paper, rendering the document useless.

Other applications

The same type of processes that are used for bank and company checks are also used to produce other semi-security documents such as insurance, tax, and trade documents and receipts, certificates, licenses, passes, bankbooks, and other voucher and security tickets.

Relative costs

Printing checks costs considerably more than printing conventional items, the additional costs depending on the level of security that has to be built into the checks. Both paper and inks will cost at least 50 percent more than conventional materials.

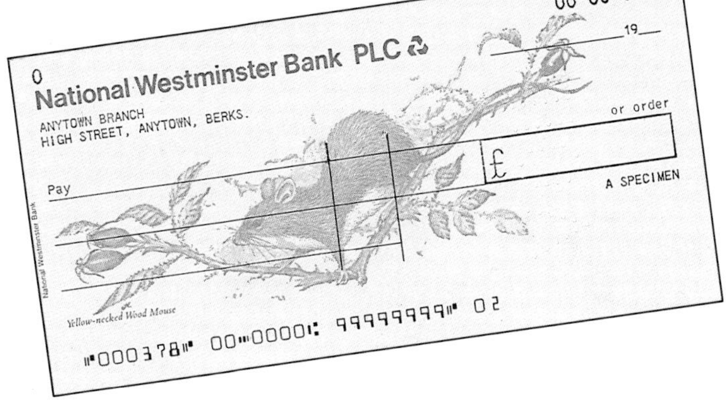

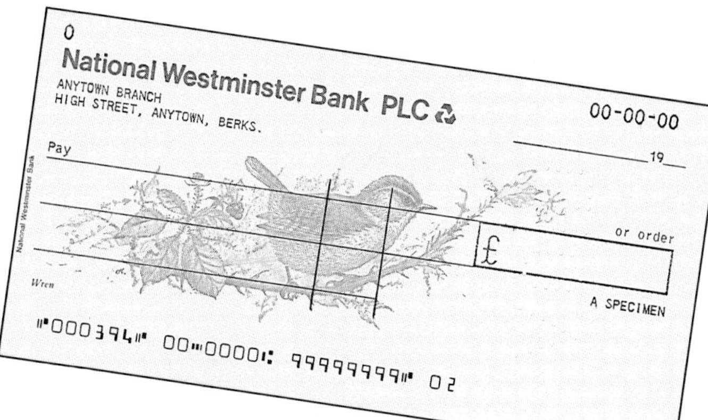

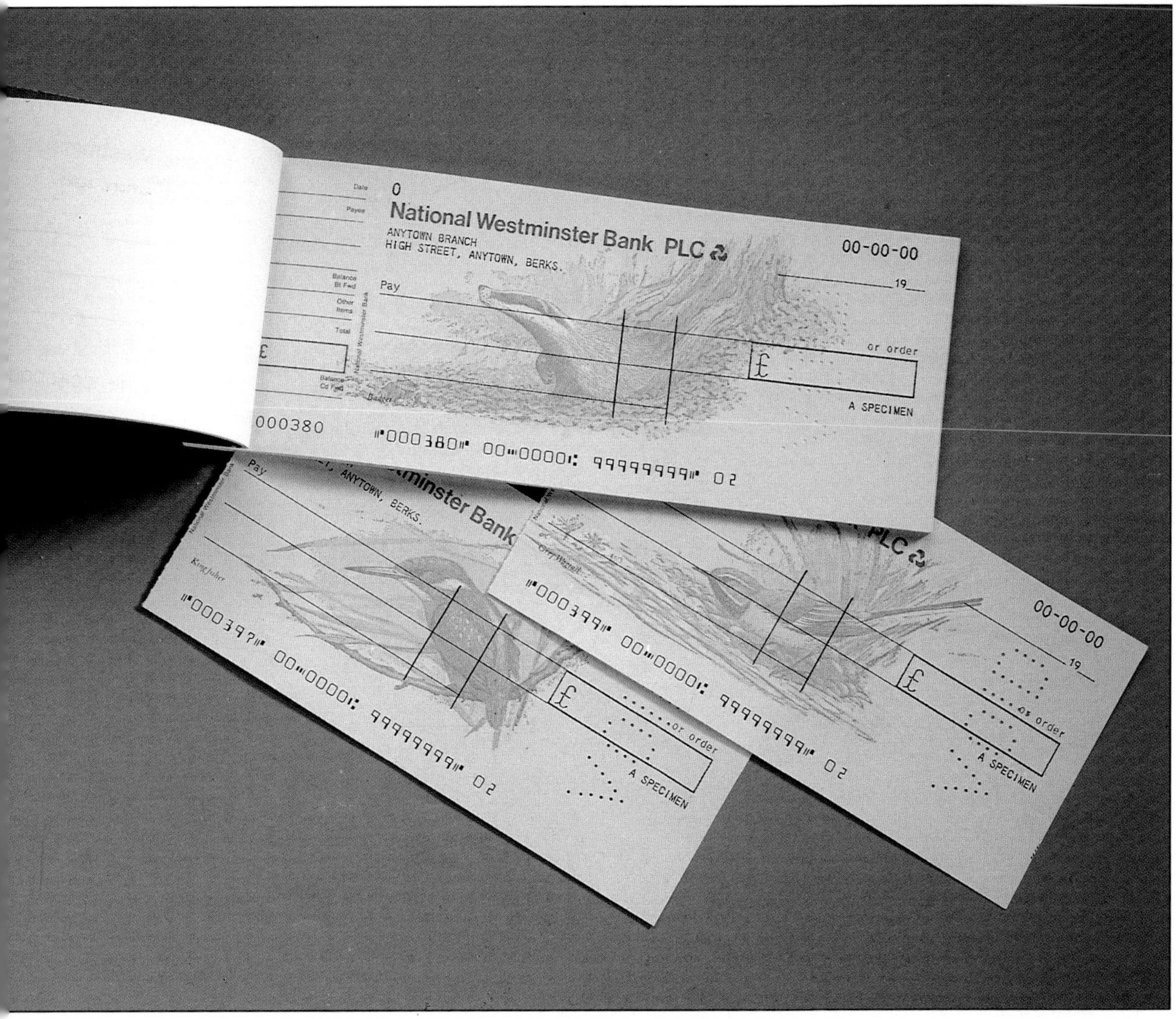

National Gallery
TRAFALGAR
DUNCAN
ST.
CHARING CROSS
SQU.
Nelson's
cabcharge
43298 ABC 5678
MR J P SMITH
01/91
EXPIRES END

SECURITY PRINTING CREDIT CARD

The production of credit cards has developed in the last 20 years from nothing to the point where it is now a major industry. The best known cards are the Visa/MasterCard type, which are issued by banks and which have to incorporate a number of stringent security devices, but the majority of cards are less complex and are used, for example, by stores for their charge account customers and by clubs for their members.

The cards are printed either by silk screen, lithography, or rotary letterpress. Silk screening is used for short-run work, but it is not capable of reproducing fine detail. Lithography can be used for medium to long runs, and it can give a finer quality in process colors. However, the lithography machine can sometimes leave marks on the card. Rotary letterpress prints well onto plastics.

Designing for plastic cards

When you are designing for plastic cards, if possible use line color only, since four-color work on such a small image area is very susceptible to misregister. Four-color images can be printed, of course, but line work is far easier. Reverses are also difficult to reproduce, but, if you are using lithography or letterpress, even small type should come out well. If brightness of color is important, screen printing will give the best results. Try to avoid bleeding the image on the card area, because this can lead to cracking around the edge of the card, where the bond will be looser, and flaking as the card is used. Leaving a natural border around the image area eliminates these problems.

Paler colors tend to work to greater effect than dark ones. Black looks impressive as the cards come off the press, but black cards soon appear to be covered with fingerprints. Golds and silvers work well.

The credit cards that are issued by banks are polished to give them a high gloss finish. The security numbers are embossed, and security features, such as holograms and magnetic strips, are adhered last of all. Low-security cards of the type used by stores and clubs are simply printed and varnished.

The scheduling time for credit cards will be anywhere between four days and four weeks, and the minimum press run can be very low if the cards are being screen printed.

Credit cards of all types have proliferated over recent years. Although good process color printing is not always easy to achieve, it can produce excellent results, as this illustration of Nelson's Column on a London taxi's credit card shows. The design for this card actually breaks most of the rules for trouble-free production — the four-color process, reverses, and an image that bleeds are all potential problem areas.

Other applications

High-security credit cards are used by all the major banks and finance companies for electronic cash transfer. Low-security cards are used by stores, clubs, and almost any company or organization that wants their customers to continue spending money with them and is prepared to give credit to facilitate this.

Relative costs

Printing plastic cards is not a cheap operation, because you pay a premium to the printer for knowing about the process. Plastic costs substantially more than paper, and the inks and varnishes are more expensive than those used on paper.

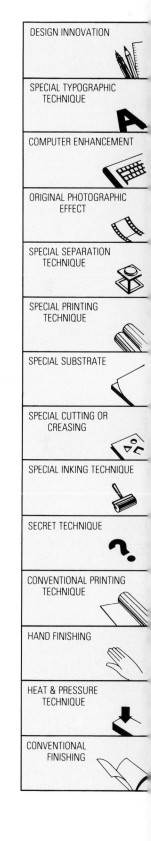

PRINTING ON GLASS BOTTLES

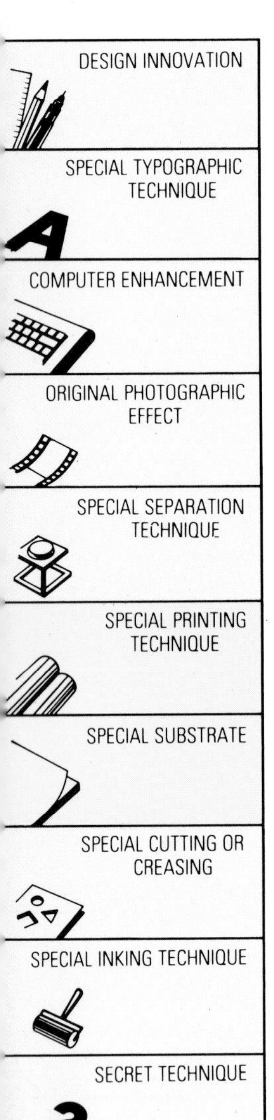

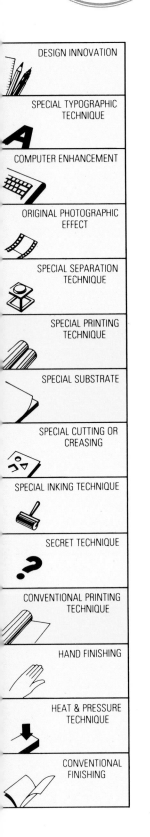

There are several ways in which it is possible to print on bottles. Self-adhesive labels (see pages 48-49) are, of course, an obvious and popular solution, but there are two other methods — direct printing and film transfer.

Direct printing is by screen or pad printing. For screen printing the artwork is converted into a stencil, ink is placed in the screen, and the bottle is held in a jig. The screen moves to the bottle, the ink is forced through, and the screen moves back, ready for the next bottle. In theory, there is no limit to the number of colors that can be printed, but in practice the maximum is six. Avoid including halftones in your design, which should be confined to line work, since the reproducible resolution does not allow the successful printing of halftones. Small type can be quite successfully reproduced. Film transfer can be achieved either by lithography or by screen printing, and lithography can be used for halftones. However, clear transfers can be used only on bottles with a single radius; tapered bottles are not suitable for this process.

You can screenprint solid golds, but metallic colors are very difficult. You should also bear in mind that bright colors are often not available in the PANTONE range of screen inks. Pink is a strange color because often the printer will not be able to predict exactly what it will look like when printed — it can vary all the way from light pink to almost red. Avoid pink ink if you can. Greens, too, tend to vary, and pastel colors often get paler.

If your design is multicolored, you will save a lot of trouble if you can accommodate a loose register. Because bottles are not flat, register is one of the greatest problems, and if it is not critical, the savings in time, worry, and money will be considerable.

Scheduling time will depend very much on the design. A multicolor design on a beveled bottle will obviously take much longer to print than one color on a single-diameter bottle. Simple jobs will require up to a month to prepare and print, while more complex work may need three months.

Try to avoid acid etching on bottles, because you cannot then screenprint them. You can, however, screenprint a pseudo-acid etch, which gives a frosted appearance, and you could then apply a self-adhesive label.

If you want an attractive presentation on a glass bottle there are three main options open to you: self-adhesive labels; screen printing direct; or as in the case of these bottles, a heat-seal shrink-wrap film. The films are printed before they reach the bottle, and then heat-shrunk around the bottle in a special heat tunnel. However, this is not a straightforward technique; you need to bear in mind that the film, and the graphics on it, will be distorted as they fit the irregular shapes of most bottles. Anticipating this distortion is where the skill comes in.

Other applications

Direct screen printing is mostly used on cosmetic and liquor bottles, while film transfer is becoming increasingly popular for soft-drink bottles.

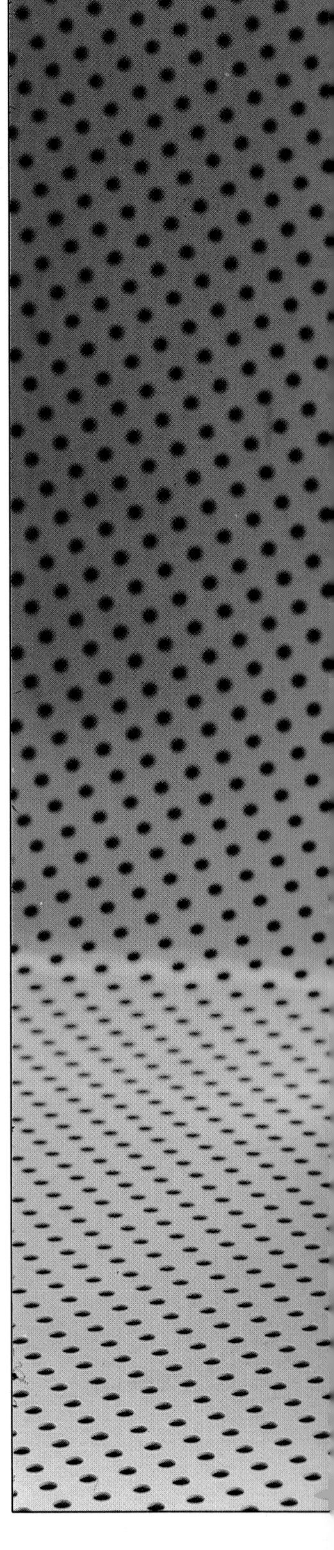

PURDEY'S FORMULA
ELIXIR VITÆ
SPARKLING HERBAL MULTIVITAMIN
DRINK
PURDEY'S
elixir vitæ
INGREDIENTS: CARBONATED SPRING WATER, A BLEND OF FRUIT JUICES FROM CONCENTRATES (GRAPE, APPLE), NATURAL FRUIT FLAVOURS, DAMIANA EXTRACT, BAYBERRY BARK EXTRACT, PRICKLY ASH BARK EXTRACT, CITRIC ACID, KOREAN GINSENG EXTRACT, VITAMIN C, ZINC SULPHATE, THIAMIN (VITAMIN B1), VITAMIN B6, RIBOFLAVIN (VITAMIN B2), FOLIC ACID, VITAMIN B12.
25cl
PURDEY'S FORMULA
ELIXIR VITÆ
SPARKLING HERBAL MULTIVITAMIN
DRINK
PURDEY'S
elixir vitæ
INGREDIENTS: CARBONATED SPRING WATER, A BLEND OF FRUIT JUICES FROM CONCENTRATES (GRAPE, APPLE), NATURAL FRUIT FLAVOURS, DAMIANA EXTRACT, BAYBERRY BARK EXTRACT, PRICKLY ASH BARK EXTRACT, CITRIC ACID, KOREAN GINSENG EXTRACT, VITAMIN C, ZINC SULPHATE, THIAMIN (VITAMIN B1), VITAMIN B6, RIBOFLAVIN (VITAMIN B2), FOLIC ACID, VITAMIN B12.
25cl

A BOOTS BEAUTY SHOP SELECTION
PERFUMERY

GRAVURE PRINTING GIFTWRAP

Producing giftwrapping paper has become big business in recent years, and the quality of print that can be achieved in this area is second to none. Giftwrap is normally printed on a gravure press, which makes it possible to have a continuous print image, unlike web offset machines, which have to have a non-image area each time the cylinder revolves. Flexography, which can also be used to print giftwrap, does not produce anything near the depth of color achievable by gravure, and it is much more difficult to maintain register on a flexo press. Web offset and flexography are suitable when the image does not have to be clear-cut, but if accurate reproduction and tight register are required, then gravure must be chosen.

Using gravure to print giftwrap will give consistent image and color throughout the length of the run. Difficult designs, even those incorporating reverses, small serif typefaces, and vignettes, create no problems for gravure. The process imposes no limits on the potential design.

Minimum print run

The minimum run length will be in the region of 130,000ft or more (40,000 m), and this will work out relatively expensive, since a substantial part of the cost of gravure printing is in the origination.

Choosing stock

The paper used for giftwrap varies from the cheap, part-mechanical, 35-40lb stock often used for Christmas wrapping to the higher quality, 45-50lb, strong white paper. The cheaper, poorer quality paper is not really acceptable for printing golds and silvers, and your printer will probably struggle to reproduce a four-color process job. Recycled paper, which is very porous and gives a flat image, does not lend itself to giftwrap, but metallized papers and films give good results. Using transparent metallic inks on silver metalized foils for example, will produce a very striking effect. If you use cheap materials, you are likely to be disappointed with the results. Printing in solid colors on a high quality paper will give exceptional results, and gravure presses should be able to print six or even eight colors on one pass.

Scheduling times are not fast. You will have to wait for up to a month for a single-color design, while complex designs can take up to three months. However, if a repeat run is required, the time is reduced significantly to a month or less. You can add almost anything to giftwrap — you can varnish, laminate, foilblock, or apply holograms to it, although, in practice, the costs would normally preclude most of these effects.

Choosing gravure to print giftwrap will allow you to produce beautiful designs that have fine tonal gradations like this one. Although flexography is cheaper and can be used for shorter runs, it cannot really achieve the sort of result shown on this gravure-printed product. Thoughtful design, such as this, can give substantial cost savings; this design is in just one color. The choice of paper is all-important in giftwrap — cheap paper will give cheap-looking results.

Other applications

Designs for giftwrap can be used for heat-transfer products for textile and clothing applications and for paper napkins. In addition, the giftwrap itself can be laminated on to a range of products, including plastic tableware.

Relative costs

Printing giftwrap is not that cheap a process, especially when gravure is used, and you generally need to produce a lot of it to make the run economic.

DESIGN INNOVATION

SPECIAL TYPOGRAPHIC TECHNIQUE

COMPUTER ENHANCEMENT

ORIGINAL PHOTOGRAPHIC EFFECT

SPECIAL SEPARATION TECHNIQUE

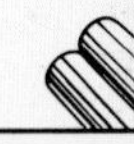

SPECIAL PRINTING TECHNIQUE

SPECIAL SUBSTRATE

SPECIAL CUTTING OR CREASING

SPECIAL INKING TECHNIQUE

SECRET TECHNIQUE

CONVENTIONAL PRINTING TECHNIQUE

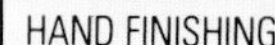

HAND FINISHING

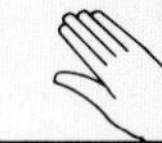

HEAT & PRESSURE TECHNIQUE

CONVENTIONAL FINISHING

SECURITY PRINTING POSTAGE STAMPS

- DESIGN INNOVATION
- SPECIAL TYPOGRAPHIC TECHNIQUE
- COMPUTER ENHANCEMENT
- ORIGINAL PHOTOGRAPHIC EFFECT
- SPECIAL SEPARATION TECHNIQUE
- SPECIAL PRINTING TECHNIQUE
- SPECIAL SUBSTRATE
- SPECIAL CUTTING OR CREASING
- SPECIAL INKING TECHNIQUE
- SECRET TECHNIQUE
- CONVENTIONAL PRINTING TECHNIQUE
- HAND FINISHING
- HEAT & PRESSURE TECHNIQUE
- CONVENTIONAL FINISHING

Postage stamps can be produced by lithography, gravure, or intaglio. In terms of cost, lithography is best for short run, commemorative work, while gravure is used for mainstream stamp printing, where quality, consistency, and legibility are the key factors. Intaglio is used for fiscal stamps, where an authoritative feel is important.

When you are designing stamps you should ideally work on an image four times the size of the end product; this will then be reduced by the printer. There is little point in thinking in terms of great detail on something so small, as it all disappears in production. For example, if you incorporate a skyscraper into the design the windows may not appear on the final stamp, because of the technique used to reduce the image.

Printing by gravure will ensure a high quality stamp, and many gravure printers will be able to give you a screen ruling of 300lpi (lines per inch).

Because of the size reduction, use overlays for text rather than incorporating it into the design itself; this will be easier for the printer. Remember to take account of the gutter between stamps, which is generally standardized at 0.12in (3mm).

There is no limit to the number of colors you can use, and postage stamps have been produced in up to 10 colors. Golds and silvers are no problem, but reproduce best on gravure. Embossing carries a cost that may be too much for one run of stamps, and holograms are almost certainly out of the question on cost grounds. Varnishing and laminating are not feasible because the postmark would not adhere. You should also bear in mind the country in which the stamp will be used; a hot, steamy, tropical country will have different paper and glue requirements from those of Alaska.

The paper that is available for stamp printing varies from 60gsm to 110gsm, and both coated and uncoated stock can be used. Coated paper gives better detail, but it is more expensive. For one- or two-color work without much fine detail, uncoated paper should be more than adequate.

Small run lengths of one to two million stamps will take between four and six weeks to produce; larger runs of 100 million or more will take two or three months, depending on the complexity. Very small commemorative runs that are printed by lithography could be ready in a few days, and they can be produced in tens of thousands.

Other applications

In addition to the major use of stamps as a receipt for a postal service given, they can also be used for a variety of fiscal purposes, including savings stamps to pay for utilities — gas, telephone, and electricity, for example — as well as receipts for money invested in savings plans and suchlike.

Relative costs

Because the cost of postage is low in most countries, the stamp itself cannot be allowed to represent too large a proportion of the cover price; that is why stamps are produced by the 100 million.

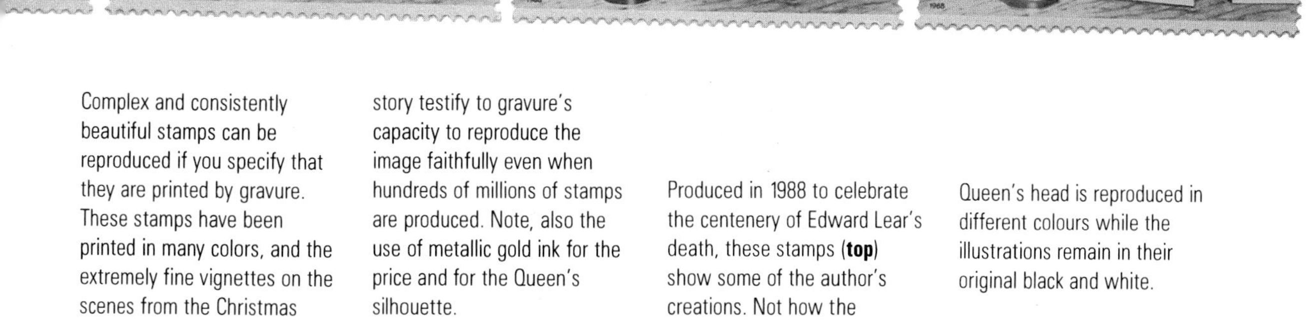

19P
The Owl and the Pussy-cat went to sea
In a beautiful pea-green boat,
EDWARD LEAR • 1812-1888
1988

27P
Yours affectionately, Edward Lear.
EDWARD LEAR • 1812-1888
1988

C. c c
32P
C was a lovely Pussy Cat; its eyes were large & pale;
And on its back it had some stripes, and several on his tail.
EDWARD LEAR • 1812-1888
1988

35P
There was a Young Lady whose bonnet,
Came untied when the birds sate upon it;
EDWARD LEAR • 1812-1888
1988

Complex and consistently beautiful stamps can be reproduced if you specify that they are printed by gravure. These stamps have been printed in many colors, and the extremely fine vignettes on the scenes from the Christmas story testify to gravure's capacity to reproduce the image faithfully even when hundreds of millions of stamps are produced. Note, also the use of metallic gold ink for the price and for the Queen's silhouette.

Produced in 1988 to celebrate the centenery of Edward Lear's death, these stamps (**top**) show some of the author's creations. Not how the Queen's head is reproduced in different colours while the illustrations remain in their original black and white.

SCREENPRINTING TEXTILES

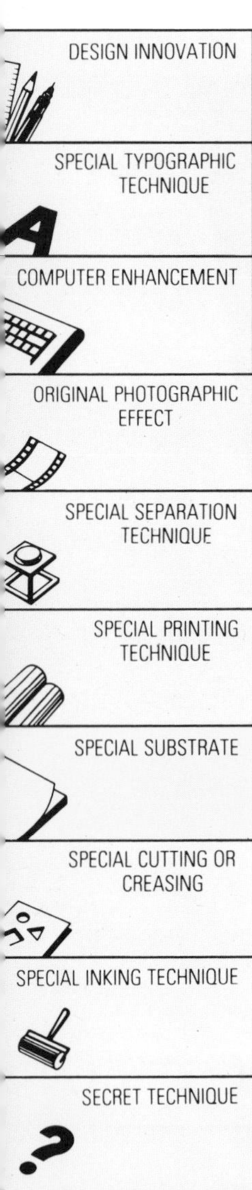

Printing designs on garments such as T-shirts and baseball caps has really taken off in the last 15 years, and it now comprises a major market in its own right. Garments are printed almost exclusively by screen printing, which, not coincidentally, has developed very rapidly in terms of quality and cost efficiency over the same period.

You can specify that a garment be screen printed in any number of colors. The largest machines can print up to 14 colors in one pass; more colors will require the fabric to go through the press again, with potential register problems on the second pass. However, this number of colors would be exceptional, and the majority of larger garment screen printers will have machines that can print up to eight or ten colors in one pass.

Most screen printers should be able to print an image up to 24×30in (60×75cm). The process lends itself to special-effect inks, such as metallics, glitters, fluorescents and day-glos, as well as to conventional inks. The colors achievable on screen-printed garments can be extremely bold and bright. It is also possible to print with a relatively high raised surface if you want that to be part of the design.

Know the limitations

It is important to understand that screen printing is not the same as lithography or gravure and the detail cannot be as fine. In addition, if you want to print in process colors rather than in solid blocks, you will very often not be able to achieve the result you would have hoped. This is certainly the case if you are printing on a black garment, such as the black material that is used for most rock concert T-shirts and merchandise. If you present such a design it is likely that the screen printer will either make a mess of it or will even break your artwork down and start again by redesigning it into blocks of solid colors, doubling your original design cost in the process! You can, however, quite successfully print process colors on to a white background. If you are designing for silks and wools, the main problem can be blotching if there are too many colors, and therefore too many inks, in one area. Vignettes can be printed successfully only across T-shirts, rather than from top to bottom, because of the nature of the printing process.

You should allow 10 days from delivery of artwork before most garments are printed. However, as with everything, if you are in a rush someone will be able to turn it around in a day. Printing onto wools and silks, which is more specialized and requires a higher quality print, will always take a lot longer. The shortest time will be two weeks, and in the normal course of events it will be anywhere from four to six weeks.

Most garments can readily accommodate other effects such as foil blocking, transfer printing and heat-sensitive inks.

Other applications

A wide variety of garments lend themselves to screen printing, including T-shirts, sweatshirts and pants, jackets, caps and hats, athletes' shirts, and shorts, aprons, and scarves. Neckties, boxer shorts, and handkerchiefs, which are printed on silk or wool, require more specialist printing, although this is still the same basic process.

Relative costs

Adding a multicolor design to a T-shirt will probably add between one third and one half again to the price of the garment itself.

Clothes are almost exclusively screen printed, an extremely flexible process. As well as conventional screen ink, these heavyweight sweatshirts incorporate a puff ink — that is, an ink that gives a relief effect. Clothing can be printed in up to 14 colors, although sensible use of just a few colors can reduce costs and look just as good. In the examples shown here, the sweatshirt on the far left has four colors, the one on the left has, five, and the shirt above has three. Line art rather than halftones will not only give more consistent results but will allow you more flexibility in the design. The typescript lettering on these garments was machine-embroidered on top of the printed image.

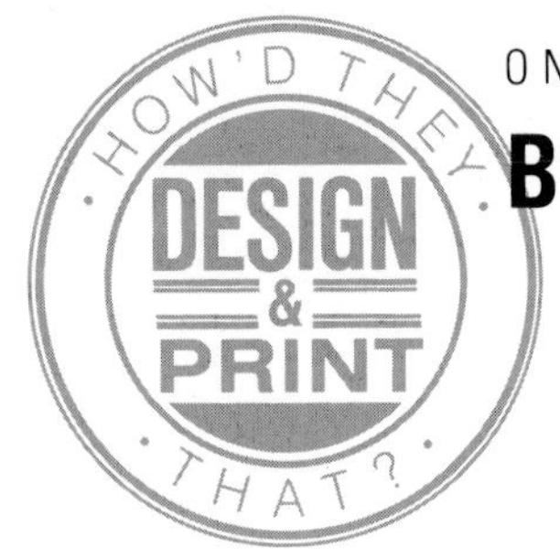

BILLBOARD PRODUCTION "TRIANGULAR" DISPLAY

Billboards are compilations of a number of small posters joined together into one large sheet. The printer uses the base artwork, type, and tints to produce a miniature printed proof. When this has been approved and corrected, the image, which is in film negative form, is projected in sections to full billboard size. From these sections plates are made, and the billboard is printed. A typical billboard may be composed of 12 or 16 of these separate sheets.

Billboards can be printed by lithography or by screen. Screen printing is usually specified for low runs or when very bright, solid colors are incorporated in the design. Lithography is not only more economical over longer runs, but it is capable of producing a much finer halftone. Vignettes, for example, need to be treated carefully in screen printing, and they may prove difficult, particularly when it comes to maintaining the register.

Choosing colors that reproduce well

It is important to remember that certain colors will not reproduce well with process litho printing; bright greens and oranges can cause problems, for example, and it is advisable to specify special colors. This is particularly necessary if the paper is uncoated. The uncoated papers generally used for poster printing will flatten the colors overall, and if you want to use rich colors, you should specify coated paper, which, although more expensive, will give a better result.

Reversing white out of images can cause problems in poster printing, so you should avoid this if possible. If the billboard is going to be up for longer than a week, light-fast inks should be used. These generally guarantee fidelity of reproduction for six weeks, and in practice they remain true for longer. If you are designing a billboard that is going to be displayed in a region with very strong sunshine, special light-fast inks will have to be used. Metallic inks can be used successfully on billboards, but they must be varnished, since they do not dry properly and will streak in the rain.

A word about the proof: this will be on high-gloss art paper, so you need to remember that the final image will look a lot different although the proof will be accurate as far as position is concerned.

Moving-triangle billboards, of the kind seen in the centers of cities, are produced in the same way as conventional posters, and then cut.

It will normally take around seven working days from artwork to finished billboard, and then time should be allowed for distribution, which is likely to be twice as long again.

Other applications

Posters can be used almost anywhere, from the huge billboards seen alongside the highway to the single-sheet versions that are displayed in bus stations and airports, and outside galleries and museums.

Relative costs

Poster costs vary widely according to the quantity printed, the number of colors used, and the types of inks. Screen printing is cheaper for short runs, but for a run of more than 100, litho printing will be more economic.

Both the billboards shown here are on moving triangle sites, where the billboard changes every few seconds. Posters for such sites are produced in the same way as for conventional billboards and simply cut to fit.

Other applications

The processes and materials used to print beermats can be used in related fields. Restaurants for example, often need place-mats in a larger format, around 18×15in (45×38cm), which are useful not only because they absorb the heat of the plate but also for showing the menu along with an illustration. Airlines are one of the major users of larger coaster-style mats.

Relative costs

Printing beermats will be slightly more expensive than normal litho printing because the press has to run a little more slowly; production time, therefore, increases. The origination and material costs should be no more than a normal job, however. A small premium will probably be charged for the scalloped edge on coasters, but any printer seriously into beermat printing will have a ready-made die on hand.

ABSORBENT PAPER BEERMATS

Beermats have their own peculiar production properties. Designed to absorb spilt beer, naturally enough they absorb ink to a greater degree than other substrates. This results in a considerable dulling of the image, so an intelligent use of colors will serve you well, as in this example where yellow has been used on blue, a highly legible combination. This design overcame a limit on the number of colors that could be used by breaking down the solid areas into halftone dots and then overlapping the percentage tints in various areas.

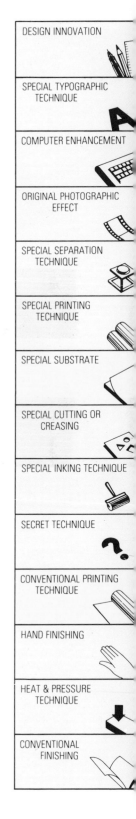

Printed mats tend to come in two formats, the thick, non-flexible type that is usually used for beers, and the thin, flexible, coaster type, usually with scalloped edge, that is used for liquor and cocktails. The non-flexible beermats are made from pure wood pulp, while the coasters are made from tissue. Both types perform two tasks: they absorb spillage from drinks and they act as an advertising medium.

Design drawbacks

Because they have to be made of highly absorbent material, mats of both types give no help whatever to the designer. The material has absolutely no lift, so colors appear flat and dead. The basic rules are to use bright colors and to steer clear of fine detail. Similarly, reversed images are very difficult to achieve. You should also expect to lose a lot of the feeling in the final product, and classic pictures tend not to reproduce well. Take care if you are reducing your artwork; if you have produced a design on a 2-foot (60cm) square board and expect the same detail to come out on a 3-inch (7.5cm) square beermat you will inevitably be disappointed.

Non-flexible mats can be printed from halftone process work, or from line art, but coasters can be printed only using line art. Coasters can, moreover, only be printed on one side, although non-flexibles can be printed on both. Furthermore, coasters can only be printed with a maximum of three colors. Both types are mainly printed by offset litho.

The scheduling time is not too long: a run of 250,000 in four-color process ink should take between four and six weeks to produce. Minimum run lengths may be as little as 10,000.

Although it is possible to varnish on top of beermats, and this may highlight the advertisement, the varnish negates the primary purpose of the beermat, which is to absorb spillage.

100w
JEREMIAH, 12
CHAPTER 12
CHAPTER 13
CAFETERIA
SANTA ANA 2
B 000890
B 000.085
B 000.085
B 000.360
B 000.180
B 000.180
VALENCIA
HORIZONS
Wine List
LA BOLOGNA

Finishing

Being able to add that extra touch to a printed product can make all the difference between success and failure, as far as the client is concerned. Making your product stand out in the crowd is part of the essence of design, and special finishes of one sort or another are often the way to achieve this.

Finishing techniques of all kinds have burgeoned over the last few years. Some techniques have been taken on board by almost everyone — spot varnishing, for example, was unheard of a few years ago but now there is hardly an item of prestige printed matter that does not incorporate it. Other finishing processes are not so well known, however, and this section discusses the modern and traditional forms of finishing, both of which need to be integral parts of the designer's armory. In addition, there is a section on special inks and special papers, an understanding of which can add considerably to the creative potential of your designs. Again, all of the processes and materials discussed have their own strengths and limitations, but appreciating these parameters will give you the freedom to work still more creatively.

DESIGN INNOVATION
SPECIAL TYPOGRAPHIC TECHNIQUE
COMPUTER ENHANCEMENT
ORIGINAL PHOTOGRAPHIC EFFECT
SPECIAL SEPARATION TECHNIQUE
SPECIAL PRINTING TECHNIQUE
SPECIAL SUBSTRATE
SPECIAL CUTTING OR CREASING
SPECIAL INKING TECHNIQUE
SECRET TECHNIQUE
CONVENTIONAL PRINTING TECHNIQUE
HAND FINISHING
HEAT & PRESSURE TECHNIQUE
CONVENTIONAL FINISHING

Thanks to computer-aided design systems and laser cutters it is now not only easier to create irregular shapes but also simpler to ascertain their design validity. Until these systems were developed, die cutting was a laborious, inflexible and relatively inaccurate hand process. However, CAD/CAM laser systems can guarantee accuracy and also offer the major benefit of enabling the shape to be changed quickly and easily. Once created on the system, the shape can be cut as a one-shot sample on a knife plotter and changes speedily made until the client is satisfied with the final output. When used in conjunction with a color thermal proofer printer, the system provides an accurate indication of what the finished product will look like.

Once approved, the final shape is laser-cut through plywood from the same computer data. Knives are added to the die, which is then placed either at the end of a press, or off-line, and litho-printed sheets passed through it. Most applications would have from 10 to 20 dies on the sheet, and the computer design ensures that each one is an exact replica of the original. If creases are required, a female die has to be made, because there has to be a recess to take the pressure.

Design constraints

Die-cut products require a certain amount of leeway in the design. The edges should bleed, and attempts to cut the image too finely, even with laser-cut dies, can put unnecessary strain on the production process, with the result that the print register is not always as accurate as it should be. The aim should be to try and keep the design around the cuts as simple as possible. Boxes for Easter eggs are a prime example of fairly complex die-cut work.

In theory, it is possible to design any shape and see it cut; in practice, however, intricate detail can cause undue complications and should almost always be avoided.

So far as scheduling is concerned, you should be able to get a sample back within 24 hours and the die the next day. It is wise to allow plenty of time when scheduling die-cut work because the client is almost certain to demand that alterations be made by the designer, the printer, or the die cutter, and usually from all three!

It is possible to die cut through products that have been laminated and varnished, and die-cut designs often benefit from foil blocking or the addition of holograms.

The favored material for die cutting is board, although you can die cut paper it is not too thin — bible paper for instance, would not cut well. Some plastic can be cut into shapes, but is less amenable to folding.

A range of packaging for a take-out food company (**right**). The word Toulouse was die cut at the same time as the box itself.

Other applications

Die cutting is most commonly used for packaging. All cartons are, of course, die cut, and some of the most ingenious work is seen in presentation packages of cosmetics and candy. Other die-cut products include promotional print, point-of-sale material, and pop-up books and cards.

Relative costs

Die cutting is an expensive process, even with the new technology. However, the new systems do make it easier and cheaper to experiment until you have the right design.

Die cutting has been made considerably easier by the development of computer-aided design and masking systems, which not only allow inexpensive mockups to be produced but also make possible extremely accurate cutting, even in such irregular shapes as these cards (**above** and **right**) which were produced as a promotion for a paper company.

DIE CUTTING POP-UPS

Pop-up books are now almost exclusively produced in just five countries: Singapore, Hong Kong, Mexico, Brazil, and Colombia. This is because so much handwork is necessary to put the books together, and the run has to be very long to be viable since costs accrued in the production process are substantial. The comparatively low labor costs and the experience available in these countries combine to make them the only real options. Pop-up greeting cards can, however, usually be produced within the domestic industry.

Pop-up books and cards are produced by litho printing on card, die cutting the printed sheets, and then hand-assembling the various pieces. The most important person in the production of a pop-up book or card is the paper engineer. This person is also the most expensive! Once the designer has made some initial sketches, the paper engineer needs to figure out all of the smart angles – that is, how the design is actually going to work and the most efficient way of putting it all together. The complications to be overcome are many and varied. It goes without saying that proofing is essential. There has to be extremely close communication between the designer or illustrator and the paper engineer. In Latin America the size of the book is limited by the paper size that can be produced, and a typical $8\frac{1}{2}\times11$in book can have a maximum of only six spreads.

Although their production is extremely complicated, pop-up books and cards can be very exciting to look at, and pop-up books can often explain in a three-dimensional way topics that are difficult to express in two dimensions. One of the best-selling books of recent years was a pop-up version of *The Kama Sutra*!

Pop-up books require a far longer schedule than conventional books: 18 months is the minimum amount of time from conception to delivery, and production can often take two years. Communication difficulties may also delay schedules, although fax machines have lessened this problem.

The minimum press run for books is 40,000 copies, so in countries other than the US there have to be international coeditions to make the project viable. Cards are much less costly and can be produced in hundreds rather than thousands.

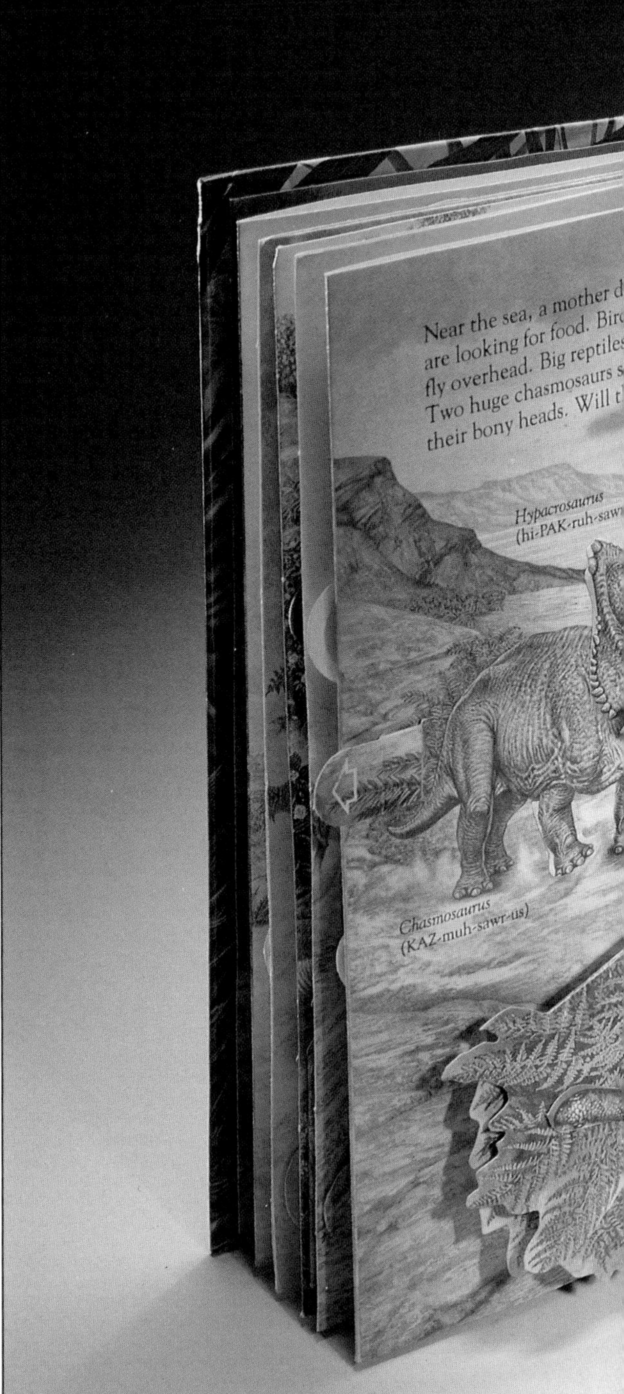

Pop-up books are very expensive to produce, and most, such as this one (**above**), have a maximum of only six spreads. *Creatures of Long Ago*, which was produced for the National Geographic Society of America, makes use of tabs to pull and wheels to turn to give the full range of moving effects – wagging tails, flapping wings, chomping mouths, and so on.

Pop-up greeting cards such as this one (**right**) can be produced commercially in runs of as few as 3,000. A rubber band and a simple V-fold are used to create the action in the bouquet, and to close the card you simply press two yellow dots. When flat, it fits easily into a conventional envelope. This card is part of a range of 45 designs, and it took 18 months to develop the paper engineering for the series.

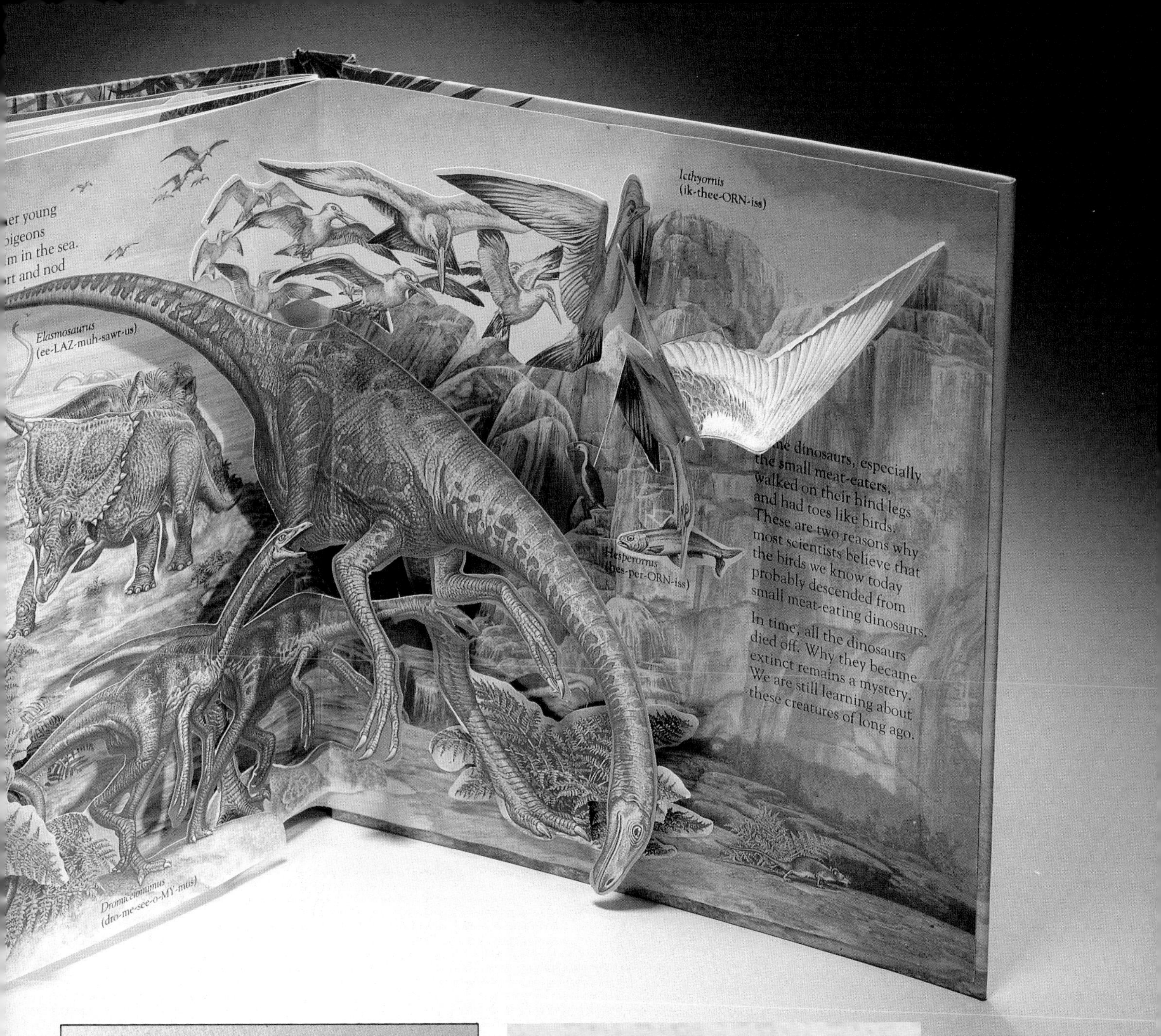

Icthyornis
(ik-thee-ORN-iss)
Elasmosaurus
(ee-LAZ-muh-sawr-us)
dinosaurs, especially
the small meat-eaters,
walked on their hind legs
and had toes like birds.
These are two reasons why
most scientists believe that
the birds we know today
probably descended from
small meat-eating dinosaurs.
In time, all the dinosaurs
died off. Why they became
extinct remains a mystery.
We are still learning about
these creatures of long ago.
Dromiceiomimus
(dro-me-see-o-MY-mus)

Other applications

Pop-up books are mostly produced for the popular educational market, and subjects in recent years have included dinosaurs, trees, jungle and insect life. The best-selling pop-up book of all time was about the inside of the human body, and more than a million copies have so far been produced. Pop-up cards are essentially part of the novelty market.

Relative costs

Pop-up books and cards are expensive! And it is worth bearing in mind that, per page, cards are more expensive than the books.

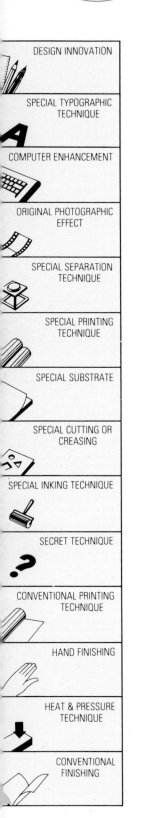

VARNISHING BROCHURE

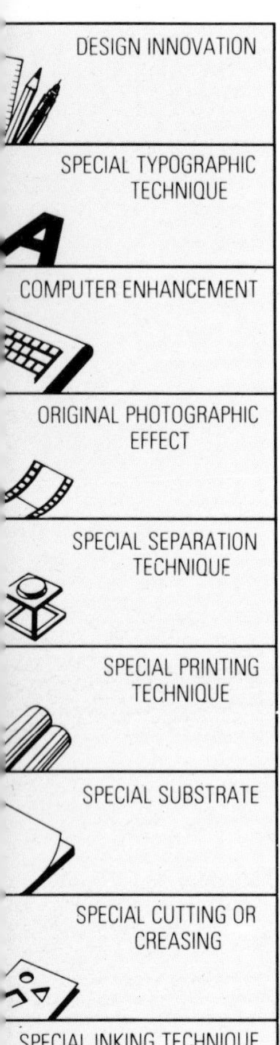

Varnishing is a relatively inexpensive way of enhancing and protecting a product. These days much varnishing is ultraviolet curable, which means that it dries instantaneously the moment it passes under an ultraviolet light, whether the work is on a press or on a dedicated machine. Varnish can be applied on the press, on an off-line varnishing unit or by silk screening, which is often used for spot varnishing. However, many hybrid production systems are also in use.

Spot varnishing has become incredibly popular in the last few years; hardly a set of reports and accounts or a company brochure is published that has not been spot varnished. The varnish is usually applied only over the color pictures in a brochure, and it gives an extremely high quality, high gloss look and feel to the publication as a whole. It can also be used on its own to achieve more subtle effects. Applying spot varnish requires a much greater degree of control over register than all-over varnishing.

The most vital point in varnishing is that the ink must be completely dry before the varnish is added. In effect, this means that you should not varnish for at least 24 hours after printing — so do not give in to an impatient client who would be even more irate upon seeing the muddy mess that would result from the cross-reaction between the inks and the varnish. However, if ultraviolet inks are used, you can varnish immediately since these inks also dry instantaneously. Applying spot ultraviolet varnish on matte laminate can also cause problems, so make sure you use a specialist.

Types of varnish

There are four types of varnish. The basic finish is the conventional oil-based kind, which is applied on the last unit of the press. It takes between two and eight hours to dry and has fair to good gloss. It is also the cheapest varnish to use.

Second, there are the water-based varnishes, which can be applied only by a dedicated machine, post-printing. Because the printer has to invest in a special machine and because its application is a separate production process, costs are higher.

Then there are the ultraviolet varnishes. These are extremely glossy and smooth; they dry instantly; they have low odor and taint levels; and they have a built-in "slip" factor so that packages do not slip around on the production line. However, it is very difficult to print ultraviolet varnishes on wet inks, so in the production process the varnish has to be applied either after the main printing of the image has dried, which adds cost and time, or onto ultraviolet inks, which are more expensive than conventional inks. Finally, there are the spirit-based varnishes which, for environmental reasons, are rapidly falling from favor.

You should be able to specify varnishing to a fine detail, although complicated work will take much more effort to get right. Again, the scheduling time should be 24 hours from the time the print is ready, although complicated spot varnish may take longer. A specialist house will be able to run at a rate of almost 10,000 sheets an hour.

Varnishing tends to be used for bulk-run work because it is both quicker and cheaper than lamination. Moreover, if there is a varnishing unit on the press, the production process adds nothing to the printing time.

Spot varnishing, which has become incredibly popular recently, can be used to give dramatic highlights to part of a design, such as these fish. Success depends on the correct positioning of the film and camera work. This piece was varnished with an ultraviolet substance, which, although the most expensive type of varnish, gives the highest levels of gloss and sheen.

Other applications

Varnishing is used to enhance a wide range of products, from magazine covers and brochures to blister packs and cartons. Spot varnishing is used in reports and accounts, in brochures, and in promotional and sales literature.

Relative costs

Varnishing costs around 40 percent of the price of laminating. Spot varnishing is more expensive because a plate has to be originated and the register tightly controlled.

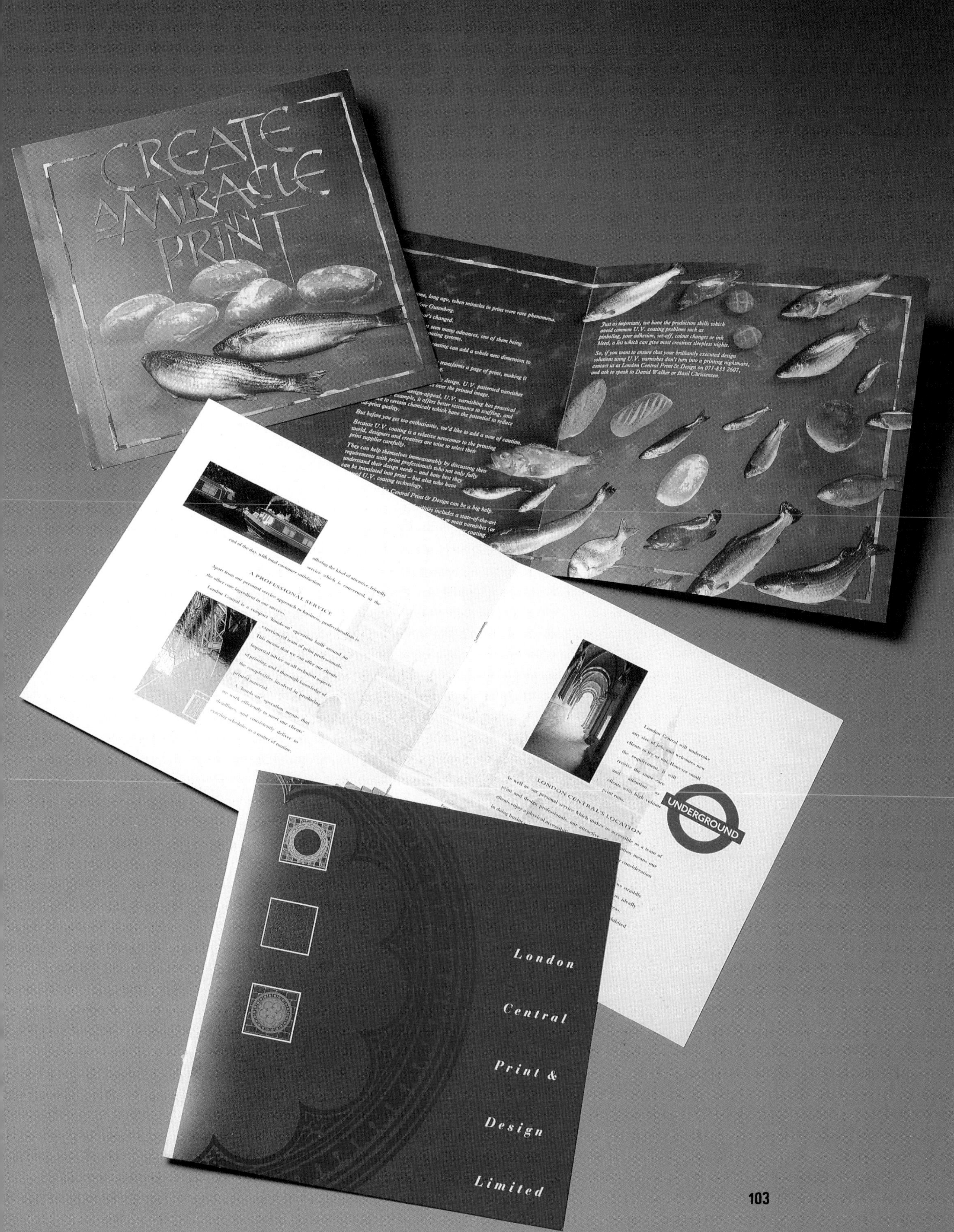
CREATE A MIRACLE IN PRINT
A PROFESSIONAL SERVICE
LONDON CENTRAL'S LOCATION
UNDERGROUND
London
Central
Print &
Design
Limited

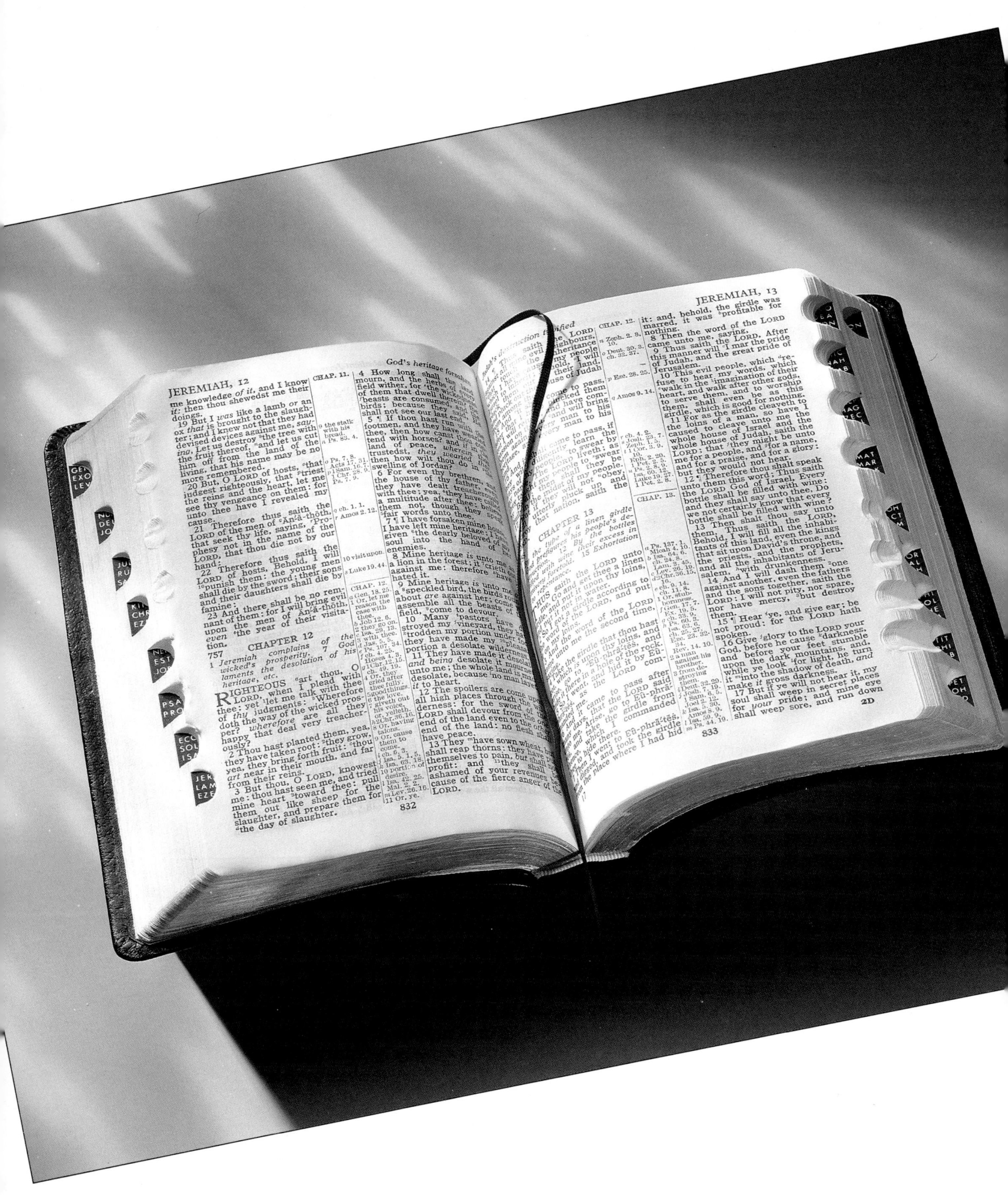
JEREMIAH, 12
God's heritage forsaken
CHAPTER 12
832
JEREMIAH, 13
CHAPTER 13
833

SPECIAL FINISHES BIBLE

Special finishes on books are exemplified in presentation bibles. Gilt or dyed edges, rounded corners, thumb indexes, ribbon reminders, and leather binding are all finishes likely to be found on bibles, and so we will use the printing processes involved in the production of bibles to demonstrate how to design these effects into any book.

It is important to remember that bibles are printed on very thin paper, with weights as low as 30lb and often lighter than that. These days the printing is by lithography. Black is the only ink that will adequately meet the opacity requirements of such lightweight papers. Although black shows through to some degree, this is virtually unnoticeable when compared to the effect of other colors. The gold or colored gilt which covers the edges of the pages is sprayed on before the cover is attached. Round cornering and thumb indexing, as shown in the illustration, are extremely laborious hand operations.

The golden rule for page design when special finishing features are to be included in a book is not to bleed pictures or illustrations at all. It looks absurd if the round cornering chops off part of a picture, and if gilt edging is added to paper that is already inked, there may be problems.

All of these features increase the scheduling time considerably, since none of them can be accomplished with any speed. Thumb indexing, for example, whether it is for an alphabetical letter in a dictionary, or a book in the bible, is carried out by hand in most parts of the world, and it is a highly labor-intensive job. In addition, not many binderies will have every facility, so you may find your book traveling between two or more separate factories for all the effects to be added. Allow at least eight weeks post-printing if you are going for the full range of features.

The minimum press run depends very much on how much you are prepared to pay. Special presentation books often command a substantial price premium since they are there to be displayed rather than read. However, you are unlikely to find it economical to include special features for a run of less than a few thousand.

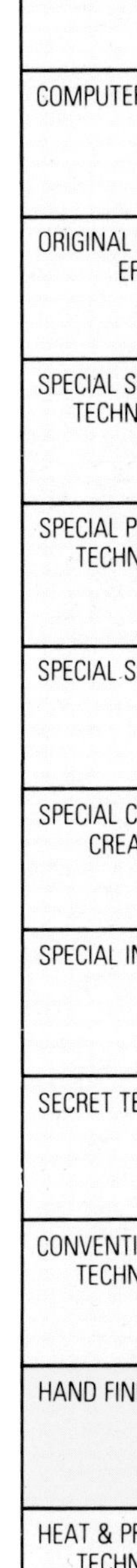

Presentation books such as this bible are often prime candidates for a whole range of special finishes, which add tremendously to the quality of the product. This bible has sewn binding, gilt edges, round corners, and ribbon reminders, and it is bound in full leather. Designing such books is often a complex business, and these special finishes add considerably to production time and costs. There are, however, only one or two golden rules to observe, and although the production processes are laborious, they are straightforward.

Other applications

Other types of book that may have some of these finishes include dictionaries, calendars, diaries, encyclopedias, reference books, and special series books, such as the complete works of Shakespeare.

Relative costs

By specifying special finishes you are adding considerably to the final cost of the product, and if you include everything, you may double the production costs.

LAMINATING BOOKS

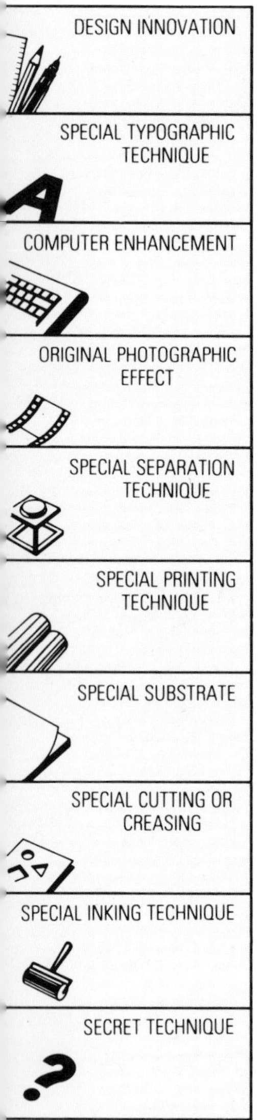

Laminating a printed product is an effective way of enhancing or protecting it, or both. The process offers a high-gloss finish, gives a high degree of scuff and tear resistance, and lengthens the product's shelf-life.

Laminate comes in rolls, and it is applied to the printed sheet as a whole piece of film through a combination of heat and pressure. Most lamination is applied to printed sheets rather than to the web. It is impossible to spot laminate, that is, to laminate discriminately — it has to be all or nothing — unlike varnish, which can be applied in specified areas.

Laminate can be either matte or gloss, and it can be combined with spot varnishing. For example, you may want to spot varnish on top of a laminated product to give a high quality feel. There are dangers in doing this, and you need to choose the correct materials or the varnish will slip around.

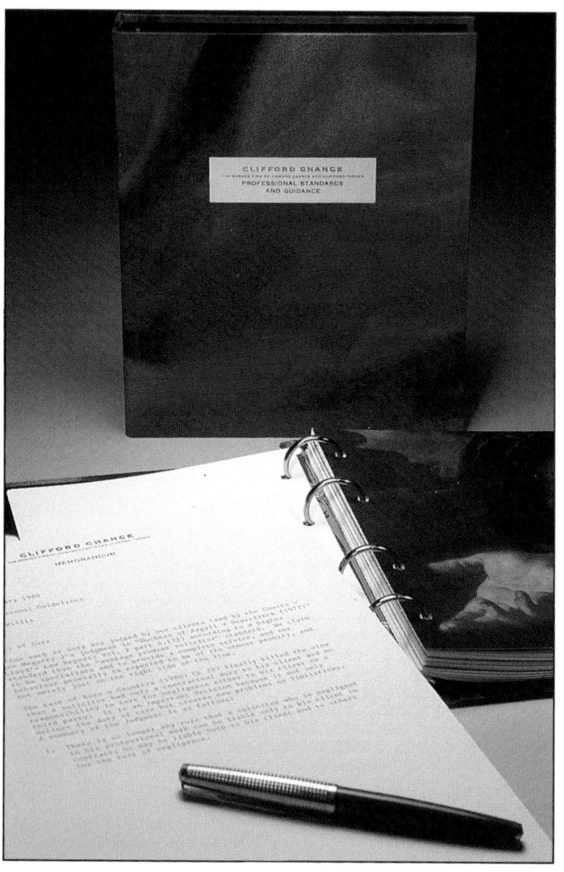

Avoiding the pitfalls

There are plenty of pitfalls the designer must be aware of. Laminating over a crease is bound to cause problems, while laminating over screen-printed products that have had a heavy deposit of ink requires care in case the laminate film does not adhere to the substrate in the well between two image areas that are close together. Air bubbles will disrupt the laminate. Avoid metallic inks when laminating, because they are liable to flake and float around under the laminate.

You can laminate virtually any substrate, from 55lb paper to 65 ppi micron board, as well as synthetics and plastic. The rougher the surface the more problems you will have. Uncoated board, for example, does not take laminate well, and you may end up with lots of air bubbles. Laminating over holograms and foil blocking protects the effects and should not adversely affect their impact, although it is possible to apply both effects after the lamination process.

The scheduling time for lamination is short. Any self-respecting trade house should be able to offer a 24-hour turnaround. Minimum runs can be very short.

Other applications

Lamination is applied to a wide range of products, including cartons, brochures, paperback book covers, reports and accounts, small-circulation magazine covers, greeting cards, menus, and maps.

Relative costs

Laminating will cost more than twice the price of varnishing, but it does offer greater protection and a glossier finish.

This handbook, which was produced for in-house use by Europe's largest firm of lawyers, is matte laminated on the cover and on every page (**left**). The client wanted the handbooks to be given the maximum possible protection because they would be used daily over a number of years by a variety of lawyers. The handbooks were produced in ring binder form so that changes in the law could be easily incorporated. The illustrations are taken from various paintings by Old Masters, and the designer has generally used the part of each painting that shows a hand. The cover of *The Creative Director's Source Book* is gloss laminated all over (**right**). The material is a heavy board, and the type is foil blocked. Foil blocking is always carried out before lamination, and it should benefit from the protection lamination affords.

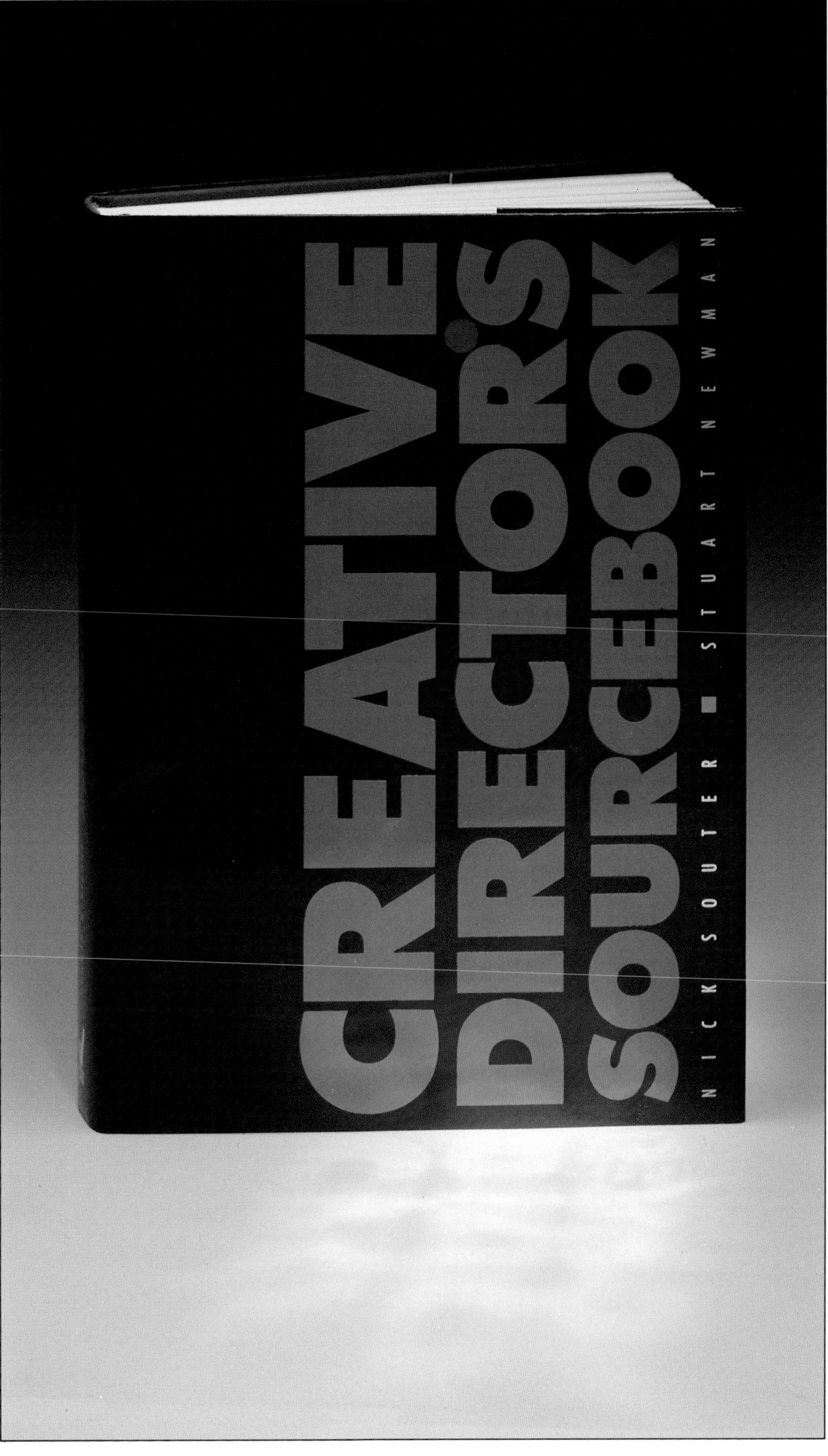

MAZDA
style
LIGHT
Decor Round 126mm
150w

MAZDA
style
LIGHT
Decor Spot
100w

MAZDA
style
LIGHT
Decor Spot
SMALL SCREW CAP
40w

MAZDA
style
LIGHT
Par 38 Floodlight
100w

HOW'D THEY
DESIGN
&
PRINT
THAT?

BLISTER/SKIN PACKAGING
HOUSEHOLD GOODS

Blister and skin packaging consists of a base of litho-printed cardboard and a plastic blister or skin that adheres to the cardboard, covering and enclosing the product. Blisters are pre-molded, while skins are molded as they are produced. Blisters and skins are generally made from some type of PVC, although recently environmental considerations have led to the increased use of some polystyrenes, which are regarded as being less ecologically harmful.

Skin packs tend to be regarded as the poor relation of the process, but they are cheaper to originate, because there is no tooling, and skins can be used to make packages for a variety of products at once. For example, it is possible to skin nine auto components onto one piece of cardboard with a generic background, cut the cardboard into the nine relevant pieces and apply self-adhesive labels to identify each particular component.

The design process involves creating the roughs, producing a mockup dummy, which is usually made of wood, and discussing the project with the blister packager. This is one process where communication with the client is essential. Not only does the designer need to know exactly what product is to be packed inside the blister, but also where and how it will be displayed, how heavy it is, and whether there are any legal requirements or constraints. Packing is also an important consideration. If the blister pack is designed in such a way that it can be "topped and toed" in transit, substantial savings can be made. Blisters or skins can usually be no larger than 30×20in (75×50cm). The designer also needs to know if it will be possible to follow the shape of the product — this is not always feasible — and to determine if the blister is for protection or solely to secure the product to the card.

Scheduling time for blister packaging is between four and six weeks. This time is considerably reduced for second runs since the blister tool already exists. Skin packaging should take less time. The minimum run will depend on how much the client is prepared to pay.

Gold blocking is used extensively in blister packaging, and all blister cards are varnished, since the process is used to heat-seal the blister onto the card.

Most blister packaging is done on carton board, but in theory it is possible to blister onto plastic or metal. In addition, two items can be blister-packed together with the base substrate omitted altogether and the products trapped between the two shells.

Other applications

Blister and skin packs are used in hundreds of ways. Many hardware and household repair products are packaged by this method, and so are auto components, cleaning products, and sandwiches.

Relative costs

Skin packaging is usually, but not always, cheaper than blister packaging.

This innovative light bulb packaging was possible because the specialist nature of these lights offered the opportunity for greater profits than was possible with conventional bulbs, so the manufacturer decided that more money could be spent on packaging. The bulbs are blister packed. The heat-sealing skin packaging process could have damaged the bulbs, so it had to be tested before production could go ahead. It was also necessary to test that the packaging would provide adequate protection for the fragile bulbs during transit. The bulbs are packed head-to-toe in boxes of 12 and 24. There are now 115 different bulbs in the range, and the high profile achieved by the packaging in hardware stores has meant that sales have rocketed.

DIRECT MAIL PROMOTION

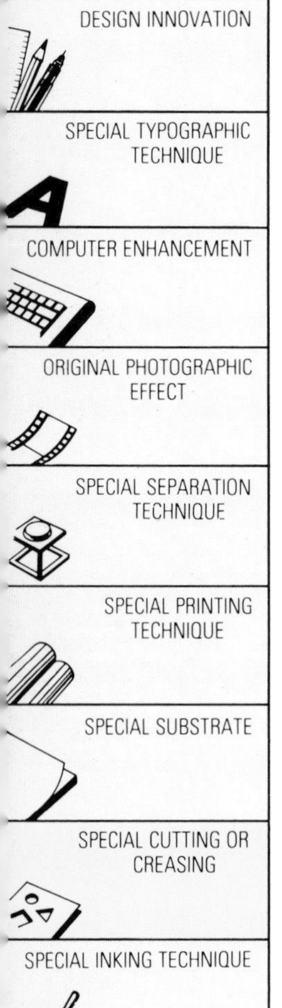

Direct mail has been the fastest growing print sector in recent times, and it still is in many parts of the world. Direct mail is usually printed by lithography, sheet-fed for short or test runs and web-fed for long runs. Any special paper folding or cutting is done on special finishing lines, which are often unique to particular printers and are either attached to the back of the press or operate as stand-alone systems.

The finishing line will die-cut, fold, perforate, glue, lay down remoistenable glue, add "rub 'n' reveal" or "scratch and sniff" features, personalize, and assemble all in one pass, enabling highly complex, personalized direct mail packages to be produced quickly by the million.

Communicating with your printer

If there is one area where the designer needs to talk to the printer, this is it. There are virtually no limits to what can be done when it comes to direct mail, and printers working in this sector are always prepared to try something new and to think through problems. You are unlikely to hear: "Sorry, it cannot be done." You are more likely to hear: "Have you thought about this feature you could add," or, "If we did it this way, you could have such and such there." If you give him the opportunity, the printer is likely to fire your imagination. There is a mass of technical problems that cannot be considered here, because each job is different, but the entire philosophy of direct mail is to look for the potential and opportunities rather than to be deterred by the problems. The actual design will be printed by lithography and can, therefore, be of a very high quality.

Once you have sorted out the design and any additional features with the printer, the actual production time is not as great as you may think, because most of the time is taken in setting up the finishing line, and if you have worked closely with the printer to prevent any unforeseen problems, a run of a million should take only a few days to complete from presentation of artwork. However, this schedule is possible only if you are using ink jet printing for personalizing. Laser printing, which does give better quality, will take much longer. The minimum press run for a direct mail package is now down to about 100,000.

Although more a piece of commercial direct marketing than consumer-oriented direct mail, this product uses several of the devices featured in direct mail products. Note the accordion fold, with 16 parallel folds, and the paper itself glued to the box at both ends. The use of glues, both cold-set and remoistenable, is one of the key tools of direct mail production, as is complicated folding. This product was one of a limited edition of 500, but direct mail products are more usually associated with runs into the millions, although that figure is now decreasing through better targeting.

Other applications

Direct mail is used, with great effect, to target certain groups of people – everyone between the ages of 20 and 30 living in a certain part of the country, or everyone with a mortgage, or households with children, for example. Financial institutions, consumer sales organizations, and government agencies are all likely to benefit from using direct mail.

Relative costs

Producing direct mail is one of the most expensive printing processes there is but, compared to other methods of reaching a target group, it is very effective. The costs vary greatly, but economies of scale clearly come into play.

WIGGINS TEAPE FINE PAPERS LTD
Paper samples: for the rush jobs where overnight samples are required, contact
Swatchbox:
board on offer
PLEASE PAY AT THE DESK
This limited edition box was specially designed for
Wiggins Teape Fine Papers Limited to commemorate
The Design Fair 1990. A limited edition of 500.
limited edition
Box
Conqueror Vellum Laid 220gsm
Concertina
100% Cotton 110gms

FOIL BLOCKING WINE LIST/PACKAGING/PROMOTION

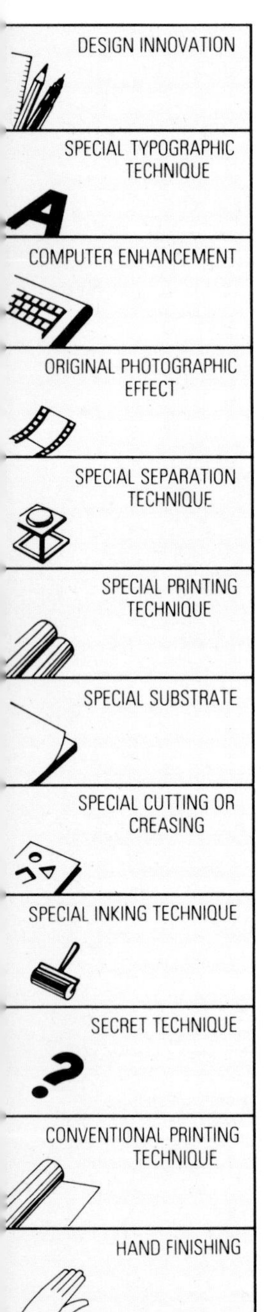

Foil blocking is more of an art than a science. There are no strict rules governing how the foil will look when it is applied or even what materials it is best applied to, and there are many apparent contradictions in the process. Aesthetically, foil blocking is one of those processes that can be used to give a product a tremendously high-class feel, while it can, just as easily — in fact, more easily — give a horribly cheap and nasty effect. Used sparingly, however, it will, more often than not, enhance a product.

A foil block is created by producing a die from artwork supplied through a photo-etching process. The foil is applied to the product through a combination of heat and pressure, which melts the glue in the foil and causes it to adhere to the substrate.

Potential problems

The designer's major problem in preparing artwork for production is to ensure that the foil bleeds. Even assuming that there will be a litho fit can lead to problems, and reversing a dead fit can be very difficult. Other problems will occur if foils are laid on top of laminates and varnishes: all of these materials have surface tensions, and trying to stick a foil onto something as smooth as a laminate will prove to be difficult if not impossible; certainly ultraviolet varnishes cannot be foil blocked. If it is essential to foil block on top of a laminate, specify an acetate laminate. It is, of course, possible to laminate or varnish over a foil.

All these stamps incorporate foil blocking. They are part of a promotional book that was produced for a specialty printer. The book was case-bound with a leather spine, and a slipcase was also made. The illustrations show how foil blocking can be used in conjunction with other techniques, including sculptured embossing, single-level embossing, foil embossing, engraving, thermography, four-color lithography, blind embossing, and foil blocking.

Choosing stock

A far better shine will be achieved if you foil onto a gloss art paper rather than onto matte stock. Whatever you choose, however, try to get a test proof. If you are foiling over an already printed product, make sure that the printer does not use spray powder on the press to help dry the ink, and also make sure that he does not foil over wet inks, because the foil will not adhere and will pull off some of the ink. In effect, this means that, once the ink has been printed, at least a day should elapse before foiling.

Foils over 3ft (1m) wide are now available, although if such a large area is foil blocked the die and make-ready times are likely to add considerably to the overall cost.

Foil blocking itself is not a fast process, but it does not take long to prepare. If you are in a hurry, it should be possible to find somewhere that will turn the job around in a day, depending, of course, on the complexity of the design. A tight register with spot ultraviolet varnishing on top will obviously take longer. The minimum run length will depend on how much the client is willing to pay — the shorter the run, the more expensive it will be.

Foil blocking can be combined with embossing to give an eye-catching and aesthetically pleasing effect.

You can foil block onto paper, board, rigid and flexible plastics, self-adhesive labels, beermats, and bookbinding cloths — in fact, just about anything that can be fed through a foiling machine can be used.

Foil blocking is achieved through a combination of heat and pressure. A die is created to the chosen design and then heated. The foil is applied to the substrate and pressed onto it by the die. The superfluous non-heated foil can be brushed away.

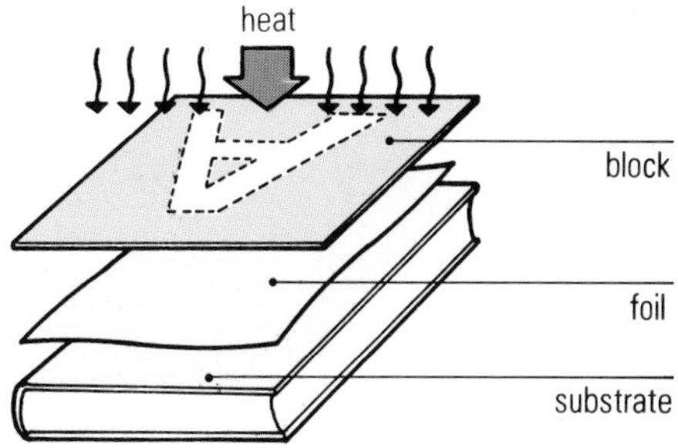

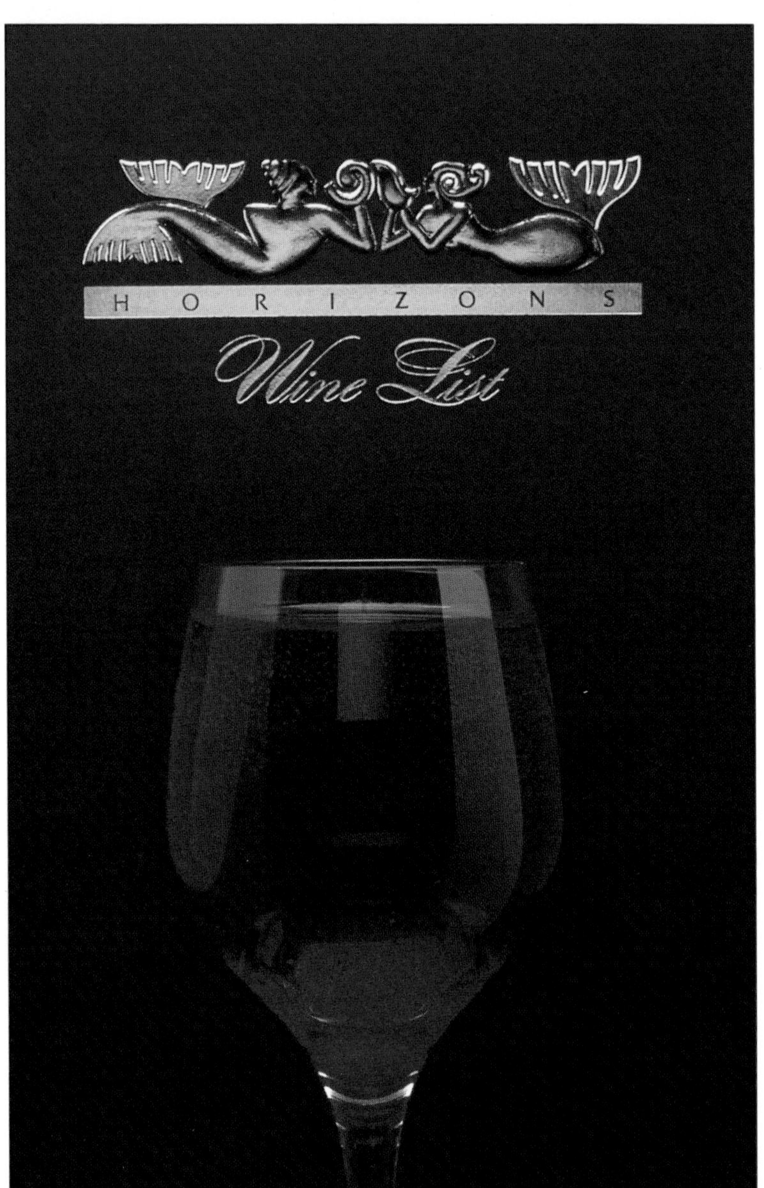

Other applications

Greeting cards are perhaps the largest area in which foil blocking is used, although the process is becoming increasingly popular across a range of products. The cartons used to package cosmetics and candy are enhanced by the addition of foil blocking, and the process is also used on drinks labels, annual reports and accounts, promotional literature, letterheads, book jackets, and video and computer-game packaging. Combined with embossing, it is also widely used on popular paperback book covers.

Relative costs

Foil blocking is not as expensive as it may seem. The process is unlikely to contribute more than 2 or 3 percent to the final selling price of a greeting card or a box of candy. The major cost is the foil itself, and there tends to be a substantial amount of wastage. For example, if you use foil blocking to frame an illustration, everything in the middle of the frame area will be wasted. Designs that minimize this kind of waste will help to keep the costs down.

Foil blocking, or stamping as it is sometimes known, is undoubtedly one of the best ways of enhancing a product's appearance. This wine list (**above**) has been embossed and then foil blocked, which gives both a quality look and feel to the finished article. Gold foil blocking often looks best against a sleek, dark background, such as navy blue or maroon, or against black as on the bottle packaging (**right**). It is possible to foil block down to fine detail, as shown by the type on the carton. Although it is by far the most popular, gold foil blocking is not the only way to foil block — this gift presentation pack (**far right**) has silver foil on a foil board.

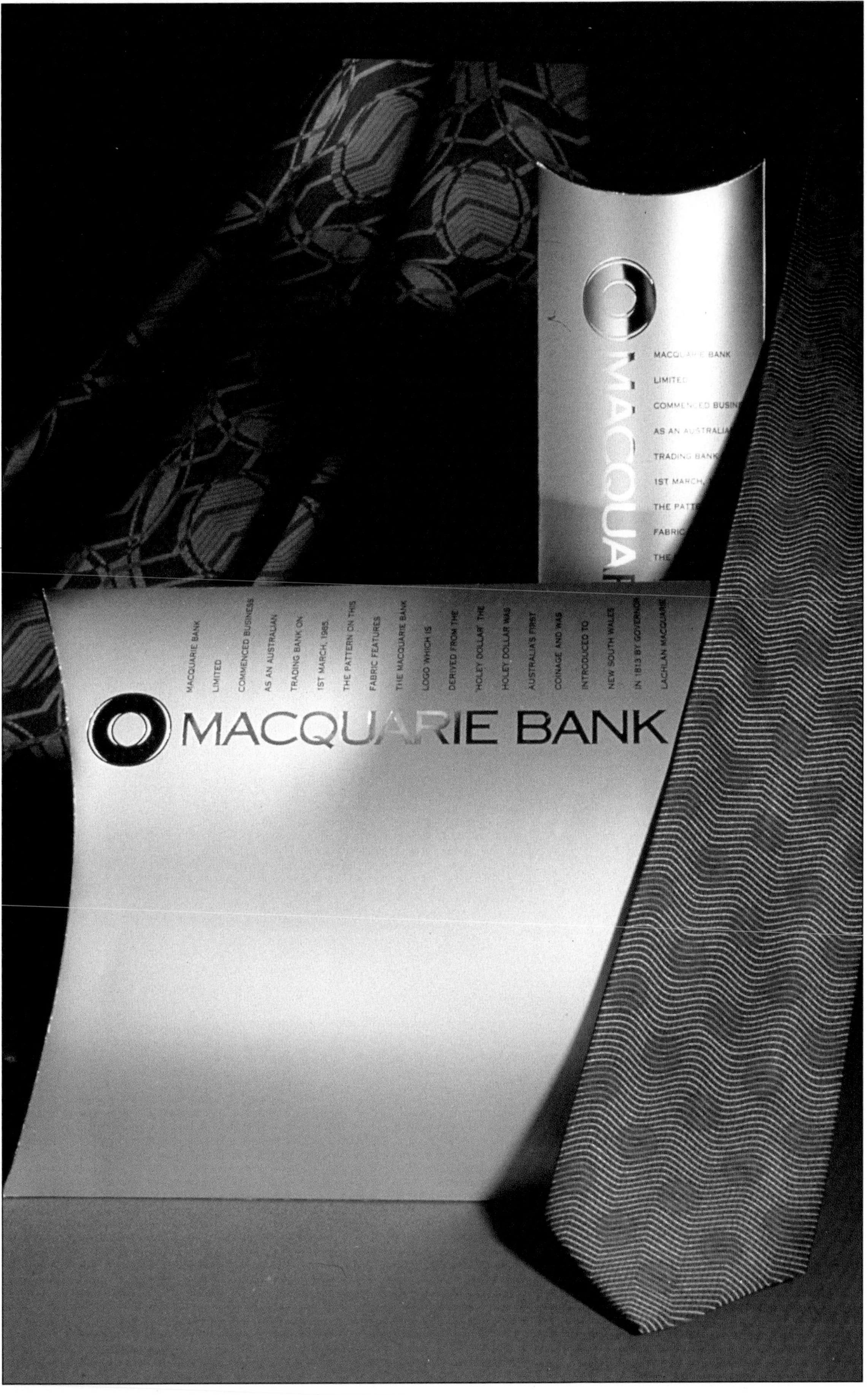
MACQUARIE BANK
MACQUARIE BANK
LIMITED
COMMENCED BUSINESS
AS AN AUSTRALIAN
TRADING BANK ON
1ST MARCH, 1985.
THE PATTERN ON THIS
FABRIC FEATURES
THE MACQUARIE BANK
LOGO WHICH IS
DERIVED FROM THE
'HOLEY DOLLAR' THE
HOLEY DOLLAR WAS
AUSTRALIA'S FIRST
COINAGE AND WAS
INTRODUCED TO
NEW SOUTH WALES
IN 1813 BY GOVERNOR
LACHLAN MACQUARIE

Blind embossing has enhanced this already stimulating stationery range for a US design agency. The registration of the embossing had to be very tightly controlled.

This award-winning example of blind embossing was designed for the full range of stationery for a small software company. The text lines were printed first. The typeface had to have exaggerated serifs so that the characters could be easily identified. In addition, the cloud effect had to be beneath the letters, because it is very difficult to read a word from just the bottom half of the characters although it is relatively easy to work out what is meant from the top half. A textured paper was chosen to emphasize the contrast.

BLIND EMBOSSING STATIONERY

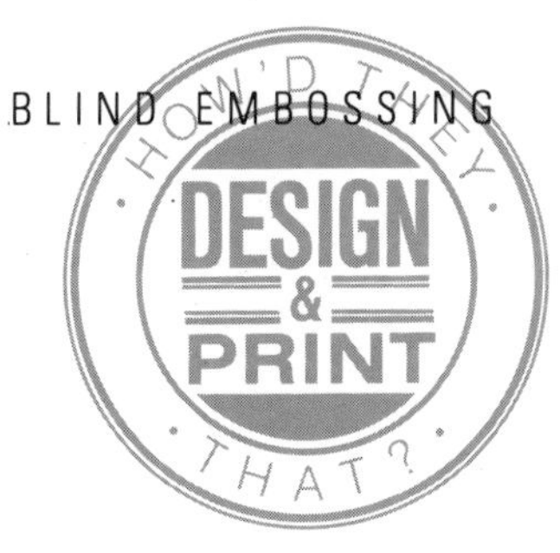

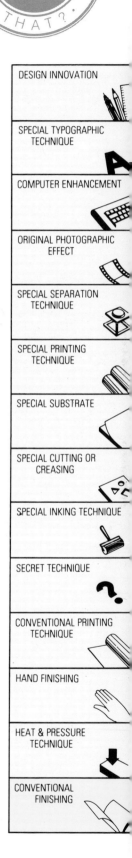

Blind embossing is a similar process to die stamping but, instead of the raised area being inked, it is left plain. As in die stamping, steel dies are used, and these can be photo-engraved if only text is needed, although hand engraving is necessary for illustrations. For example, if you want to emboss a rose to show the shape of the petals and the inner stamen, hand engraving has to be used because you cannot photograph artwork in three dimensions.

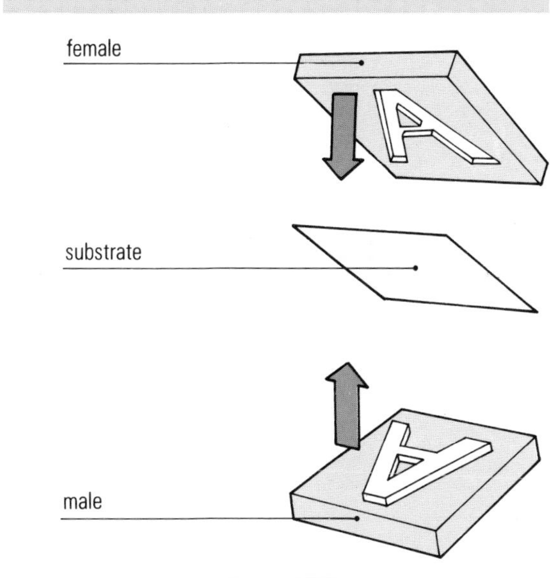

Potential of blind embossing

Blind embossing has tremendous potential for design, although many embossers feel that it is not fully appreciated by designers. It gives a product a high-quality feel with subtlety. In addition, it can be used creatively with other effects; when combined with foil blocking, for example, it creates a tremendously eye-catching effect, which is used to advantage on cartons and especially on the covers of the popular paperbacks found at airports, stations, and hotel bookshops.

Scheduling times for blind embossing are less than for die stamping because no color printing is involved, although they are still determined to a large degree by the design. If hand engraving is needed, allow longer.

Run lengths can be from as little as a couple of hundred up to hundreds of thousands. As with die stamping, laminating and varnishing may cause problems, and you should always try to emboss after varnishing and laminating. Laminating, for example, needs a flat surface, and if the surface is embossed air bubbles may develop between the embossed image and the laminate.

It should be possible to emboss on virtually all types of paper and board, except for very fine tissue and bible papers. Theoretically, there is no limit to the maximum sheet size that can be embossed.

Other applications

Embossing can be used in a wide range of applications — the only limits are those imposed by the designer's imagination. Embossing can set a product apart from its rivals in overcrowded markets. Greeting cards, business stationery, presentation folders, and the areas of packaging that need to look expensive, such as those for confectionery, cosmetics, and alcohol, all benefit from embossing.

Relative costs

Embossing will cost roughly the same as the actual printing. So whatever you pay to have, say, a greeting card printed, double the price to include embossing.

HOLOGRAPHY MAGAZINE

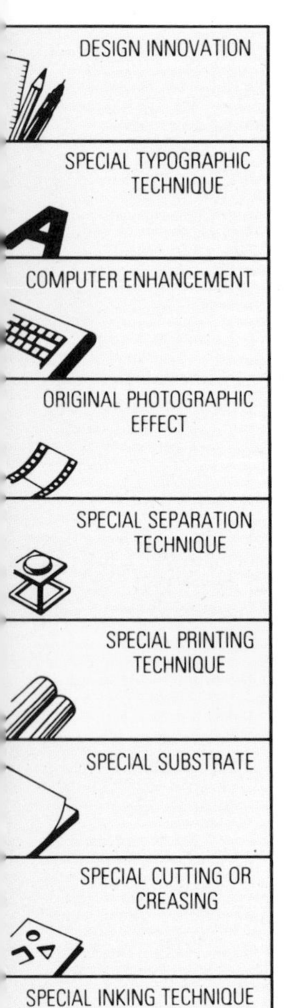

Holograms are improving in quality,all the time and are being used in an increasing number of ways. They are essentially a recording of light waves in much the same way that compact discs are a recording of sound waves. Holograms have to be produced in a totally isolated laboratory environment, for even human body heat will upset the process. The object to be reproduced in the hologram is recorded by laser from 300 different positions onto an extremely fine-grain emulsion. A complicated series of operations then takes place, as the laser-recorded information is transferred into a minute ridge-and-groove format. You can proof a hologram, but by then you would have spent 50 percent of the production costs.

Holograms can be derived from actual objects, as well as from type (which has to be back lit), photographs, and computer-generated graphics, which give especially good effects. The size of the actual object is vital: it has to be the same as the hologram, and if it is larger, a model has to be made. At present the maximum practicable hologram size is around 6in (15cm) square. A further limitation is that living organisms cannot be holographed except by prohibitively expensive pulse laser, so the recording has to be of a totally motionless object. If it moves more than one five-millionth of a millimeter during the recording process there will be no hologram.

The scheduling time will depend on the complexity of the job, and whether a modelmaker has to be used. A rough guide is that it takes about six weeks to get to the proofing stage and another six weeks to produce the hologram. Of course, you could probably find someone to produce a hologram for you in a week if you were prepared to pay for it. Once the original embossing master, or shim, has been made, reprints are a lot quicker, and there is virtually no limit on the number that can be produced — several million have been made from a single master. The minimum quantity will depend on how much the client is willing to pay, but a couple of hundred is the bare minimum.

Holograms can be applied to most surfaces, although they do not work especially well on rougher surfaces; they have, for example, been tried without notable success on cereal packeages. The best results are achieved on a varnished carton board or on a coated paper or plastic. Laminating over holograms is both possible and desirable, since it protects the image from scratching during handling and transport.

When the magazine is angled away from a direct light source, the globe on the cover cannot be read as a 3-D image.

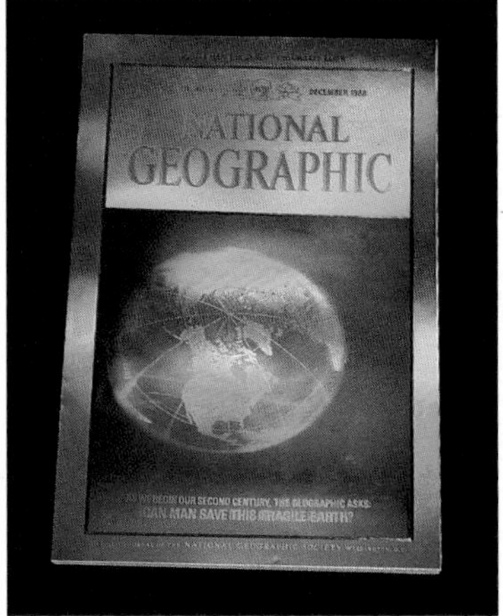

When the magazine is tilted toward the light, the globe appears as a 3-D image standing out from of the jacket. (The limitations of litho printing — used for this book — make it impossible to convey this 3-D image effectively.)

This hologram of the world that appeared on the cover of *National Geographic* magazine was created from more than 300 laser light recordings of the object. Holography as a technique gives rise to two of the biggest mysteries in the entire printing industry. The first mystery is, how does it work? The second is, why has it not taken off in the major way that its proponents have prophesied over recent years? Mystery number one is solved on the opposite page. Mystery number two remains unanswerable. We do know that holography has remained comparatively expensive, that it is not suitable for use on uncoated stock, and that it can be unimpressive — there can be few people who have not spent time squinting at a book cover, trying desperately to figure out what effect was intended. Holography is, however, very well suited to some kinds of work — as a security feature on plastic credit cards, for example — and when it is well done, as on this magazine cover, it looks extremely impressive.

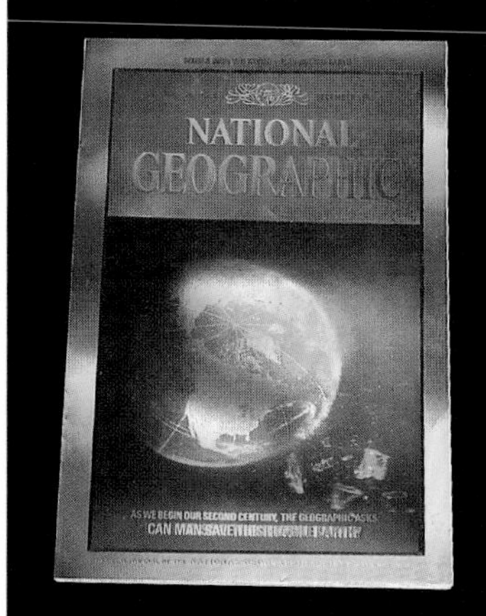

Moving the magazine in different directions gives the reader the impression of observing the globe from different viewpoints.

Other applications

Holograms have been used successfully in security printing applications, and most major credit cards incorporate a hologram. They are also used on book covers — especially mystic or science fiction titles — children's toys and food packaging, exclusive tickets and membership cards.

Relative costs

Although the cost of holograms has fallen in real terms over the years, they are still by far the most expensive extra that can be added to a printed product. However, if the unit cost of the product itself is high, the holograms need not be proportionately expensive.

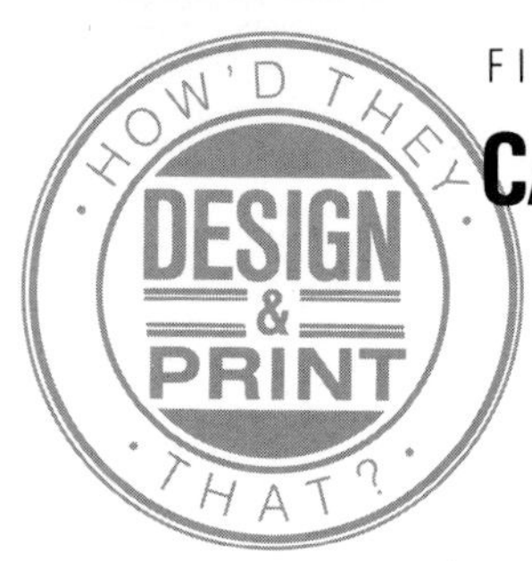

CASED BOOK BINDING QUALITY REFERENCE

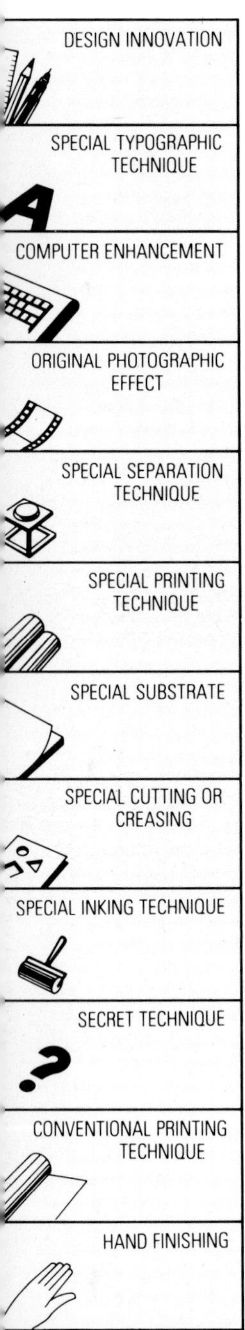

Two types of spine can be specified for a case-bound book: round–backed, known as ordinary hollow, and square-backed, known as broad hollow. Broad-hollow binding is most commonly used for children's annuals and large format, thin books, whereas round-backed is used for almost everything else. The signatures in the book itself are usually sewn together, or they can be glued into the spine in the process known as perfect binding. Sewing is more expensive, but if the book is going to be used for more than a few months, it is by far the best choice, since perfect binding tends to disintegrate with use.

Case binding is constructed from gray cardboard, which is glued to cloth; endpapers are glued to the other side of the cloth, and the book block is glued to the endpapers. The book block does not actually touch the spine. For additional strength and decorative purposes, head- and foot-bands can be added to the spine; these are normally pieces of striped material, which give a quality look.

Square- and round-backed spines

There is no real cost difference between square- and round-backed spines; the most important factor to bear in mind when specifying the spine style is the width of the book. A 32-page children's annual will look far thicker with a square back, while a 256-page novel will not need a square back and will open better with a round back.

Case binding a book, as distinct from paperback binding, will add another three or four weeks to the production schedule. The minimum press run for case binding is 1,000 copies, although you may find a bindery that will handle as few as 500 copies if work is slack.

Case-bound books are usually blocked with gold foil to enhance their appearance.

Other applications

Almost all books are case-bound or hardcover, as they are generally known — for the first edition. Some books — reference books and encyclopedias, for example — are always case-bound.

Relative costs

There is no real difference in price between square and round binding, but sewing signatures will cost at least 10 percent more than perfect binding. Case binding is considerably more expensive than paper binding, and you will normally have to specify a dust jacket as well, which adds still further to the cost.

The diagram illustrates how a square-backed case will give a book of few pages considerable extra bulk.

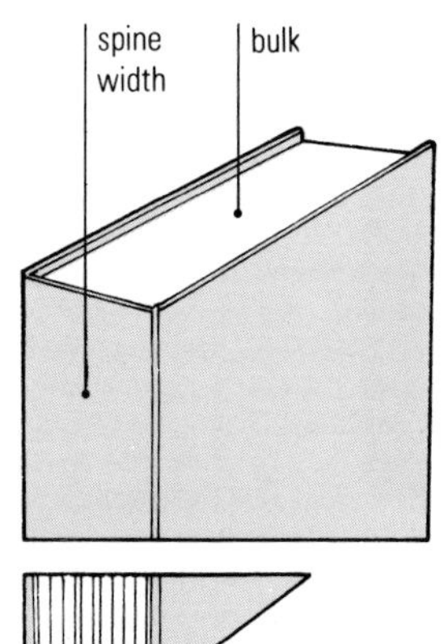

This book about distinguished people was a natural candidate for a high quality case binding coupled with gold foil blocking on the cover.

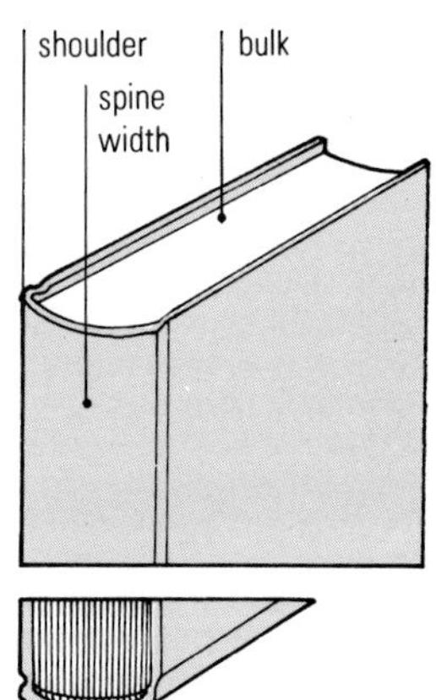

Debrett's
Distinguished People
of Today
Debrett's
Distinguished
People
of Today
1990

SPECIAL INKS MAGAZINES/PROMOTION

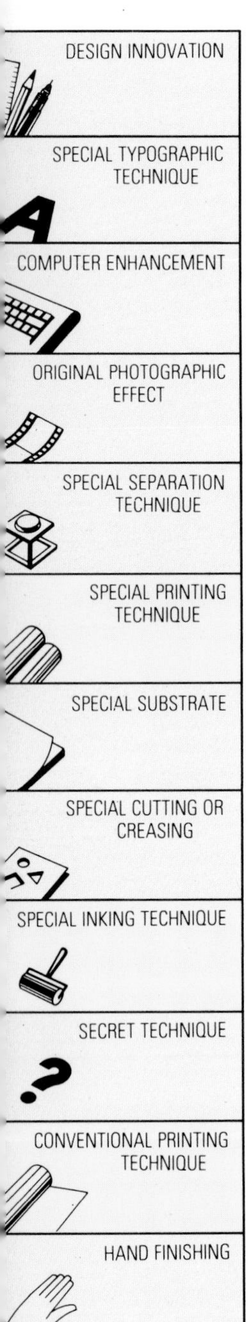

The creative use of inks is a subject worthy of a book of its own. Did you know, for example, that some ink manufacturers offer more than 100 types of black ink alone? However, here we will consider only popular special inks that are found in work printed by lithography. Inks used for the other processes are quite specialized, and if you are preparing work that will be reproduced by other means, make sure that you talk to your printer about any design limitations they may impose.

The main special inks used in lithography are metallic, fluorescent, ultraviolet and, for security work, invisible. With the exception of invisible inks, none of these special inks can be treated in the same way as conventional litho inks, and you must be aware of their potential and the restrictions they impose when considering whether to use them in a design.

Specifying inks

Apart from the color, of course, there are several factors that you need to check before you specify an ink for an individual project. The kind of information you will need and the degree of detail that will be necessary will depend on the type of product being designed. For example, if you are legally obliged to include a health warning of some sort on the side of a package, you must be sure that the ink you specify will not become washed out when it is exposed to sunlight as, for example, PANTONE©★ Warm Red does.

In addition to light fastness, you may also need to be aware of an ink's product resistance, rub resistance, and taint and odor levels, which are, of course, crucial in packaging for food and children's toys. Pantone Warm Red contains barium, for example, and in many countries that element is banned from use in all packaging for products for children. The fact that a child would probably have to eat approximately 100,000 toy boxes to get sick is irrelevant. You must check before you specify to avoid making an expensive mistake.

Metallic inks

Metallic inks, usually golds and silvers, can be printed on paper or board, but if you are designing to print on plastic or foil, you must specify the use of ultraviolet metallics, which will dry on top of the substrate. Metallic inks are best used on coated rather than uncoated papers and boards, but even some coated stock is unsuitable, so check first.

To gain maximum brilliance with metallic inks you must specify that the printer uses the fullest possible ink film. However, if your design has a large, solid area and a small area of fine detail both of which you want printed in metallic, there will almost invariably be problems, because the fine area will fill in. If you have to have both, the printer should use two separate printing units, one for the solid and one for the fine area.

You cannot overprint metallic inks and, although it is possible to varnish to give maximum rub resistance, the varnish will certainly diminish the brilliance of the metallic finish. Metallic inks are often used to enhance a product by giving it a quality look much more cheaply than by gold blocking. Sets of report and accounts, brochures, and whiskey, candy and cosmetics packaging are among the main areas for the use of metallics. The inks themselves are only about one third more expensive than conventional litho inks, so there is a relatively wide range of applications available for comparatively little extra cost.

This European magazine has made the use of fluorescent and metallic inks on its covers something of a trademark. Fluorescent inks have a tremendous brilliance, but they tend to become dull very quickly if left exposed to sunlight for too long. To achieve the greatest possible levels of brightness with fluorescents, each item needs to go through the press twice. A much greater degree of consistency will also be achieved by printing metallic inks twice.

© Pantone, Inc's check standard trademark for colour reproduction and colour reproduction materials.

2/91
SKY
MAGAZINE
FEBRUARY 1991 £1.30
Canada $3.50
rap on a roll
FEATURING:
LL COOL J
MONIE LOVE
RUN DMC
BIG DADDY KANE
PUBLIC ENEMY
Val Kilmer is Jim Morrison
THE DOORS - 1991's HOTTEST BAND, 1991's HOTTEST MOVIE
SKY
MADONNA BY MONDINO
ROB LOWE ABOUT THAT NIGHT
SUPERMODEL!
FIRE POWER!
INSIDE: THE WORLD'S TOP 20 MALE AND FEMALE MODELS

Fluorescent inks

Fluorescent inks can give brilliantly colorful results, but they have several flaws. First, to achieve that strength of color and brilliance, there have to be two printings — that is, the same color is printed on top of itself, either by two passes through the press or by two units of the press laying down the same color in the same place, one after the other. One pass will not lay down enough ink film weight to give the desired result. Second, fluorescent inks have extremely poor light fastness, so they are unsuitable for outdoor use. Even two weeks in a Scandinavian winter will wash out all the color, and the same will happen in about two hours in a Caribbean summer! Most litho printing of fluorescent is, therefore, for point-of-sale material that is for indoor use, and it can be extremely eye-catching. Fluorescent inks cost approximately twice as much as conventional litho inks.

Ultraviolet inks

Ultraviolet — UV — inks are rapidly gaining in popularity, particularly in the printing of packaging of all kinds. There are two main reasons for this so far as the print buyer is concerned: these inks have very low odor and taint levels, and they can be printed extremely quickly because they dry instantaneously. From the designer's point of view, using ultraviolet inks eliminates the need to compromise. For example, if you have designed a deep purple package for a candy bar, you may not be able to achieve the necessary depth of color with a conventional litho ink because it would not be possible to lay down that amount of color within the commercial production parameters — there has to be a compromise somewhere. Ultraviolet inks, on the other hand, are characterized by a very high color density.

In some countries ultraviolet inks are now used on almost half the cartons that are produced. They are also used for album covers, book jackets, food packaging and labeling — on almost anything, in fact, on which the image needs to stand out. Ultraviolet inks cost about two thirds more than conventional inks, and your printer will probably also charge a premium for having his press equipped to print with ultraviolets.

Other inks

Invisible inks, which are used almost exclusively for producing security documents and papers, can be printed in exactly the same way as conventional litho inks, but they cost five times as much.

Other special inks include thermochromatic inks, which change color according to the surface temperature with which they are in contact. So, for example, a design on a coffee cup can change according to whether or not there is hot coffee in the cup. For best results, designs using thermochromatic inks should be rendered on a dark background. Colors can be any within the spectrum.

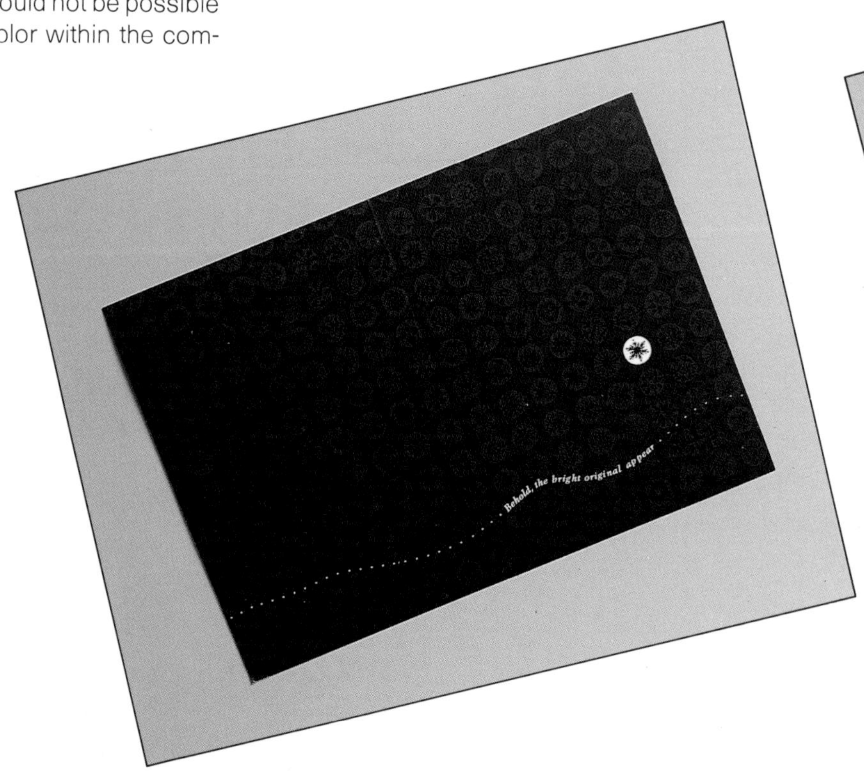

This is an example of the use of thermochromatic inks — that is, inks that change color according to the temperature of the surface with which they are in contact. The inks will vary from colorless to red, through the colors of the spectrum, to blue/violet and back to colorless again as the temperature of the substrate rises. The temperature at which the effects start to appear can be anywhere between -22° and 158°F (-30° and 70°C), and the color-change band can be as narrow as 1.8°F (1°C) or as high as 37.8°F (20°C).

Pantone Matching System

The Pantone Matching System (PMS) is universally accepted as the primary means of communicating color between designer and printer. However, there are several important factors to bear in mind when you use the Pantone system and these will help avoid many potential problems.

First, as a designer you should always use the Pantone book rather than a simple swatch when specifying a color. The book is composed of pages of tear-off strips of colors, and you should attach the appropriate strip to your artwork. The Pantone swatches can show variations in density, and by using the strip from the book you are giving the printer an absolutely definite specification that will eliminate any errors.

Second, you need to ensure that the printer matches your color faithfully. It is not good to look at the printed result under one light source; you must view it, together with your original design, under several kinds of light, such as daylight, neon, and tungsten. If the color remains true through all the viewing conditions, it is a pure match.

Third, use the information chart in the front of the Pantone book to assess the ink's suitability to the job you are designing. The chart gives information about the characteristics of different inks, such as their light fastness and alkali resistance, and whichever color you choose from the thousands within the book, it will have the characteristics of the base color. Never specify an ink without consulting the chart.

Fourth, remember that the final color as printed and seen is greatly affected by the substrate itself. The final color can vary widely in appearance if it is used, for example, on a high gloss art paper or on an uncoated board.

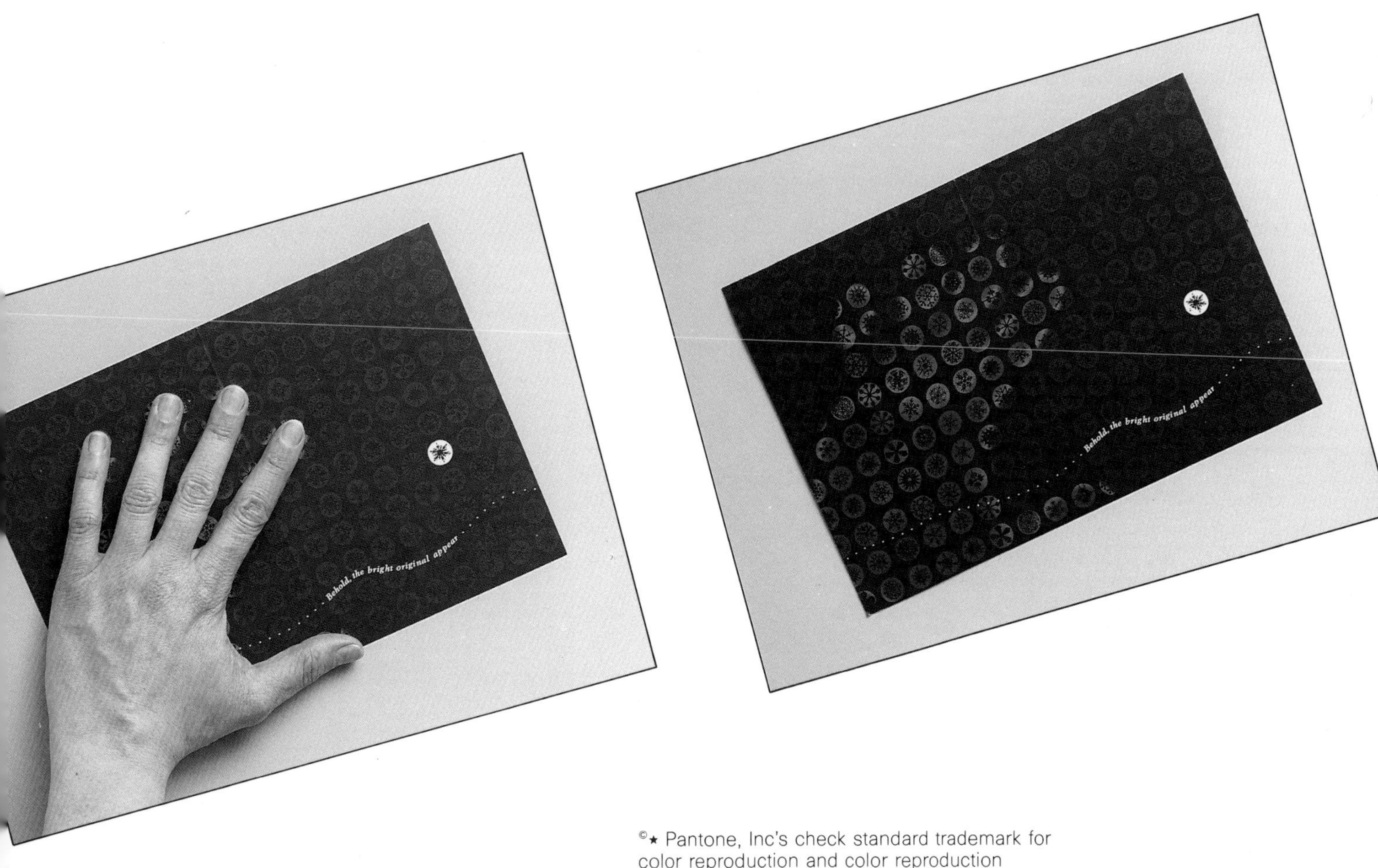

©★ Pantone, Inc's check standard trademark for color reproduction and color reproduction materials.

Litho printing was used in two different ways to achieve the effect of marbled paper for these cook books (**above**). In the top book a very subtle, pale effect was required for the overall background of each page, so a black and white print was made of a sheet of marbled paper, and this was marked up for four-color origination, the color specification being 30 percent magenta, 20 percent yellow.

The designer of the bottom book wanted a muted, dark background. This time a hand-marbled paper was photographed and developed as a color print. The photographic studio was then instructed to darken and resaturate the colors. Several tests were necessary before the correct balance of tone and color was achieved.

MARBLED PAPER BOOK/STATIONERY/MENU

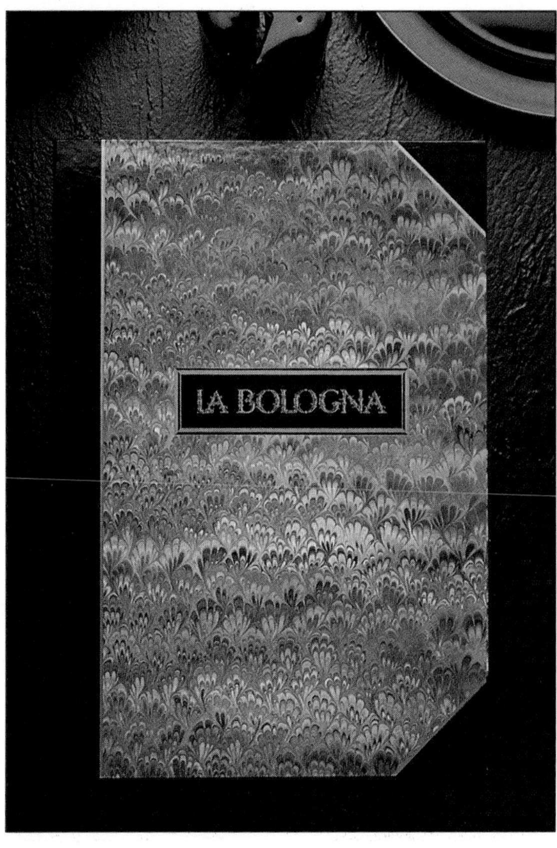

Marbled paper can be produced by hand or by machine. Production by machine is cheap and fast, but the advocates of the traditional method claim that machine-made paper looks cheap.

Marbling paper by hand is a highly skilled operation. The marbler creates an image in ink, water, or oil, which sits on the surface of a tub of glue. A sheet of paper is laid on top of the image for a couple of minutes to allow it to soak into the paper. A skilled worker can produce six or seven sheets of paper an hour, with a usual maximum size of about 25×20in (63×50cm) — which is why it is expensive.

An image created from oils has a soft look; watercolors give a clear, crisp appearance; and inks appear slightly dull. The paper used is generally between 60lb and 75lb.

Designs for reproduction on marbled paper usually incorporate gold-blocked lettering laid directly on to the background. However, you can create your own solid background, giving the marble the effect of a border. Black backgrounds, with halftone illustrations and gold lettering, work extremely well on marbled paper.

The main applications of marbled paper are as endpapers in hardcover books, and they are also sometimes used as cover materials on books.

Hand-marbled paper costs around 20 times more than litho-printed paper.

This restaurant menu (**above**) is a four-color, litho-printed reproduction of a piece of hand-marbled paper. Using machine-printed reproductions of marbled paper will save considerable amounts of money.

It takes a skilled craftsman an hour to produce six or seven sheets of hand-marbled paper. This stationery set (**left**) is marbled in four colors — red, pink, cream, and green. Although in theory every sheet of hand-marbled paper is different, a competent marbler should be able to produce 1,000 or more sheets that look almost identical. Hand marblers also produce sample books.

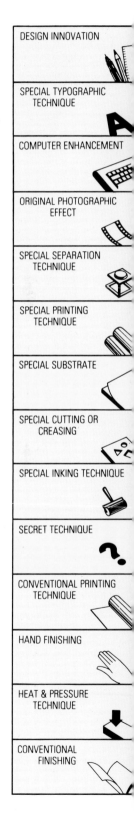

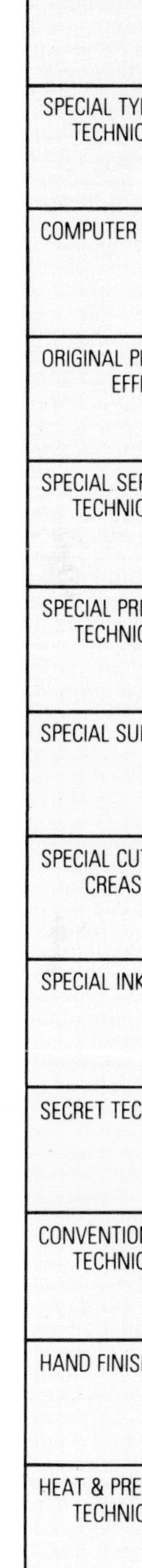

The original artwork prepared for a watermark (**above left**) and the finished watermarked sheet (**above right**).

registered

WATERMARKED PAPER STATIONERY

Using a watermarked paper gives an impression of quality. In addition to the off-the-shelf brands available, it is possible to specify your own watermark.

The papermaker will take your design, convert it onto a type of die, and place it on a mesh roller — a dandy roll — on the papermaking machine. The die comes into contact with the wet paper and creates the watermark. There are two types of watermark. A line watermark is a straightforward outline of the design created by a convex die, which displaces paper fibers so that the resulting image is lighter than the background paper. The other type is known as a shadow watermark, which is created by embossing the wet paper with a concave die, which causes more fibers to come into that area, so making it darker than the background.

These methods are used on modern papermaking machines, but older, mold-type machines are still used extensively for producing paper for bank notes. These machines give extremely high quality paper, but at a price to match.

There are four basic positions for a watermark. First, registered, where the watermark appears in the same position on each sheet. Second, staggered, where the watermark appears somewhere on the sheet, although in no guaranteed position; staggered watermarked paper may have several marks on, or bleeding off, the sheet. The third position for a watermark is repeat, where the design is repeated vertically as often as you like. The final position is cut ahead, a random placement.

Three possible positions for a watermark (**below**). In the registered design the watermark always appears in the same place; for the staggered design, at least one watermark always appears somewhere on the final sheet, although there are no guarantees as to the final position; in repeat design, the design is repeated as many times as you want vertically throughout the paper.

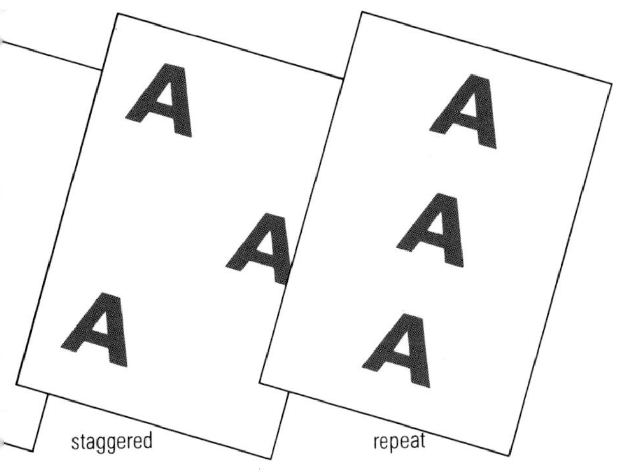

Rules for design

The three main guidelines for designing a watermarked paper are: do not make the design too fine; do not make it too thick, or else it will weaken the paper; and avoid tight corners.

If you want to incorporate your own watermark you will have to order a minimum of one or two tons of paper and buy the dandy roll. Obviously, the more watermarked paper you order the cheaper it becomes. Scheduling time for a specially watermarked paper is from eight to ten weeks from delivery of artwork.

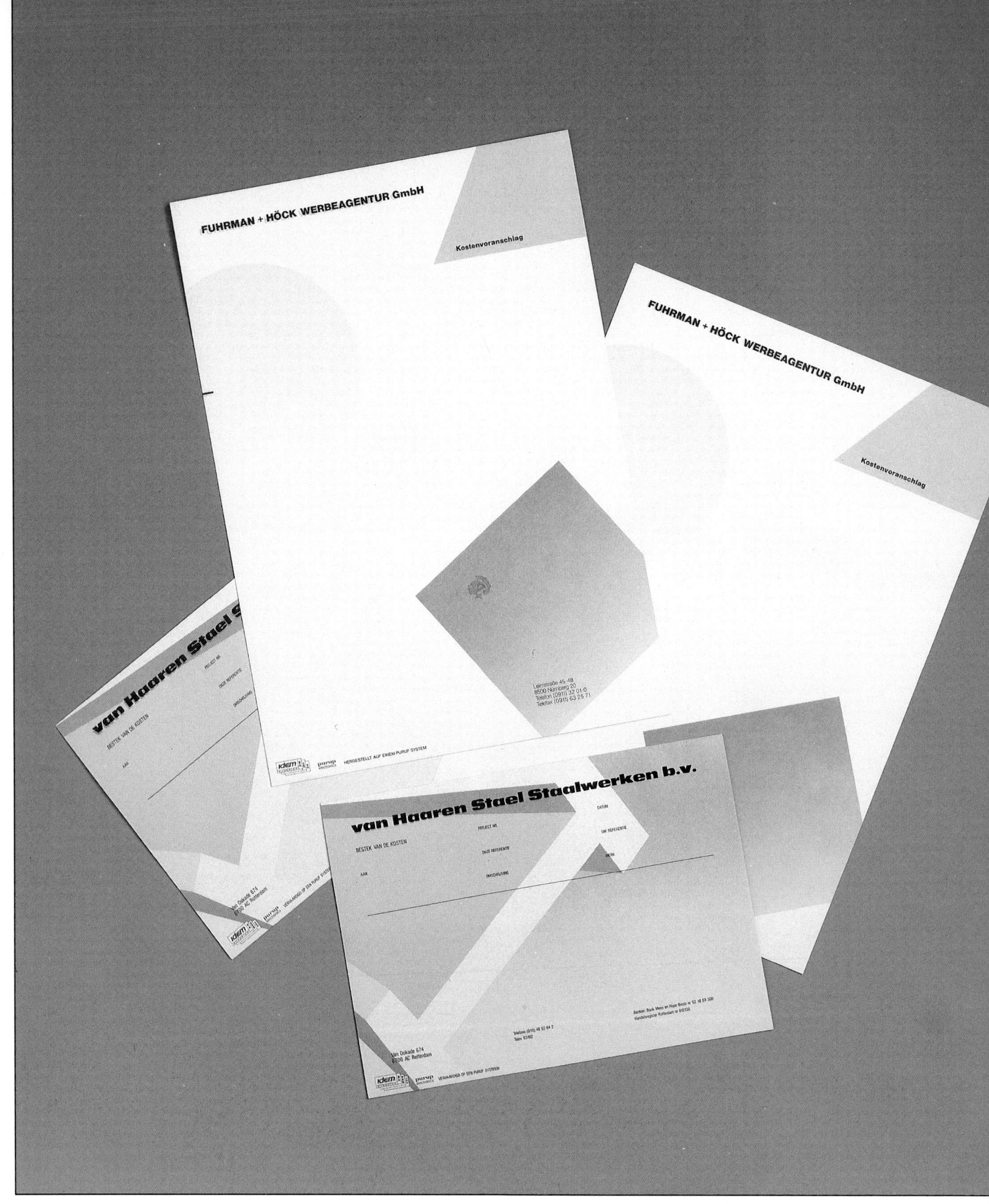

Vignettes can be used to very good effect on carbonless papers, and creative design should be able to exploit this. The top sheet of this form for Dutch steelworks is printed in just two colors — blue and black. The German form (**above**) is a beautiful example of the way in which carbonless forms can be transformed by an imaginative design.

CARBONLESS PAPER BUSINESS STATIONERY

Carbonless papers are used to produce a copy of the original document without the need for a messy layer of carbon paper between the sheets. The back of each sheet, apart from the bottom one, is composed of hundreds of tiny capsules of dye. When pressure is applied to the paper, by pen or printer, for example, the capsules burst, depositing the dye on the surface of the sheet below, where it is absorbed onto its coating, which is usually clay in Europe and resin in the United States and Japan.

Most carbonless papers come in sets of between three and six parts, although you can specify up to 15 parts.

Standard carbonless papers are not particularly suitable for four-color process printing because of the high absorbency level of the paper, and whatever image you design will look considerably duller than on conventional paper. However, most manufacturers of carbonless paper do supply a higher quality top sheet, which has a matte coating that permits four-color process printing. Solid colors work well on standard papers, as do vignettes, and you can achieve excellent results on carbonless paper by using just two colors in a variety of tones. You should be able to print the smallest type size on carbonless paper.

Avoid metallic and fluorescent inks, particularly on non-coated stock – the fluorescents will lose much of their brightness, the gold will look bronze, and the silver will appear gray. You can die stamp and emboss, but if you want to varnish, be sure to use ultraviolet varnish or it will run into the sheet.

Practical considerations

There are a couple of practical points to consider when designing for carbonless paper. First, if the sheet is going to be folded, make sure you include an image at least $\frac{1}{10}$in (3mm) wide, along the line of the fold, otherwise a dirty black mark will appear where the capsules have burst along the line during its time in the folder. Your design should anticipate this and incorporate a feature to mask it. Secondly, if the set is going to be mailed, try to design it so that the part of the sheet that will be under the post office's franking machine has an image on it to hide the area affected by any capsules that burst.

A range of stock can be used to produce carbonless paper, both laid and wove, as well as watermarked. They are available in various tints, and range in weight between 30lb and 60lb for the under sheets and 40lb and 100lb for the top sheet. Boards up to 135lb or 170lb are also available. Special carbonless papers can also be produced for banks and similar institutions, but the minimum order is likely to be around 50 tons.

Some carbonless papers, known as self-contained, react with themselves. These are useful if you want information to be written on a substrate that cannot accommodate the dye capsules.

Other applications

Apart from their obvious uses in regular documentation, carbonless papers are now being used in new areas. One manufacturer has launched a semi-gloss art carbonless paper that can be used when two or more copies of a transaction are required and when one party wishes to leave the other with an attractive presentation pack. Vacation and financial brochures are examples of this. In a vacation brochure, for example, the art coating means that the front and back covers can be printed with high gloss, four-color pictures of the vacation spots, while the inside – the other side of the paper – is not coated but has the same surface layer as a conventional carbonless stock, to which is attached a top sheet. When the customer reserves a vacation, the salesperson fills out the top sheet, which can be torn out, leaving the customer with the bottom sheet, so that the brochure is, in fact, complete, not only with the individual reservation details but also all of the vacation details in one, single package.

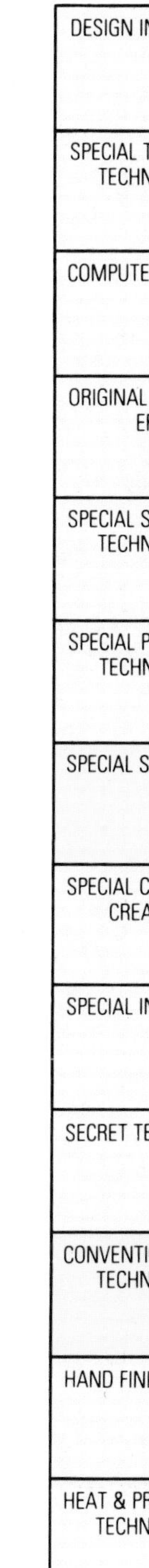

RECYCLED PAPER PACKAGING/PROMOTION

Image-conscious companies are turning increasingly to the use of recycled paper for their stationery. There are, in fact, several types of recycled paper but not all papers that claim to be "recycled" strictly deserve the name. The most environmentally sound recycled paper is made from paper that has been returned to the mill after use, and has had the ink dispersed within it, so there is no waste. Other recycled stock is de-inked by being washed in caustic soda or a detergent, a process that results in slightly better quality, but produces a waste, which has to be disposed of.

Most recycled papers are some shade of gray. It *is* possible to obtain a white paper, although this will have been made by recycling either non-printed wastage in the mill itself, or from printers' offcuts, neither of which have ever actually been printed on before. Many countries now produce recycled paper in various categories. Always use the highest classification and ensure that the paper is wood-free.

Recognizing the limitations

The overriding rule when designing for recycled paper is to treat it as it is and not to try to achieve the kind of result you would aim for on a glossy art paper. Remember that there will be no brilliance in the reproduction, and that recycled paper is very porous and cannot hold fine detail. In addition, mid-tones tend to fill in, so if you are planning to include a moody transparency you are going to be disappointed with the results. If you can, try to avoid using transparencies altogether and stick to line illustrations. Also, try to steer clear of areas of solid color, because recycled paper is prone to flaking, and your solid color will end up with a lot of the ink missing and the paper showing through. Similarly, fine type, particularly with serifs, will reproduce badly.

Precise matching is difficult on recycled stock — litho dot gain is far more than on conventional paper and a 70 percent screen is likely to come out solid. Four-color printing can be attempted, but more satisfactory results will be achieved from line and two-color work. Recycled paper is often dyed to disguise its grayness, so you can make good use of the background color in a design.

If you are designing for recycled paper it is essential that the color separation company knows what it is doing, since many of the pitfalls of the paper can be overcome, or at least mitigated, by a knowledgeable color separator.

Attempting to use special effects on recycled paper will prove more difficult than with conventional paper, as the roughness of the finish will always be a problem.

Printing process color on recycled paper is far more difficult than on conventional paper since the paper tends to produce dull tones. Excellent results can, however, be achieved, as can be seen in the three images on this spread. The *Voyage of All Time* poster **(far right)** was the most ambitious; it was printed with the four process colors and six extra colors, and the line work was silk screened and sculpture embossed. In addition, the edge of the poster was die cut.

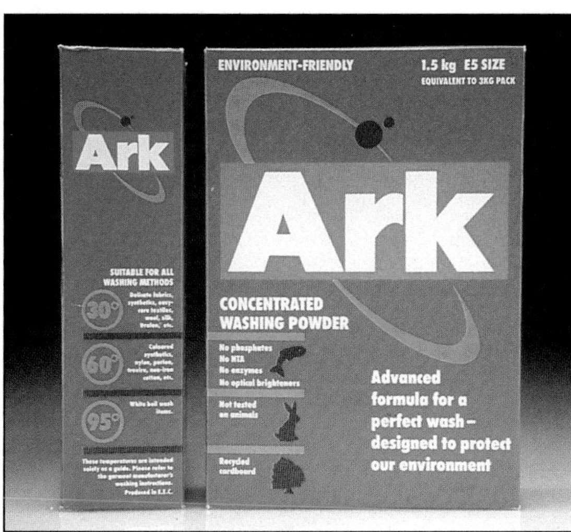

Other applications

Recycled paper is now acceptable for a wide variety of applications. It is used to print brochures for companies that specialize in environmentally friendly products, report and account folders for companies that want to demonstrate their commitment to the environment (or, want to give the impression of being committed), letterheads and magazines of environmentally concerned organizations and societies.

Relative costs

Recycled paper should now cost no more than virgin paper. Of course, if you buy only a little, it will work out more expensive, but if you order a ton or more you should get a good price.

LISBOA
MADRID
VALLADOLID
ZARAGOZA
BARCELONA
VALENCIA
CORDOBA
SEVILLA
CADIZ
MALAGA
GRANADA
MURCIA
ALICANTE
CARTAGENA
TANGER
MARSEILLE
MARRAKECH
Sardegna
CAFETERIA
SANTA ANA 2
000.890

INDESTRUCTIBLE PAPER MAP

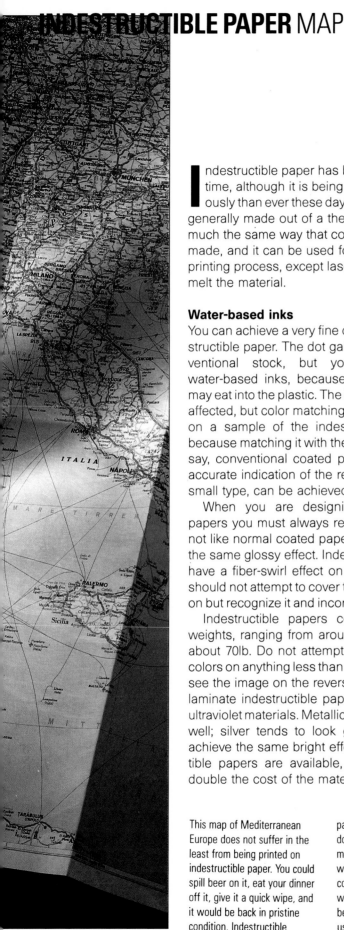

Indestructible paper has been around for some time, although it is being marketed more vigorously than ever these days. This kind of paper is generally made out of a thermoplastic material in much the same way that conventional papers are made, and it can be used for virtually any type of printing process, except laser printing, which may melt the material.

Water-based inks

You can achieve a very fine quality of print on indestructible paper. The dot gain is less than on conventional stock, but you must print with water-based inks, because solvent-based kinds may eat into the plastic. The brightness of ink is not affected, but color matching should be carried out on a sample of the indestructible paper itself, because matching it with the results of printing on, say, conventional coated paper, will not give an accurate indication of the result. Fine detail, even small type, can be achieved with flexography.

When you are designing for indestructible papers you must always remember that they are not like normal coated papers and will never give the same glossy effect. Indestructible papers also have a fiber-swirl effect on the surface, and you should not attempt to cover this up by piling the ink on but recognize it and incorporate it in the design.

Indestructible papers come in a variety of weights, ranging from around a very thin 20lb to about 70lb. Do not attempt to print with process colors on anything less than about 35lb as you may see the image on the reverse. You can varnish or laminate indestructible papers provided you use ultraviolet materials. Metallic inks do not reproduce well; silver tends to look gray and you cannot achieve the same bright effect. Coated indestructible papers are available, but using these will double the cost of the material.

This map of Mediterranean Europe does not suffer in the least from being printed on indestructible paper. You could spill beer on it, eat your dinner off it, give it a quick wipe, and it would be back in pristine condition. Indestructible papers are often used if documents or other printed matter are going to be used where adverse weather conditions are expected, or when the product is likely to be damaged through rough use.

Other applications

Indestructible papers are used for items such as labels and tags for outdoor plants, or for the labels used on chemical drums which are exposed to the weather. They are also used for horse racing notes and other outdoor sports information, and for maps, signs and placards, security envelopes, and promotional clothing.

Relative costs

Indestructible papers cost between eight and ten times more than conventional papers, and you may also have to use ink that is more costly than would be the case for conventional stock.

LASER-CUT PAPER STATIONERY

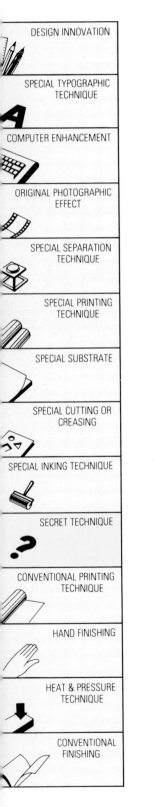

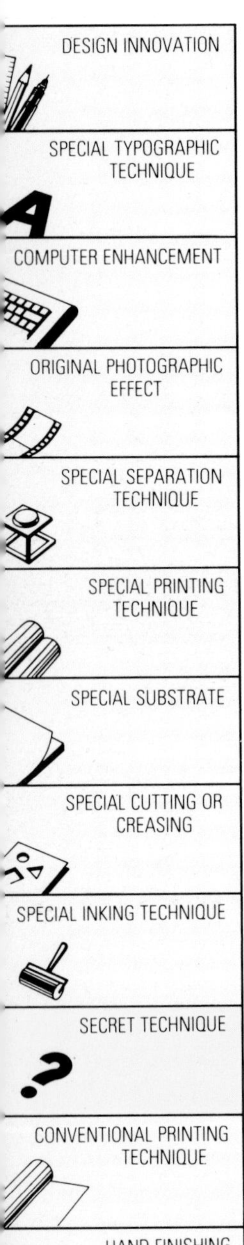

Laser cutting is a new technology that offers the designer a relatively quick and cheap way of cutting out sections of paper to a high degree of accuracy and fineness. The only comparable technology is die cutting, which, in comparison, is an extremely crude process, unable to attain anything like the intricacies achievable with laser cutting.

The only limitation on laser cutting is that there must be a minimum 0.02in (0.5mm) cut. The process is best used on uncoated stock, between 45lb and 200lb. It is possible to use coated papers and synthetics, but these tend to leave small amounts of residue around the edge of the cut. In most cases there will be a little smoke discoloration on the reverse side of the cut and some papers may show a certain amount of discoloration on the front. Check with the laser specialist before you specify the paper.

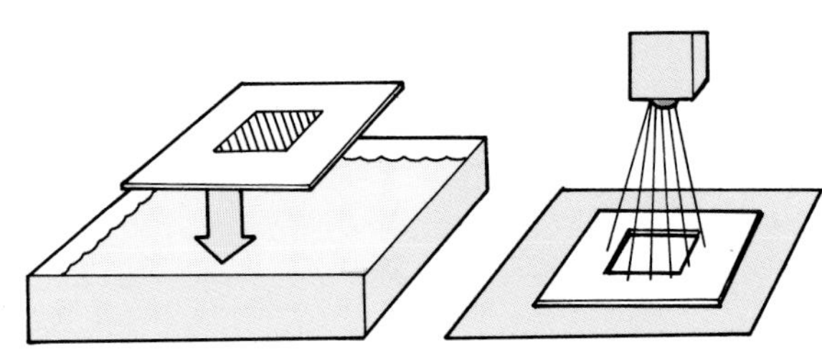

This range of products has been laser cut. This new process allows a hitherto unavailable degree of intricacy to be achieved in cutting out shapes. Artwork is scanned into the computer system, and from it a laser beam cuts through the stock. Although the process is neither fast nor cheap, it is highly effective.

Preparing the artwork

There are several factors to take into account when designing a piece of artwork for laser cutting. First, you must be aware of the background — what will be seen through the cutout. Second, bear in mind that contrast is the key to a successful laser-cut effect — the greater the contrast, the greater the impact. Avoid dark top and back-up sheets and having full-color images on the inside and outside. Excellent results can be achieved by using vignettes on both pages, one reversing the other — i.e., the top page vignette runs from top to bottom, while the back-up page runs from bottom to top. White on white, or white on pastel gives a lovely, understated elegance. Laser cutting is similar to embossing in that the less printing there is, the more sophisticated the end result appears to be. For laser cutting, your artwork must be in black and white, camera-ready form.

It is likely to take at least four weeks between delivering your artwork and receiving your laser-cut paper. The minimum economic run will not be much less than 5,000, and the maximum sheet size is 20×20in (50×50cm).

Other applications

Laser cutting works well on most kinds of stationery, reports and accounts, greeting cards, invitation folders and promotional material, and, in fact on anything that needs a sophisticated, high-class look.

Relative costs

Laser cutting paper should work out at roughly double the cost of die stamping. Costs can be reduced by keeping all the laser cutting within the smallest possible area, and by using as low a weight of stock as possible, since the laser takes longer to cut higher grades. Papers with a high mineral or chemical content will engrave more slowly.

SEASON'S GREETINGS
THE GUTENBERG FESTIVAL
LONG BEACH · 1984 · CALIFORNIA

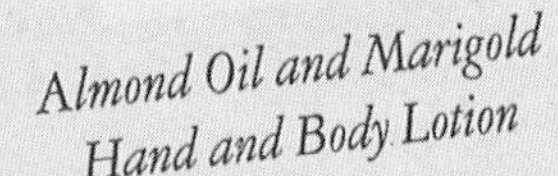
Almond Oil and Marigold
Hand and Body Lotion
Sweet Briar and Violet
Body Lotion
SKINCARE PRODUCTS
Sea Mineral and Kelp
Facial Scrub
Oatmeal and Avocado
Face Mask
Willow and Arnica
nditioning Shampoo
HAIRCARE PRO
d China Bark
ir Shampoo
Yarrow and Melissa
Shampoo for Dry Ha
allow and Quince Blossom
onditioner for Dry Hair
UCTS
oba Oil Conditioner
or Normal Hair

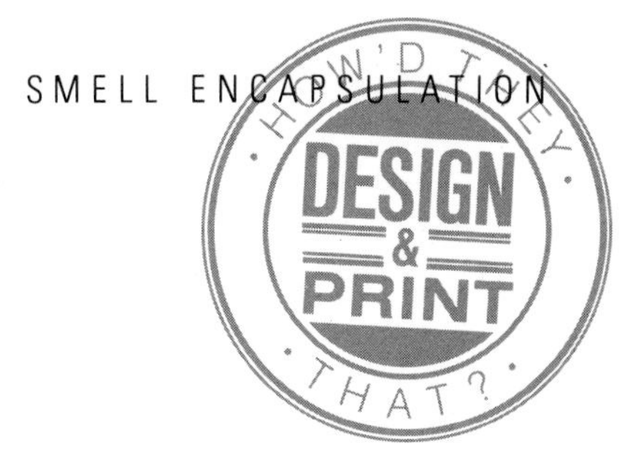

SMELL ENCAPSULATION PROMOTION

Smell encapsulation, or "scratch and sniff," as it is perhaps better known, has been around for some time. The technology that makes it possible was developed from carbonless papers, and it works on the same principles. In this case perfumes are encapsulated in tiny water-soluble capsules, which are printed — usually by screen-printing technology — on a given area. When the area containing the encapsulated perfumes is rubbed or scratched, the walls of the capsules are broken and the smell is released. Although application by screen printing is the commonest method, the medium containing the capsules can be sprayed or roller-coated onto a given area.

Scratch and sniff is widely used to promote perfumes, but there are good examples of it being used to promote other products. For example, one manufacturer of microwave ovens used it in an imaginative way to promote their ovens: they gave potential purchasers three delicious food smells to help them envisage the appetizing meal coming out of the microwave. Manufacturers are able to create a host of different smells, and there should really be very few fragrances that they would not be able to reproduce.

If you want to incorporate smell encapsulation into a project you should allow an extra three or four weeks in the production cycle. This is partly for the printing itself but mainly, of course, because the scent has to be custom-made. The process works best when it is printed over litho paper and board.

Clearly, if you are using smell encapsulation there is little point in adding another effect on top of it; overprinting with the scent should be the last process. It is difficult to print with the medium onto varnishes and laminates because the resin can "crawl" and form globules. In addition, care is needed because some underlying inks will not accept water-based screen inks, and they may give poor adhesion. Any paper and board, however, should accept scratch and sniff. Designers should also be aware that the human nose can become confused if different fragrances are placed too close together on the same design.

Other applications

Smell encapsulation can be used for a host of effects, limited only by the designer's imagination. Although cosmetic promotion is an obvious area, the process can be used for washing detergent and fabric softener promotions, drawer liners and greeting cards, and for a range of novelty products, including many promotional items, packaging, stationery, gift wrappings, and children's books.

Relative costs

The process will add considerably to the cost of the product, although the extra expense is not necessarily caused by the cost of the scents, which are often comparatively inexpensive. The additional costs arise from having to screenprint the whole run in order to lay down the smell.

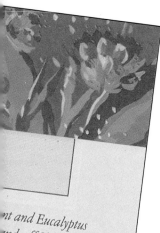

Smell encapsulation can be a useful design tool, especially in retailing. When a major UK supermarket chain wanted to launch a new range of hair-care products, it felt that sales would increase if customers could smell the products' perfumes. However, it did not want the bottles on display to be continually opened because they would be damaged and some of the product would be lost in the process. The supermarket produced "scratch and sniff" cards for each product, and these were displayed alongside the bottles on the shelf. Customers scratched, sniffed, and liked the products, and the range went on to become highly successful.

HOW'D THEY
DESIGN
&
PRINT
THAT?

GLOSSARY

Terms that have their own entry are written in *italics*.

Basis weight The weight of a ream (500 sheets) of a paper or board in a basic or standard size. For example, 25 × 38in is the standard size for book papers, so basis 50 book paper means that 500 sheets of size 25 × 38 weigh 50lb. Also known as substance weight. See also **gsm**.

Bindery The area of the print factory in which the job is finished — that is, where the printed sheet is manipulated into its final format by such processes as folding, stitching, gluing, and guillotining.

Bleed (1) Printed matter designed to run off the edge of the paper. (2) Ink that changes color or mixes with other colors, which is sometimes caused by lamination.

Caliper The thickness of a substrate or the device used to measure it.

Coated Term used to describe paper or board that has a top layer of china clay to give a smooth finish. Coated stock reproduces a sharper dot than *uncoated* substrates and usually has a higher level of gloss. Glossy magazines, for example, are printed on coated paper. Also known as enamel paper.

Cora (Computer Orientated Reproducer Assembly) The traditional, and very fast, high-level typesetting language. See also **Densy**.

Corrugated board Board that has flutes of paper within the outer layers.

CYMK (cyan, yellow, magenta, black) The four printing colors. All color printing is produced from these four colors. Cyan, yellow, and magenta are the three subtractive primaries; black makes up for their deficiencies.

Dedicated The word used to describe any item of equipment that has been specifically designed for one single task.

Densy The traditional, and very fast, high-level operating language. See also **Cora.**

Die Metal object in the shape of an image that will cause the substrate to conform to that image when it is pressed against it; usually operates with a male and female, relief and recess, working together.

Digital/digitize A means of transporting information by breaking it up into computer-accessible language. Original artwork can be scanned into a system, digitized, then manipulated and transported around that system in digitized form before being output as *hard copy* again.

Dispro A function on some electronic repro systems by which the final film is disproportioned to take account of the fact that the printing plate will be wrapped around a cylinder.

dpi (dots per inch) The term used to describe the resolution obtain on film negatives or positives. As a rough guide, traditional high level film output will be 2800 or more dpi.

Embossing The process of pressing an uninked block or *die* against paper, which raises or recesses an image by causing the dimensions of the paper to conform to the die.

Enamel paper See **Coated**

Finishing The final stage of the production process during which the printed product is made ready for use. The processes, which include cutting, stitching, gluing, and guillotining, are carried out in the *bindery*.

Flexography Commonly known as flexo, this is one of the major printing processes. It is a relief process using rubber or plastic plates on web-fed offset presses. Although the quality achieved is improving, results are not as good as those from *gravure* or *lithography*

Font A set of type characters of the same design; for example, Times or Helvetica.

Four-color process The term used to describe color printing by means of the three primary colors (yellow, magenta, and cyan) and black. See also **CYMK.**

Gravure One of the major methods of printing. The process uses chrome-plated cylinders that have been etched by laser to hold ink in recessed cells. It gives the most consistent and highest quality results; it is also the most expensive method and is economic only for long runs. Also called rotogravure.

gsm (g/m^2, grammes per square metre) The method, widely used outside the *US*, of indicating the substance of paper or board on the basis of its weight, regardless of the sheet size. Magazine paper, for example, is usually between 80 and 120gsm. See also **Basis weight**.

Halftone A photograph printed by any of the major printing processes, which, although they cannot actually print intermediate tones, can adequately represent them by using dots of various sizes generated by a scanner or halftone screen. A mid-gray is thus depicted using a dot that is 50 percent of solid.

Hard copy Typed or printed copy from a computer or wordprocessor on paper or film, as opposed to the *soft copy* on a VDU.

Highlight The term used to describe an area of a *halftone* where there is little effective image, so the dots are very small — that is, less than 10percent. The converse is *shadow*.

Hot metal A system of typesetting, developed at the end of the 19th century, that revolutionized the print industry. The process has now been superseded by computerized typesetting in most of the world, but hot metal is still used in some developing countries because it is cheap and the system can be easily repaired.

Interface The point at which two systems meet and where different computer languages and protocols or operating systems have to be reconciled.

Leading Originally strips of metal, less than type high, that were used in *hot metal* setting as general spacing material. In typesetting systems, to lead is to add spaces between lines of type.

Letterpress The original printing process and, until about 20 years ago, the predominant printing method. It involves the use of a relief plate (of wood, metal, or a synthetic substance), which is coated with ink. The stock is passed over the inked area and the image is transferred to the substrate.

Linen tester A magnifying lens used to check halftone dot patterns.

Linework The term used to describe artwork for reproduction for which four-color separations are not required.

Lithography A printing process in which the image and non-image surfaces are on the same plane (a planographic process), while the paper makes contact with the entire plate surface. The printing area is treated to accept ink and the non-printing surface is treated to attract water or another dampening solution so that it rejects ink. Lithography is probably the most widely used of all printing processes.

lpi (lines per inch) Also known as screen ruling, the term refers to the quality of reproduction. Newspapers, for example, may be 60 or 80 lpi, while fine art reproduction may be 200 or more lpi.

Macintosh Also known as the "ubiquitous Mac." The Macintosh has revolutionized the entire graphic arts industry since the mid-1980s. It is available at comparatively low cost and, in the right hands, is able to provide high-quality pages at reasonable speed.

Masking A reproduction technique for color correction in the preparation of separations on a camera or enlarger.

Metal decorating Printing on a stock such as tin.

Mid-tones The term used to describe the areas in a printed reproduction that are generally composed of between 30 and 70 percent dot.

Non-corrugated board Board that has no flutes between the outer layers.

Off-line The term used to describe a section of the production process that takes place away from the main production line. The connection is made by transferring a disk or other magnetic medium between the devices. See also **On-line.**

On-line Computers and phototypesetters are on-line when thay have direct access to another piece of equipment. See also **Off-line.**

Pass A cycle of a press or phototypesetting system. To print in one pass means that all the colors are laid down as the stock travels once through the press; to print in two passes means that the stock has to travel twice through the press, and so on.

Plotter A computerized machine that records images by means of a laser. It may be either an output device of film separations or a device to cut out the *dies* to produce cartons.

Point size A means of measuring type. In the Anglo-American system the point is 0.013837in or 0.351457mm; 12 points make a pica or pica em. In Europe the Didot system is used; the point is is 0.376065mm (0.0148in), and 12 points make a cicero.

Porous Word used to describe stock, such as newsprint or poor quality cardboard, that readily absorbs ink. Such stock tends to give a dull, flat image, and fine detail may be lost.

PostScript The now-standard operating language through which *desktop page makeup* (DTP) systems operate. Pre-press systems are now described as PostScript-compatible or not.

Process colors See **CYMK.**

Proof Before the final press run is carried out, the artwork and/or text are reproduced as a representation of the finished item so that any last corrections can be made. Only wet proofs give an accurate representation of the final appearance; other systems — film, thermal, ink jet, or toner — have, because of the nature of their processes, compromise to some extent.

Register For the printed reproduction of work, all four process colors must be in register — i.e., they must fit together perfectly. It is easy to tell if print is out of register by looking at the edge of the image through a magnifying glass. If you see a line of cyan, magenta, yellow, or black dots, that color is out of register.

Reverse out The term used to describe the process by which the image is not itself printed but the surrounding area is, so that the image is actually the surface unprinted.

Rotogravure See gravure.

Sans serif A class of typefaces without *serifs*. Both the main body text and the captions in this book are set in a sans serif face.

Scanning The method by which original artwork is separated into the four printing colours (cyan, magenta, yellow, and black). Four films (known as separations) are output in halftone dot format. A plate is made from each film, and the image is re-created on the printing press by virtue of the dots' ability to convince the brain that together they form one continuous tone picture.

Screen ruling See **lpi**

Serif The small terminating strokes on individual letters and characters except in *sans serif* faces; most newspapers, for example, use serif *fonts*.

Shadow The term used to describe the area of a *halftone* where the image is particularly strong; the dots may be 80 percent or more. See also **Highlight.**

Signature A section of a magazine or book printed on a web-fed press. Signatures are usually in configurations of 8, 16, 24, 48, or 64 pages, according to the press size.

Soft copy The display on a VDU rather than a proof of copy on a substrate. See also **hard copy.**

Solids Solid areas of a single color; these are often surprisingly difficult to print successfully.

Split ducting The process by which two inks are placed in the same printing unit, one on either side. It is a very complex procedure that is used for security reasons.

Transparency A photograph, especially a positive color image, on transparent material. Available in several formats, transparencies are, at present, the best means of conveying images to the pre-press system.

Uncoated Term used to describe paper or board that does not have a top layer of china clay.

Vignette A graduated tint. The effect applied to halftones that, instead of being squared up or cut out, have the tone etched gently away at the edges.

INDEX

Page numbers in *italic* refer to illustrations and captions

CREDITS

Quarto would like to thank the following for providing photographs, and for permission to reproduce copyright material. While every effort has been made to trace and acknowledge all copyright holders, we would like to apologize should any omissions have been made.
Key a = above; b = below; l = left, r = right; c = center.

p10br L & M Machinery; **p11** Phil Abel, Hand & Eye; **p12 & 13** Karen Welman, Michael Peters Group USA; **p14 & 15** Banks & Miles; **p16** Music Sales; **p17**bl Quarto Publishing; **p18 & 19** O'Brien Associates; **p21** Skolos Wedell Inc. USA; **p22**t Jim Mortimore, Electric Icon; **p22**bl Jim Mortimore, Electric Icon with kind permission of 'Newbridge Network'; **p24 & 25** Nov. 1990 and Jan. 1991, editions of Captain America Copyright © Marvel Entertainment Group Inc.; **p26 & 27** Purup Electronics; **p28** World Publications; **p29** Quarto Publishing plc; **p32-33** Bang on the Door; **p33** br Bang on the Door; **p33**tl, tr, cr (x2) E-Zee Studios; **p34** The Ian Logan Design Co., Designer: Adrian McKay, Illustrator: Paul Hampson, Design Director: Alan Colville, Client: W.H. Smith Ltd; **p35** Phil Baines, Paschal Candle Design 1990, & Crafts Council; **p36 & 37** With many thanks to M.A.N. Roland; **p38** McVities; **p39** The Sunday Times Magazine, Art Editor: Pedro Silmon, Inside Illustration: Christopher Brown, Cover Supplement Photography: David Woolley 18th March 1990; **p40** The Ian Logan Design Co., Designer: Alan Colville, Illustrator/Artist: Brian Cooke, from 'Book Jackets from the 1930's', Batsford Books; **p41** The Ian Logan Design Co., Designer: Stuart Colville; **p42 & 43** Clothes Show Magazine; **p44** Today Newspaper; **p46 & 47** Trickett & Webb Ltd; **p48 & 49** Denny Bros; **p50 & 51** Toray; **p52 & 53** Studio 82, Hull; **p55** Arti Grafiche Motta, Italy; Quarto Publishing plc; **p56 & 57** Duffy Design Group USA; **p58 & 59** Duffy Design Group USA; **p60**b The Partners; **p60**t Cato Design Inc. Aus; **p61** Cato Design Inc. Aus; **p62** Edwin Gretton of Charles Openshaw & Sons Ltd. (Diagrams); **p62/63**c Duffy Design Group USA; **p63** S.D. Warren Co. USA; **p64** Fasson UK; **p66** Smith & Milton Ltd; **p67** Michael Peters Ltd, Creative Director: Glen Tutssel, Designer: Pat Perchal, Illustrator: Harry Willcock, Photographer: Bryce Atwell; **p68** Lewis Moberly; **p70 & 71** Shin Matsunaga Design Inc. Japan; **p73** The London Design Partnership Ltd; **p74 & 75** The Langston Corporation; **p76 & 77** The Partners; **p78 & 79** Der Nederlandsche Bank N.V.; **p80 & 81** National Westminster Bank plc; **p82 & 83** Trickett & Webb Ltd; **p84 & 85** Purdeys; **p86** Trickett & Webb Ltd; **p88 & 89**b Trickett & Webb Ltd; **p89**t Stamps using original drawings by Edward Lear, Designed by The Partners, Stamp Designs © Royal Mail Stamps. Reproduced by permission of Royal Mail Stamps; **p90 & 91** The Duffy Design Group USA; **p92**br DMB&B, Burger King; **p93**t Young & Rubicam, Legal & General; **p93**bl Courtesy of Gallaher Tobacco Ltd (All Billboard photographs supplied by Mills & Allen, The Outdoor Media Group); **p94 & 95** The Partners; **p98 & 99** Duffy Design Group USA; **p100/101**t 'Creatures of Long Ago: Dinosaurs', National Geographic Society USA, Art Director: Jody Bolt, Illustrator: John Sibbick, PE: John Strejan and James Roger Diaz; **p101**b Explosive Pop-Up Greeting Card, Published by Second Nature Ltd, UK. Design & Engineering: Kevin Perry, 3rd Dimension, London; **p103** London Central Print & Design; **p104** Collins, Publishers; **p106** The Partners; **p107** Quarto; **p108** Ziggurat Design Consultants Ltd; **p111** Platform Design; **p112 & 113** Duffy Design Group USA; **p114**tl Cato Design Inc.; **p114**br Lewis Moberly; **p115** Cato Design Inc.; **p116**tl Skolos Wedell; **p116**tr The Partners; **p116**b The Partners; **p118 & 119** United States Banknote Corporation, National Geographic Society USA; **p121** Debretts; **p123** Sky Magazine; **p124 & 125** Grey Matter; **p126/127**b Compton Marbling; **p126**t Quarto; **p127**t Cato Design Inc.; **p128** Wiggins Teape; **p130 & 131** Wiggins Teape; **p132** The Jenkins Group; **p133**tl David Davies Associates; **p133**tr Duffy Design Group USA; **p134 & 135** Du Pont de Nemours; **p136 & 137** Lasercraft USA; **p138** J Sainsbury plc